Caterflies & Butterpillars

Caterflies & Butterpillars

Front Cover Photograph
Courtesy of Laura Hildebrand, Morden, MB

E. Tyler Rowan

AuthorHouse™
1663 Liberty Drive
Bloomington, IN 47403
www.authorhouse.com
Phone: 1-800-839-8640

Published by AuthorHouse 12/10/2012

ISBN: 978-1-4772-9762-9 (sc)
ISBN: 978-1-4772-9761-2 (e)

Library of Congress Control Number: 2012923411

This book is printed on acid-free paper.

Contents

Introduction xiii
Too Busy? 1
The Interesting thing about Men 3
Out of Control 5
Ten Guidelines from God 8
Sorry, I'm bad at this 11
Priorities 13
On Attitudes 14
Complacency 16
Family Funnies 18
Growing Pains 19
Growing Roots 21
Understanding Jesus—1 23
Understanding Jesus—2 25
Understanding Jesus— 3 27
Understanding Jesus—4 28
Understanding Jesus—5 30
Family Funnies 32
Friday Friends 34
All That I Can Say 35
You're IT! 37
Family Funnies 40
When I Grow Up 41
A New Message 43
Got Faith? 44
R.E.S.P.E.C.T.—1 46
R.E.S.P.E.C.T.—2 48
R.E.S.P.E.C.T.—3 50
Undeserving 51
Lessons from the Road 54
Pinching Those Pennies—Groceries 55
A Rebel Without A Cause 58
Reading Rainbow 62
A Bunch of Handy Little Lists 66

My Anniversary Gift 68
Keepin' It Real 71
Oh Canada, Our Home and Native Land 73
Thankfulness 75
I Couldn't Have Said It Better 76
This Is Why I Do It 77
Children Aren't All That Different 79
Family Funnies 81
Big Bang? 82
My Prerogative 84
Beauty 85
My Heart for Women 87
Family Funnies 90
Doing Life Together 93
Good-Bye Plan B 95
This Settles It! 97
Spiritual Warfare —1 98
Spiritual Warfare—2 100
The Neighbours from Heck 102
Called? 104
The Earth is Square 106
The Heart of Worship 107
Filling of the Spirit 108
Christmas Appreciation 111
Accountable for His Flock 113
Do As I Say, Not As I Do 115
How Do Your Pages Read? 117
On Earth, As It Is In Heaven 119
My New Year's Resolution 120
Selfish 121
My To Do List 123
Holiday Randomness 125
God in the Flesh 127
Oh, the Anticipation! 129
Think Generous 130
Keep Keepin' On 132
But Have Not Love 135
Excuse Me, I Seem to Have a Little Something in My Eye 137

There's a Party in Heaven 139
Update, More Heavenly Partying 141
Jude 17-23 (Msg) 143
Pondering in my Heart 144
The Daily 145
Nothing 146
Questions on the State of Our Hearts 147
Be You 149
A Time to Weep 151
Refreshment 153
Time is in His Hands 154
All the Growing Up 156
MIA 158
Family Funnies 160
Happy B'Day to the B-Boy 161
A Bridal Love Story 163
Understanding Jesus 166
The Setting of the Sun 168
My God Chronicles 169
Time Management Works for Me (Usually) 172
Grandma 174
Lead Your Heart 177
The Hard Work 179
On the Horizon 181
Read the WHOLE Book! 183
Giving IS Frugal 184
God's Small Stories 186
The Crazy Mom 188
Gold Nuggets 190
God is in the Quiet Whispers 192
Getting Ready (Pre-Prayered) 193
The Anticipation is THICK in the Air 195
Questions that Keep me up at Night 196
Ragged Beauty 198
Parched without Prayer 200
Steps of Fear FAITH 202
How to Pray Your way Through Temptation 204
Day 24 206

Unsettle Me 208
The LORD is There 211
A Special Day for a Special Gal 213
Rest is Good for the Heart 215
What is Joy? 217
God In-cidences 218
Family Stuff 221
Making Friends 223
Aching Heart 225
The Crooked Mat 227
Morning Solitude 229
Consider it Pure Joy? 232
Feet First 234
And Again, as I Hop Back on the Wagon 236
The Tree 238
My Shoulders are no Longer Hunched over by the Weight of the World 240
From Dishonour to Freedom 242
Pondering 244
The View from Up Here 246
The Moral of the Story 248
On the Loose 250
Traditionally Speaking 252
Year in Review, 2009 254
Be the Centre 256
When I Wander 257
Start Dating Again 259
All or Nothing 261
Building Your Ministry—1: What Your Team Really Needs from You 263
Building Your Ministry—2: How to Love on Your Team 266
Really Random Facts 270
Stirring up the Embers 272
The Writing on the Wall Headstone 274
Unexpected Blessings are the Best Kind 275
Parenting is Tough 277
Our Greatest Weakness is NOT Knowing Our Own Strengths .. 280
My Will or His? 282

Get Serious 284
Maturity, does it equal boredom? 285
Family Funnies 287
The Tragedy of the Unopened Gift 288
Are You Burying Your Talents? Or Do You Even Know What They Are? 289
On Daddy's Shoulders 291
Framed and Stoned 293
I Don't Have the Energy for That 295
A Couple Life Lessons I'm Learning 297
I am an Orphan 299
Kids Say the Darndest Things 301
Secrets to Make a Marriage Last 302
Don't be a Moses 305
The Perfect Mom—1 308
The Perfect Mom—2 311
Just my Imagination? 315
My Kids Robbed the Bank 317
If I Only had a Brain 319
No amount of discipline will make up for a lack of training! 321
How to See 324
Obsessed by Unbelief 326
Seven Steps to Stop Anger in its Tracks 328
How we made it through alive 331
Thing Six: What to do when you mess up 333
How to Repair a Cracked Vase 337
Hypocrisy 340
I'm Just a Yeller 343
Giving starts right here 346
How to be Superwoman (or not)—1 349
How to be Superwoman (or not)—2 352
How to Change the World 354
Good Fruit: Patience 356
Year in Review 357
Good Fruit: Joy 359
When You've Lost Your Faith 361
Stuck in a Rut 365
Bumped off Self-Centre 367

Living Life with Purpose 369
To have eyes of Wonder 373
Things my Grandma Taught me 375
Unconditional Love 377
(Im)Perfect Family Devotions 379
Changing the Way our Family Works 382
Who Are You? 384
How to Have a Good Day 386
Categories of Crazy People 389
If You Can't Get it All Done 391
Impress or Influence? 393
A Life of Purpose 395
Preparing our Kids for the Reality of Marriage 397
Counter-Culture Decisions 400
Protection? Or Presence? 403
Just a Mom—1: It's Okay to Want More 405
Just a Mom—2: 5 Key Principles to Getting Started 408
Just a Mom—3: Practical Tips for Getting Out of the Slump 411
Just a Mom—4: It's Not About You 414
Just a Mom—5: Finding Your Calling 417
Just a Mom, Q & As 421
Just a Mom, Q & As—continued 425
Preventing Road-Trip Rage 428
Wrestling with God for my Broken Marriage 430
When You Don't Agree with Your Husband 434
Camping 101 436
Never Say No 438
Christianity hates women and so do I 441
Getting Over Myself 445
For the Overworked and Overwhelmed Woman—1 447
For the Overworked and Overwhelmed Woman—2 449
How to Bring the Romance Back 453
You are Loved 455
Don't Put The Kids First 457
Laughter, Sunshine, and Joy 459
And my heart turns violently inside of my chest 461
Listening to God—Where to Start 462
Crave God, Not Food—1 464

Crave God, Not Food—2 466
Making Your Faith Real 468
Messed Up 471
It's Not About Me 473
Too Comfortable? 476
Hosting a Banquet 479
Life, Interrupted 481
Tapping into His Strength—I 482
The God Chronicles 484
Pondering in my Heart 486
The Daily 487
Questions on the State of Our Hearts 488
All the Growing Up 490
An Important Reminder About Priorities 492
Be Glorified 493
Time is in His Hands 494
God Makes Time 496
Criteria for Choosing a Husband 498
He Equips 500
The Heart of a Man, The Heart of a Woman 501
Life Changing 504
Equilibrium 505
Hard Lessons, Soft Blessings 508
We Never Walk Alone 512
Taking the Longer Walk 514
Marriage Builders 516
Unbalanced . . . 2 519
There is more than one Path 522
Asked and Answered 525
The Ugly Duckling 528
Riding the Roller-Coaster 531
Here I Come 535

About The Author 537

Introduction

E. Tyler Rowan is a girl on a journey—a journey with purpose (and a bit of attitude!). With her quirky sense of humour, she shares what it's like balancing your spiritual identity as a child of The King with having five kids, a husband, and a dog. And a temper problem. And a self-control problem. And worrying about whether you're a good enough mother, a good enough wife, a good enough anything.

In other words, Tyler's going through the struggles that most women face today, but she's not afraid to do it in public, where it can touch people, so that God's grace can reach even across the keyboard and on the screen. As she says, "it's not about me." It's about Him.

As you read these words you'll develop a picture of this woman that I already know a bit in real life. But as you read it you'll find yourself getting a fuller picture of the woman—Tyler as she banishes the TV from the main family room with trepidation; Tyler as she realizes that one of the rough parts of being a Christian is feeling conviction so quickly when you do something wrong (and have to apologize to your husband); Tyler as she struggles with letting God write her to-do lists. And Tyler as she struggles with weight loss, hitting the big 3-0, and learning how to budget.

As I read through her blog, I saw myself there, that constant tug-of-war between two MEs: the one ME that is wants to be so super disciplined with my time, and my money, and my housework, and my weight; and the other ME that just wants to revel and enjoy the beauty that God has given me, and the wonderful people He's put in my path.

Women feel that struggle. We all want to be superwomen, who have it all together, who can decorate and budget and mother and cook. Yet life rarely works out that way. Grandmothers get sick. Emergencies happen. And all that discipline sometimes seems for naught. Should we be struggling like this? Is this what God asks for us?

As Tyler tries to answer those big questions, her posts are interspersed with the whispers from God, like whispers in a storm. Whispers showing her that the Bible is not meant to make us feel guilty or heavy-burdened, but is meant to make our burden lighter. The Bible is really God's love letter: a love letter that every mom with kids underfoot needs so desperately to read and understand and LIVE.

That's what Tyler is trying to do, little by little. She has let herself feel grace. She has let herself calm down. And her wonderful post "10 Guidelines from God" probably sums up this journey best. In it, God tells Tyler what He wants her to do—what He wants all of us to do:

Quit Worrying. Put it on my list (no, not your to-do list; God's to do list!). Trust Me. Then leave it alone. Talk to Me. Have faith. Share. Be patient. Be kind. And most of all, love yourself.

Are you able to love yourself today, despite feeling like you're not a good enough mom, not a good enough wife, not a good enough Christian? Maybe you need to take this journey with Tyler, where you'll find that God really is enough. And He has made you enough, too!

Sheila Wray Gregoire
Speaker, blogger from To Love, Honor and Vacuum (http://tolovehonorandvacuum.com), and author of The Good Girl's Guide to Great Sex.

Too Busy?

Ever feel like you're simply too busy? Too much to do, not nearly enough time. Clean the house, cook the meals, help with homework, spend time with hubby, have coffee with friends, drive from here to there 40 times a week, take kids to soccer/ballet/art class, do ministry work, do service projects, go to Church, Bible study, life group . . .

It's weird, but I often go from one extreme to the other. One day I'm so busy I can't even think straight, the next day I'm bored out of my mind (not usually for lack of something to do so much as lack of motivation to do anything). When I'm sitting at either end of the spectrum one thing is consistent—I find excuses to skip out on my time with God. Too tired, too busy, I deserve a rest, taking the day off, other very important Godly things to take care of . . .

The funny thing is, any time I skip out, my whole day suffers. I feel either rushed or completely lacking in 'get up and go;' I am either frantic or frustrated; I feel angry, sad, cranky, lonely, irritated—all at the same time! I want to be left alone, but hate feeling isolated.

God has called me to spend time with Him each morning. (Morning might not be everyone's time, but I do know that He wants time from each of us, whether morning, evening, mid-day.) It seems counter-intuitive, but the days where I'm up at 6:00 or 6:30am are my best days. Even if I was up with a baby 14 times that night. Even if I have 6 million things to do, plus errands to run, plus misbehaving children. Although, I've even noticed that the kids' behavior is better on these days (or maybe it's just the mom's disposition).

* Here's a quote I read today that spoke to my heart:

It's so easy to be caught up with the busy things of life that we overlook tending our inner lives. Then we often find chaos in our heart and mind and wonder why God seems distant. During those times we will most likely find our Bible starting to gather dust. God's Word is nourishment for our souls. ~ Gail Rogers

It's crazy! I would never risk not eating the food my body needs for survival (and enjoyment, lol). I don't risk driving without my seatbelt (and my cell phone in case of emergency). I can't imagine hopping on a motorcycle without a helmet (okay, if you know me I know you're thinking, "come on, Tyler, you would never get on a motorcycle to begin with!" true). So why do I take risks with the very ESSENCE of my life?! Nothing is good without Christ at the heart of it. My best intentions at life—parenting, housekeeping, ministry—none of it is worth anything if I've done it on my own. My very soul cries out against it!

"Keep God's Word at the very core of your life. As a Christian you simply cannot risk living otherwise." ~ Gail Rogers

The Interesting thing about Men . . .

Recently, my husband suggested to me that we pick up a marriage book and work through it together . . . As most women would, I responded with glee! My husband cares enough to work on improving our marriage, sigh, happy face. Now, imagine for a moment that I was the one making the suggestion—the more likely response from him would be: a) ignore the suggestion; b) reject the suggestion; c) ignore the suggestion; d) take offence at the implication that he is a less-than-perfect mate; or e) all of the above! (On a side note, this is not a commentary on my darling husband in particular, but more a general observation about the differences between men and women.)

Incidentally, the book we intended to study is available in DVD format, and being offered by the marriage ministry in our Church—being the kind of folks that we are (that is, just slightly this side of completely lacking in motivation, lol), we went for the easy route. Tonight marks week 2 . . .

The author/speaker, Dr. Emerson Eggerichs, has quite the humorous take on how the genders view things differently. Take, for example, the statement "I have nothing to wear." What does this mean? When I say it, it probably means I have nothing NEW to wear, or possibly I have nothing THAT FITS to wear. Heard from Pat, on the other hand, it likely means I have nothing CLEAN to wear. LOL!

Now, indulge me for a moment as I ponder the title of the book . . . "Love and Respect: The Love She Most Desires, The Respect He Desperately Needs." Huh? I *get* the love part—we all need love, right?! It's up there next to food and water on the hierarchy. But respect? Seriously? Shouldn't respect be EARNED??? According to Eggerichs, no! Unconditional love for the woman (that is, love that is not contingent upon actions and performance, but simply for *being*) is equivalent to unconditional respect for the man (that is, respect and honour for who he is and what he does, even at those times we feel his performance is lacking). I must say, this concept is almost beyond my ability to grasp!

An example? I recently picked up a picture of little Kai for our wall of fame (Pat's actually quite good at photography, and we posed the baby all nicely). Unfortunately, the picture was slightly off-center. Pat comments on this flaw (I wonder if he's hinting that it's somehow my fault . . .) and my reply is this, "yeah, I noticed those pictures you took for my blog are a bit off-center, too," with a chuckle. And we move on to living life with 5 kids . . .

A couple hours later, Pat enlightens me—somehow, in my casual observation, he has interpreted a slight to his ability. What he heard—"you are terrible at taking pictures . . . you are a failure . . . you should never take pictures again." Again I say, HUH? My comment (or perhaps a better word is criticism) made him feel disrespected. Until that moment, I had interpreted the word 'respect' to mean ("you are a good person who does good things")—nope! Respect really means "you are capable, you are able, and you do a good job." Ah-hah! No wonder my husband figured we needed a marriage book . . . (On another note, I have realized this to mean that every time I comment on, or God-forbid *correct* the way he parents, I am disrespecting him. Which is essentially the same as if he were not loving or appreciating me—for example not answering with a resounding "NO!" when I ask if something makes me look fat.) Shoot. I've got a lot of work to do!

Out of Control

self'-control', n. restraint of oneself or one's actions, feelings, etc. also known as . . . self-discipline, self-possession, restraint, poise, composure, reserve (see resolution) . . . determination, will, decision, strength of mind, resolve, master over self, moral courage, tenacity, doggedness also referred to as . . . "denying one's flesh" (the flesh, or the human nature and its desires are often driving human choices . . . Scripture says to deny the flesh—or refuse to give in to our human desires—and instead seek God's will)

I have been on a binge! A binge of selfishness and greed. I have been out of control!

While pregnant with this last beautiful child (Malakai), I ate what I wanted when I wanted it. The result—a weight gain of 49 pounds (not something a woman nearing 30 can afford to do to her body).

I spent the last year (or many years, really) of my life spending money on what I wanted when I wanted it. The result—every single bill behind (some unpaid for 3 months), creditor phone calls, NSF cheques and the accompanying fees.

While I know I should be up each morning reading my Bible, praying, and connecting with my Lord, I hit the snooze button more days than not. I'd rather sleep. When my kids ask me to play games, colour, read, or just hang out, I say "not right now" more often than not. I'd rather clean (or cook, or do the banking, or be on the phone, or be on the computer . . .). If someone is misbehaving and I should go conduct some discipline, yelling from where I'm currently seated/standing/working seems to the modus operandus. The list could go on, and on, and on.

I have no self-control, no discipline, no will. (Proverbs 25:28 *Like a city whose walls are broken down is a [woman] who lacks self-control.*)

We live in a culture that tells us we can all have whatever we want whenever we want it, and without having to work for it . . . we deserve it . . . why wait, when we can have it now . . . we can have MILLIONS of dollars working only hours a week . . . we can have a Cindy Crawford body only exercising 10-minutes a day . . . "I'm worth it!"

God's world can be so counter-intuitive! He wants me to deny my desire to be lazy (and hit snooze, or yell) . . . He wants me to deny my desire to shop more and pay bills less . . . He wants me to deny my desire to stuff my face with all the yummy and unhealthy things I crave. Why?

Titus 2:3-5 *Likewise, teach* ***the older women*** *to be reverent in the way they live, not to be slanderers or addicted too much wine, but to teach what is good. Then they* ***can train the younger women*** *to love their husbands and children,* ***to be self-controlled*** *and pure, to be busy at home, to be kind, and to be subject to their husbands,* ***so that no one will malign the Word of God***.

Ah-hah! I am supposed to learn self-control in my life so that other women can learn from me (from my mistakes and my successes). I am supposed to learn self-control in my life so that no one will think badly of God or His Word (and my selfish and greedy nature will not cause anyone to reject the Gospel of Christ). *(LOL, not that I consider my almost-30 self an 'older woman,' but that I have more years of Spiritual growth under my belt, if you know what I mean.)*

This year, I am committed to getting things back under control. Not through my own strength, not by my own will—but with the help of the Only One who can truly teach me to deny my flesh. I believe that if we are obedient in the small things, obedience in the bigger things just naturally occurs. So by practicing on my small issues (eating, spending) I believe it will be easier to work out my big issues (time in the Word, yelling).

Here are the steps I've taken so far: I'm on Weight Watchers and have a membership at the gym. AND, my beautiful friend Christine spent HOURS with me figuring out a budget that works (and most importantly gets the bills paid and kept up-to-date) . . .

Here's what God has been doing to help me with the other issues: I have been virtually unable to sleep past 5am for 2 weeks (it's not the most pleasant wake-up call, as my back pain has been terrible, but the agony typically eases by about 9am)—what else does one do at 5am besides drink coffee and read the Bible?! AND, I have been really noticing how the children yell at one another and at us (Pat and I) . . . when I hear it I can hear my own tone of voice and words echoing back at me (yikes!).

My hope and prayer is this: may I submit myself to the will of God for my life (rather than the selfish desires of my human nature and what the world tells me I should focus on), and through this "denying of my flesh" may other women think good things about God, and may my children see and love the Jesus that lives in my heart . . .

Ten Guidelines from God

Effective Immediately, please be aware that there are changes YOU need to make in YOUR life. These changes need to be completed in order that I may fulfill My promises to you to grant you peace, joy and happiness in this life.

I apologize for any inconvenience, but after all that I am doing, this seems very little to ask of you.

Please, follow these 10 guidelines:

1. QUIT WORRYING: Life has dealt you a blow and all you do is sit and worry.

   Have you forgotten that I am here to take all your burdens and carry them for you? Or do you just enjoy fretting over every little thing that comes your way?

2. PUT IT ON THE LIST: Something needs done or taken care of. Put it on the list.

   No, not YOUR list. Put it on MY to-do-list. Let ME be the one to take care of the problem. I can't help you until you turn it over to Me. And although My to-do-list is long,

   I am after all . . . God. I can take care of anything you put into My hands. In fact, if the truth were ever really known,

   I take care of a lot of things for you that you never even realize.

3. TRUST ME: Once you've given your burdens to Me, quit trying to take them back. Trust in Me. Have the faith that

I will take care of all your needs, your problems and your trials. Problems with the kids? Put them on My list. Problem with finances? Put it on My list.

Problems with your emotional roller coaster? For My sake, put it on My list. I want to help you. All you have to do is ask.

4. LEAVE IT ALONE: Don't wake up one morning and say, 'Well, I'm feeling much stronger now, I think I can handle it from here.' Why do you think you are feeling stronger now? It's simple. You gave Me your burdens and I'm taking care of them. I also renew your strength and cover you in my peace. Don't you know that if I give you these problems back, you will be right back where you started? Leave them with Me and forget about them. Just let Me do my job.

5. TALK TO ME: I want you to forget a lot of things. Forget what was making you crazy. Forget the worry and the fretting because you know I'm in control. But there's one thing I pray you never forget. Please, don't forget to talk to Me—OFTEN! Love YOU! I want to hear your voice. I want you to include Me in on the things going on in your life. I want to hear you talk about your friends and family. Prayer is simply you having a conversation with Me. I want to be your dearest friend.

6. HAVE FAITH: I see a lot of things from up here that you can't see from where you are. Have faith in Me that I know what I'm doing. Trust Me; you wouldn't want the view from My eyes. I will continue to care for you, watch over you, and meet your needs. You only have to trust Me. Although I have a much bigger task than you, it seems as if you have so much trouble just doing your simple part. How hard can trust be?

7. SHARE: You were taught to share when you were only two years old. When did you forget? That rule still applies.

Share with those who are less fortunate than you. Share your joy with those who need encouragement. Share your laughter with those who haven't heard any in such a long time. Share your tears with those who have forgotten how to cry. Share your faith with those who have none.

8. BE PATIENT: I managed to fix it so in just one lifetime you could have so many diverse experiences. You grew from a child to an adult, have children, change jobs many times, learn many trades, travel to so many places, meet thousands of people, and experience so much. How can you be so impatient then when it takes Me a little longer than you expect to handle something on My to do list? Trust in My timing, for My timing is perfect. Just because I created the universe in only six days, everyone thinks I should always rush, rush, rush.

9. BE KIND: Be kind to others, for I love them just as much as I love you. They may not dress like you, or talk like you, or live the same way you do, but I still love you all. Please try to get along, for My sake. I created each of you different in some way. It would be too boring if you were all identical.

10. LOVE YOURSELF: As much as I love you, how can you not love yourself? You were created by me for one reason only: to be loved, and to love in return. I am a God of love. Love me. Love your neighbors. But also love yourself. It makes My heart ache when I see you so angry with yourself when things go wrong. You are very precious to me. Don't ever forget it!

Sorry, I'm bad at this

So here's my little food for thought today (borrowed from Alicia Britt Chole):

The thunder sounded in the distance as my dad and I exchanged smiles. Hearing the summons, we both rose and took our places on the deck. Side by side we sat in silence relishing the first movements of nature's symphony.

The wind carried to us the sweet promise of rain. The lightening danced to a rhythm it alone could hear. The clouds rolled like an ocean over our heads.

While the storm proclaimed nature's untamed beauty, I sat in perfect peace in daddy's arms and tears of contentment collected in my eyes.

From the beginning, Dad was determined that his child would not inherit fear. "There is nothing to fear," he would say as he scooped me up and carried me out to our chair. Over the decades, I grew to savor storms—they were an invitation to rest with my daddy.

Dad's arms can no longer hold me—I am reminded of that reality every time I hear a distant thunder. But Another still sits near me when the winds beat against my life.

Life's storms are rather impolite. They neither consider our calendars nor consult our hearts. Without requesting permission they simply come.

But each time they come, our Father God smiles and whispers, "There is nothing to fear."

As the earth shakes and our dreams crumble, God extends to us His strong arms. As the wind howls and our faith trembles, God offers to hide us in Himself.

Life's storms issue to us an invitation to rest with Father God. Nestled securely in His eternal embrace, even the most furious storm cannot crush our fragile hearts.

Priorities

"The person whose calls you answer every time, that's the one you're in a relationship with." This is roughly quoted from a movie Pat and I watched last night. It's a striking truth. The people we spend our time talking to and hanging out with, the activities we engage in most often, these are like a mirror, reflecting our life's priorities.

If asked (well, I'll tell you even if you don't ask, lol), my list of what's important to me goes something like this: God, marriage, family, friends, ministry, fun, money. But if I asked someone else, based solely on their observations of how I spend my time (let's say they can see everything), they might suggest my priorities are: driving around, talking on the phone, working on the computer, reading novels, running interference for the kids, ministry, shopping, cleaning, cooking, yelling (hard to know where to place that one on the list), budgeting, coffee with friends, prayer/Bible reading, husband, TV (this one has only been bumped down on the list recently, since we abolished TV from the main living room), health/fitness . . .

Hmmmm.

On Attitudes

I have been super grouchy lately. Not to the point where I'm nasty to be around (though you'd have to ask Pat to be sure), but just where I'm scowly and grumbly.

For example, our retreat committee met yesterday to do some assembly for the craft. Basically, we needed to put all the pieces together in a Ziplock bag so when the women at the retreat want to do their craft everything they need is already together. Now, if you don't know me you might not be aware of my 'quirks.' One of these quirks is my utter lack of craftiness. I am terrible at anything craft-related! Not only that, but I just don't enjoy it. (Give me a bunch of walls to paint and I'm in my glory, but DO NOT ask me to create a lovely handicraft!) I digress . . . Anyway, we're there to work and to fellowship, so you'd think I could deal. Nope. Hated it. So un-fun. The worst part is, though, that this 'hated it' attitude was written all over my face for 4 hours!

I know in my heart that, in spite of the unpleasantness of the task, I could have chosen to enjoy my time with 9 totally great women. I could have taken joy in the throng of children in and out of the room, rather than feeling irritable about how rambunctious they were. I could have done the work with a song in my heart and a smile on my face. But I didn't. What's even worse is that I am noticing this attitude issue cropping up all over the place.

Maybe I need more sleep (after all, waking up 4 times each night is probably not quite what my body needs). Maybe I need Christine (my BFF who is working full-time for a few months . . . we normally talk about *everything* several times a day, now we talk about nothing once a week). Normally, I'm a fairly optimistic gal; I like to encourage others to see the good in things. I don't really know where all this crabbiness is coming from, but that's not really important. I need to figure out how to change it!

So I was thinking, what would I do (if I were feeling inspired and creative) to help my children learn about having a good attitude? Ah-ha! The answers to all life's questions can be found in one precious Book . . . Here's one little tidbit of God's advice to me on attitudes:

Colossians 3:23-24 *Whatever you do, work at it with all your heart, as working for the Lord, not for men, since you know that you will receive an inheritance from the Lord as a reward. It is the Lord Christ you are serving.*

I really like how the Message puts it . . .

Servants, do what you're told by your earthly masters. And don't just do the minimum that will get you by. Do your best. Work from the heart for your real Master, for God, confident that you'll get paid in full when you come into your inheritance. Keep in mind always that the ultimate Master you're serving is Christ. The sullen servant who does shoddy work will be held responsible. Being a follower of Jesus doesn't cover up bad work. [or a bad attitude]

Complacency

Do you ever start to feel complacent, apathetic even, in your faith? I know there are times when I do . . .

When life is rolling along smoothly—no major issues with any of the kids, marriage is feeling solid, ministry is growing—it's almost as if God gets nudged back in my life. My time is filled with going to Church and Bible study, serving in ministry, reading good books about God. But time spent, just God and I, slips away.

I tend to develop this mindset of, "God has me so busy at home and in ministry, and I really grow through the act of serving, so it's all good." I keep on plugging ahead, and I'm certain I really am learning, growing, and changing . . . but I'm missing something vital—connecting, knowing His heart for me. Though my Spirit is shouting at me that it needs more, my flesh tells me that this is enough. I get 'settled' and become complacent. Sound familiar?

Did you know that the Bible isn't just a good book or a bunch of words that God wants us to read? Recently I learned that His Word is His love letter—to me! That's kind of hard to grasp, I know. Take a moment to consider your first big crush . . . He's theeee cutest boy in school, and he likes YOU! You go to your locker and discover an envelope stuffed inside, with a note in it! What do you do? You might eagerly tear it open right there, unwilling to wait even one minute before drinking in his adoring words. Maybe you tuck it away to read in the quiet stillness later, when you can really savor each precious phrase.

God has given us a love letter like that—how can we go to His Book with anything less than eager anticipation of how His words of love can fill our lives? Oh, I'm so sad to say that I often open my Bible with a sense of duty rather than excitement. I can just imagine the look on my husband's face if he gave me a Valentine's card and I opened it with the attitude, "well, I'll read it because I have to, sigh." His very Spirit would be crushed. And yet I do this to my LORD!

Father,

I pray that I will not have a complacent faith. Give me a passion and excitement to be with You, to bask in Your Presence, and especially to read the beautiful love letter You wrote just for me. Forgive me, Lord, for the way my attitude has hurt You. I love you so much, God! Please, change my heart so that my actions and time spent reflects how deeply I love you.

In Jesus Beautiful Name,

Amen

Family Funnies

Driving along one day, Meg (4) asked why the snow on the road looks dirty. Thinking I should jump on this learning opportunity, I delve into an explanation of road gravel, traction, and so on . . . In spite of Meg's less than enthusiastic participation, I quietly hope that she's grasping the concept. Later, to test her comprehension, I ask if she remembers the big word we talked about earlier. With a slightly irritated look on her face, Meg demands, "Why are you trying to teach me?!" *LOL! This, people, is why God has not called me to home school.*

Abbey (6) to her dad, "Dad, William—not William in my class, but William on the bus, you know . . . the one who's in grade 2, he's 7-years-old—" (deep breath) "he said he has a crush on me." Dad asks, "Do you know what that means?" "No" (giggling). Dad, "Well, what did you say to him?" Abbey, "I laughed." *How straightforward . . .*

Braeden (9) to dad, "Dad—you took Mom for a date? Where'd you go?" Dad, "Sure did buddy. We went to see Riverdance." "Aw Dad, that's so cute! I'm proud of you!" *Really, how does a 9-year-old know that watching people dance around for 2 hours is less than fantastic to most men?!*

Growing Pains

My baby is growing up too fast! When you know (well, are pretty sure) you've had your last baby FOREVER, the mommy clingy factor seems to go up a bit.

My plan for this last child, sweet baby Kai, was to breastfeed till at least 6 months. It seems, no matter my intentions, my other 4 babies were 'off the boob' (yes, I'm sometimes known for my less-than PC vernacular) somewhere between 4-6 months. Various life circumstances would inevitably create a situation where switching to the bottle was the best option for the family. I never really had a problem with this, until now. Now, with the deep-seated knowledge that I will never hold another baby to my breast, I am mourning the loss.

If you've been around my home for the past (almost) 5 months, you may have noticed that our 2nd born boy child, 5th born overall child is ~~the fussiest baby on the planet~~ um, not entirely content. A *million* people suggested that I try giving him more bottles (Christine, Pat, mom), but I was adamant, "he doesn't need more to eat! My body is made to feed him, and I know he's being well fed. For goodness sake, the child is over 16 pounds!"

Pat, love of my life, father extraordinaire, had had enough crying to last him 2 lifetimes—so he insisted I must try this bottle thing. So I would nurse, burp, rotate infant to other side, nurse, burp . . . satisfied that he was satisfied, I'd put him in one of his many large and brightly-colored contraptions for some play time. Cry, cry, cry. So I'd warm up a 4 oz bottle, just knowing that he wasn't really hungry. A few seconds later, once he finished gulping those 4 ozs back and had burped, and was still looking for more, I heated up another 4 oz bottle. This pattern continued for 3 days until I finally conceded—for reasons completely foreign to me, my body was not creating sufficient nutrition for this chubby little guy. Shoot!

By day 2 of the 'breast-breast-bottle-bottle' ordeal, a new Malakai had emerged. Content to play, full of smiles, shrieks, and giggles, mellow . . . ah, the peace! As I'm sure you are wondering—how long does a feeding take with this ordeal? Well, folks, too darn long! So we've mostly moved on to the bottle—which is filled to 6 oz every time, almost always drained and more added to finish out the feeding. He's happier, Pat's happier, the siblings are even happier, and in many ways I am too. But I am also just so sad . . . Never again. It's like the end of an era (lol, okay—that may be a bit on the ~~ridiculous~~ dramatic side)! Sigh.

Growing Roots

I like to think that I have a fairly strong faith. That when life tries to get me down I'll turn to God for strength. That my belief in Christ is so deeply planted in my spirit that it will not fade away during difficult times. But thinking is one thing—I'd like to be sure!

This morning, I read the parable of the sower (Luke 8:4-15):

While a large crowd was gathering and people were coming to Jesus from town after town, he told this parable: "A farmer went out to sow his seed. As he was scattering the seed, some fell along the path; it was trampled on, and the birds of the air ate it up. Some fell on rock, and when it came up, the plants withered because they had no moisture. Other seed fell among thorns, which grew up with it and choked the plants. Still other seed fell on good soil. It came up and yielded a crop, a hundred times more than was sown."

When he said this, he called out, "He who has ears to hear, let him hear."

His disciples asked him what this parable meant. He said, "The knowledge of the secrets of the kingdom of God has been given to you, but to others I speak in parables, so that, 'though seeing, they may not see; though hearing, they may not understand.'

This is the meaning of the parable: The seed is the word of God. Those along the path are the ones who hear, and then the devil comes and takes away the word from their hearts, so that they may not believe and be saved. Those on the rock are the ones who receive the word with joy when they hear it, but they have no root. They believe for a while, but in the time of testing they fall away. The seed that fell among thorns stands for those who hear, but as they go on their way they are choked by life's worries, riches and pleasures, and they do not mature. But the seed on good soil stands for those with a noble and good heart, who hear the word, retain it, and by persevering produce a crop."

How do I KNOW if the seeds of God's Word were planted in good soil? Better yet, how can I prevent them from simply 'falling on rocks' or 'growing among thorns?' Is there something I can do to help my faith take root?

I've seen people go either way—for some, life goes crazy and they grow deeper into their relationship with the Lord; for others, they begin to question what they've believed and doubt who God is. So what's the difference? And what can I do to solidify my faith, so that when tough times come (which they will—James 1:2 says WHENEVER you have troubles, not IF you you have troubles), my faith won't fall away or get choked up?

Understanding Jesus—1

I've been reading through Matthew these days, and I'm surprised to find that it's taking a while. It seems that everywhere I go there are words that are more to me than they were before. I have this desire to dig deeper into these words and understand more clearly what they mean—what Jesus means when He speaks them. Hopefully you can bear with my fumbling learning curve as I work through some parts of the sermon on the mount, starting with the beatitudes (Matthew 5:3-12) . . .

Blessed are the . . .

I think it's important to first figure out what Jesus means by the term 'blessed.' In my everyday life, I often equate blessings and things. For example, "What a beautiful home you have," "Thank-you, we're very blessed." Or, "God has blessed me with these children/ this marriage/these friends." To be honest, I really don't think that's what Jesus is getting at here. I really can't imagine Him sitting on this big hill, chatting with his disciples while a crowd of people listens in, telling them "Now, if you are poor in spirit, meek, merciful, etc., I assure you that you will have a life full of great things that you can give Me credit for."

I think the key to 'blessed are those' is found at the end of each verse: *for theirs is the kingdom of heaven . . . for they will be comforted . . . for they will inherit the earth . . . for they will be filled . . . for they will be shown mercy . . . for they will see God . . . for they will be called [daughters] of God . . . for theirs is the kingdom of heaven* . . . and finally—*because* ***great is your reward in heaven***. Jesus isn't telling me how to get everything I want or need here, but He is telling me how to get the ONLY thing I really need! He cares so much that I receive this 'blessing' that He provides me with a thorough list of the character attributes He wants me to develop, in order to receive His great heavenly rewards.

. . . poor in spirit

Okay, I must confess that I initially read over this the same way I would skim a phrase in a novel that I didn't completely understand. Like understanding that one phrase probably won't affect the overall impact of the story. In fact, I flew all the way through Matthew's fifth chapter, and it was only once I reached the end that I realized I didn't truly grasp any of what Jesus was talking about! We all know what it means to be poor, right? To do without, to have not. Or in terms of a poor performance—weak, lacking, unsatisfactory, inferior. So is Jesus really saying we will be blessed if our spirit (or spiritual lives) are weak? I couldn't wrap my head around this, because I know that Christ has called me to grow strong in Him, so I pulled out my handy Google search engine. After reviewing about 5 different takes on it, my heart settled on this: we **are** poor in spirit, imperfect and lacking. To accept this fact and acknowledge that, on our own, we are spiritual nothings, destitute—we can do nothing apart from Christ—this is what it means to be poor in spirit. Ah-hah

Isaiah 66:2b *This is the one I esteem: [she] who is humble and contrite in spirit, and trembles at my word.*

Oh, to be esteemed by God Himself! Our pastor often speaks of having a contrite heart and spirit, of putting ourselves in our rightful place (way below God). This heart attitude, a BE-attitude, will reap unimaginable rewards in heaven. Oh Father, that I would be poor in spirit and beautiful in Your eyes . . .

Understanding Jesus—2

Blessed are those who mourn . . .

I know that when we mourn and grieve, the Holy Spirit comforts us. But I also know that we are not supposed to wallow in mourning (after the loss of a loved one, for example) because those who love Jesus get to be with Him. For the past couple days I have been mulling this concept about in my head . . . why then, does Jesus seem to be encouraging us to mourn? Yesterday in Church we sang a song with the words, "Break my heart for what breaks Yours." I tend to think that the blessing (in this case, comfort) is given when we mourn for those things that Jesus mourns for: lost souls, broken relationships, starving children, aborted babies, people full of bitterness and hatred.

Blessed are the meek . . .

Isn't Jesus the funniest guy? Like really, He just keeps telling us to be different! Our world gives honor to the strong, powerful, successful . . . Jesus tells us to be meek! In my mind, this word meek is equated with 'wimpy.' Not just physically weak, but in personality too. You know, that person who stands and lets another berate her—tear a strip out of her—and simply looks at the floor and takes it, a doormat. I had to dig a bit to see if Jesus was really asking me to be a doormat.

The concordance in my Bible defines meek as 'humble before God.' Humble is a word I understand a bit better. To be humble is to not take all the glory for yourself, even if you deserve it. To be humble is to be truly repentant when you do something wrong. To be humble is to strive to do good for the sake of doing good, rather than seeking recognition.

Proverbs 11:2 says *with humility comes wisdom*. Proverbs 3:34 tells us that *[He] gives grace to the humble*. Psalm 18:27 tells us that He *save[s] the humble*. Don't we all desire wisdom? Don't we want, no **need**, grace (forgiveness)? Is there anyone who doesn't want to be saved, to be rescued? To experience these blessings here on earth, all we need to do is put Jesus first and ourselves last. We don't need to be doormats, weak and pathetic. In fact, we need to be strong enough to turn praise and glory away from ourselves and lift it up to God, who truly deserves it.

Phew, God doesn't ask much of us, does He (LOL)?! These heart attitudes, these ways to be, they can sound so simple on the first reading, but with a little exploration I am realizing that I require a total attitude overhaul . . .

Understanding Jesus— 3

Blessed are those who hunger and thirst for righteousness, for they will be filled.

I've said it before, but obviously this truth is not yet buried deep in my heart . . . God cares about my weight loss! He cares because my health matters to Him. He cares because His Spirit dwells within this body. He cares because He knows that food (no matter how yummy) will never fill me up. Him, His Word, living for Him, striving for righteousness—these things will fill me up. If my heart's desire is to be filled by the Lord, food will take its rightful place in my life. Rather than being the thing I seek when I'm stressed or lonely, food will exist for my nutrition and sustenance. When I'm stressed or lonely there is One who is so much better that can fill me up. The effect will be immediate and satisfying, and it won't add another roll to the muffin top.

Thank-you, Jesus!

Understanding Jesus— 4

Blessed are the merciful . . .

It's pretty easy to show mercy and compassion to some people. It takes little effort to give a homeless man a few coins or a sandwich. It's easy to send money to a global organization for the purpose of feeding an adorable little child. It makes sense to give of our time and money to charities and clubs that have programs for helping those who are less fortunate. Somehow, though, I suspect that Jesus is asking for something deeper, something that's not so easy to give, when He calls us to be merciful. I suspect that this has a lot more to do with loving our enemies that it does with loving those in need. For me, I can sense Him asking me to show love to people who irritate me . . . well, one person in particular. Someone who (in my mind) seems very self-centered and finds a way to make every circumstance a major dramatic and traumatic event. Someone who gets my blood boiling whenever I am asked about that person or that particular situation. This person needs my mercy, my forgiveness, and my love . . .

Blessed are the pure in heart . . .

To be sure I really 'got' this, the concordance in my Bible defines the heart as the centre of one's being, including mind, will, and emotions. My thesaurus gives all sorts of great descriptive words for pure, too: uncontaminated, wholesome, chaste, uncorrupted, authentic. To not allow my mind or emotions to be contaminated or corrupted, to keep my thoughts, desires, and actions wholesome—this is purity of heart. Not simply good intentions, but chasteness in my spirit.

Blessed are the peacemakers . . .

I am sensing a theme here! Again, the first thing that comes to mind is loving our enemies. Making peace the priority, at all costs. Sacrificing the desire to 'be right' in the name of keeping harmony. Not only submitting my own will in order to show Christ's love to those who don't know Him, but submitting in disagreements with other believers. Building unity and trust within the body of Christ . . . To again quote my concordance, "In so doing, they reflect the character of their Heavenly Father and so are called **[daughters] of God**." It just struck me that, if I am the opposite of a peacemaker (so basically, I act in any way that does not promote peace), I will also be the opposite of a daughter of God (an enemy of God). Ouch!

That's a lot to digest in one morning . . . I'm going to go spend some time with my Daddy now, because I know I can't make these changes on my own strength!

Understanding Jesus—5

Blessed are you when people insult you, persecute you and falsely say all kinds of evil against you because of me.

Seriously? I am supposed to consider it a blessing to be insulted? To be persecuted? It's hard to imagine, isn't it? Praying as Paul did, praising God during times of trial and attack—praising Him not in spite of our circumstances, but actually because of them . . . thanking Him for those circumstances. If it's in the Word, I believe it to be true, so somehow it really can be done. We really can give God praise and glory FOR those times we are persecuted. But how?!

I think that it starts with our perspective. First, I just want to consider the concept of persecution. I have always thought of persecution as other people being cruel to me because of my love for Jesus. I remember once being called a "Bible thumper"—that's pretty straightforward as far as persecution goes. Then there's the situation in schools and courts—no more prayer in public schools, no more giving an oath on the Bible (whatever book that's special to you will be sufficient)—again, pretty clear persecution of the Christian faith and of those of us who believe.

What about those times in our lives when we are getting beaten down by our circumstances? Losing our friends. Terminal illness. Divorce. In the past I've seen these as 'really bad things' that happen. These really bad things wield enough pain to cause many a strong believer to doubt, question, and even walk away from what they believe. Often, I believe that these really bad things are not simply 'bad luck,' but rather spiritual attack. Satan, the devil, the evil one—whatever you choose to call him, he's an insecure guy. He can't stand it when people are loving God and believing Him. He hates faith, and he will rally up a whole dominion of evil forces to help him wreck even one person's faith. He attacks us *because* of what we believe and Who we believe in—the essence of persecution. Here's where perspective comes in . . .

So when I feel insulted, attacked, beat down because of my faith . . . the first thing I do is take a deep breathe and ask, "why is this happening to me?" (Don't we all ask this question?) The answer is often the same—this is happening to me because I love Jesus and the enemy of Christ hates that. And even if the enemy may not have initiated this attack against me, he most certainly will take advantage of it in order to ruin my faith. How do I have victory of the enemy? How do I make sure he won't win and beat my faith out of me? There's only one way—praising God! "God's power is unleashed through the praises of His people!" (From *Spiritual Warfare for Every Christian*, Dean Sherman.) I praise God because I know He is faithful and will use even the worst circumstances for good in His kingdom. I praise God because I know He is good even if life isn't feeling so good. I praise God because I know He is more powerful than any insult or attack. I praise God, even when it feels like I should mourn and weep, because I KNOW that taking this action will bring blessing. I know it, because Christ Himself promised it—

Rejoice and be glad, because great is your reward in heaven, for in the same way they persecuted the prophets who were before you.

Family Funnies

Thanks to the lovely springish weather, the kids have spent many hours out-of-doors this week! Yay! For those not here, you wouldn't know that we live in a large close with a huge grassy space and several little groves of trees—it's about the size of 2 football fields—called a green (in these parts). So, the 3 girls are out in the green gathering fallen branches and dragging them across the road to our front yard (don't worry about the road, it's a close and everyone who drives on it lives in it, and everyone who lives in it knows we've got a gaggle of kids over here, lol). They proceeded to stick the branches in the pile of snow on our front yard. Grandma pulls up and chats with the girls to see what kind of fun they're up to. **Meg** (4 1/2) tells Grandma, "We're planting the trees. That means we're taking care of God's world, doesn't it?" *I just LOVE it when they take the things of God to heart!*

Sweet little **Shea** (2 1/2) is definitely two, with a vengeance! The child cries and screams with hysteria about practically everything. Her feelings are going through a very tender phase. Early this morning (ridiculously) I hear her shrieks from downstairs in Abbey & Meg's room. I run, imagining the worst (dresser fell on her, someone is trying to murder her, etc.). Arriving downstairs, I see no blood or broken bones—a good sign—and ask Shea what's wrong. "Abbey, Meggie, no be my friend! Waaaaaaaa!" *Oh. My. Goodness. I am going to lose my ever-living mind if this craziness doesn't end soon!!!*

Everything that **Braeden** (almost 10) had to say this week involved a scowl and a growl. Bad mood, bad attitude. No fun at all. Suggestions? *Yes Mom, I know I need to look for the positive, and I'm sure there were some great and funny things (because Braeden is the funniest kid I've ever met), but I just can't recall anything but the grouchy mood that dominated.*

Abbey (6) is in Kindergarten at our local Christian school. Their most recent class project was to adopt a polar bear. While we were praying at bedtime one night this week, Abbey pipes in, "please take care of the bears that live in the icy lands, because soon there will be no more."

Kai (almost 6 months) has been learning to shriek lately, which is both hilarious and painful on the eardrums. Hopefully I can catch him on video for next week. Oh, and can I just ask—how old were your kids when they started crawling? The girls all started around 8-9 months, Braeden was obviously later—2 1/2—due to cerebral palsy, but this little man is totally trying to crawl already! Is this normal? Or insane???

Friday Friends

I have theeeee best husband and friends! Ever!

Yesterday was a rough day. All I can say is that sometimes life is just plain hard. I was exhausted.

My sweet husband came home with flowers for me, and a card that said, "you are the greatest gal a guy could ask for." And these weren't just any flowers. Nope. Since Pat couldn't remember which I liked more—daisies or tulips—he brought both. Can I hear a nice big, 'awwwwww!'

This morning, a good friend came by for coffee. She loves me (and I love her) so she brought me a French vanilla from Tim Horton's. Time was short b/c I had lots of running around to do, so I figured we'd visit for a short while and go our separate ways. Leave it to her to surprise me! She sent me on my way and stayed home with the 3 that were here today. She brought food for lunch. She played Memory and War with them. She even baked muffins! I could've cried. (Actually, I did shed a couple tears, but then pulled it together.)

I should also mention my other friend, who has emailed and phoned and prayed for me about a dozen times in the past 24 hours. And my mom—ditto to the previous, PLUS she came over to get my organizing butt in gear. (We went through a massive amount of papers! Three garbage bags and three filing boxes worth. Whew!) And my dear friends who emailed me encouragement, prayers, and challenging thoughts throughout my day.

Seriously, you guys bless me. I'm overwhelmed. And so you know, though I'm still pretty raw, I feel better today. God's doing some tough work in me, but we're getting through it together.

All That I Can Say

You know those times in your life where it's all you can do to function? Where you tell yourself over again, "just do the next thing . . . keep moving forward . . . don't stop moving," because if you dare to stop the feeling of what you're going through would simply crush you? Where the best prayer you can offer is simply, "please, God, please"—where more is utterly impossible?

It can be so easy to forget how those times feel. We experience life smoothly for a time, and the pain from the past fades. It's easy to feel frustrated with others who seem to be 'stuck' in a place of pain and heartache. Who seem to be 'losing their faith.' It's hard to remember that the difference between a time of stability and closeness with God and a time of echoing emptiness is **one small event**.

This is my confession—I have been callous, uncaring, and impatient. I have held pride in my heart, thinking that my faith is strong and I would not go down the path of doubt. I have forgotten that it was only last summer that I could barely pray, where the pain and confusion of what I thought God had promised and my reality were crushing my spirit.

I have not been a good friend. Rather than listening, loving, caring, and praying I have pushed, prodded, challenged, and judged. I told myself that 'iron sharpens iron' to justify my harsh attitude, but God (in His mercy) has reminded me that 'the greatest of these is love.'

If I speak in the tongues of men and of angels, but have not love, I am only a resounding gong or a clanging cymbal. If I have the gift of prophecy and can fathom all mysteries and all knowledge, and if I have a faith that can move mountains, but have not love, I am nothing. If I give all I possess to the poor and surrender my body to the flames, but have not love, I gain nothing. ~1Corinthians 13:1-3

My friends, I am sorry. Please forgive me. When you needed someone to listen, I preached. When you needed someone to understand, I judged. When you needed someone to pray for your broken heart, I prayed for my own agenda. I hurt you and pushed you away, and I was wrong. I can only hope that you will be willing to give me another chance to be the friend that you need.

David Crowder's song was one of the things God used to show me how wrong I've been. It reminds me of those dark times, and all I can do is pray "please, God, please."

You're IT!

What I was doing doing 10 years ago . . .

Ten years ago I was a college student—in my first year of studies for my Bachelor of Arts in Psychology. We were probably gearing up for finals right around this time. I had a baby on March 16, took about a month off school and did my work from home, then returned for my 40-hour week to study and write exams. My 5-week old baby went to day care from 8:30am-5:00pm 5 days a week.

During this time in my life my mind was being 'opened' by all the big learning at college, I was fairly strong into women's lib, and since I knew I wanted a career putting my child in someone else's care was just something I had to do. You would often hear me saying, "there is no way I'd ever be a stay-at-home mother . . . it's just not in me . . . my kids will be better off if I'm pursuing something I love and someone who adores children plays with them all day . . . really, this will make me a better mom in the long run." I completed my degree in 2001 and joined the workforce, with an 8-month maternity leave during 2002, until 2003 (after the birth of baby #3).

I can't say that all thoughts of career have been abandoned, or that I don't occasionally explore what I'd need to do to get back in the work force—thankfully, though, the decision is not left totally up to me. I've got a great God who speaks into my life daily, and when I get too caught up in what I want He gently reminds me of what He wants. There is nothing I'd rather be doing in this world than honouring Him, and He keeps telling me to start right here at home with my 5 little monkeys. It's not easy, it's not always beautiful, but it is most definitely blessed.

5 things on my 'to do' list for today . . .

- clean bathrooms
- vacuum
- make supper
- respond to a couple ministry emails
- ~~write a blog post~~ — check!

(The housework is vital, though you might notice that it's 2pm and I've yet to start, because Pat is getting home after a week away and nothing says "I love you, honey" like a nice clean house! I finally finished this post, it's now 2:39, that took way longer than I expected. Now I've only got an hour to do the housework, and everyone's going to be waking up from nap—yikes!)

5 snacks I enjoy . . .

- chips (rip-l, salt and vinegar, dill pickle, Doritos zesty)
- chocolate (Cadbury Creme Eggs, Aero, Coffee Crisp)
- sour candies
- all types of sweet desserts
- heated appetizers
  (I think that about covers it all, don't you?!)

5 things I would do if I were a billionaire . . .

- pay off all our debts and those of our parents
- drill water wells in Africa
- build a maternity home right here in Red Deer, Alberta
- adopt children, oodles of them, from all over the world
- hire nannies to help me care for my zillions of children

5 bad habits . . .

- biting my nails
- junk food
- always playing 'devil's advocate' in conversations
- procrastinating
- procrastinating (this one's really serious, lol)

5 places I've lived . . .

- Winnipeg, Manitoba
- Morden, Manitoba
- Kindersley, Saskatchewan
- Red Deer, Alberta
- Calgary, Alberta

(Between these 5 locations, which I believe covers all of them—mom?, I would guess that there have been at least 25 different houses/apartments. We moved a lot when I was a kid, and it kinda carried into adulthood.)

5 jobs I've had . . .

(Ooooh, this will be fun!)

- Gas Station Attendant
- Bus Girl, Hostess, Waitress (I moved up the ranks, ya know.)
- Beer Tub Girl, Shooter Girl, Waitress (Ditto. Thankfully, this phase was only a few months. Good money, yucky job.)
- Group Home Worker—adults with schizophrenia; youth under government care
- Treatment Foster Care Coordinator (I think this was their fancy term for saying I was the middle man for foster parents with severe needs foster kids and social workers.)

Okay, I know it asks for five, but my current unpaid job is by far the most important one (and most difficult) that I've ever had—MOMMY!

Family Funnies

Megan (almost 5) is a fan of big words. If she hears me use a big word on some occasion, you can be guaranteed she'll try it out, too. Overheard as she was playing with her sisters this week: "Oh my, it is simply gorgeous!" (She pronounced the word with a lovely 'fancy lady' voice, so it came out more like gohahgeous.)

Shea (almost 3) is the 4th of 5 children. I am beginning to suspect that she has no ability to play alone. The other day, everyone was a school and the baby was napping, but I could hear Shea talking away. In fact, she was bossing (something she never gets to do with her big sisters), "You get over here, NOW!" A while later as we load into the van I hear her saying, "You sit here, and you sit here." When asked who she was talking to (also asked on another occasion by Grandma) she replied, "I'm talkin' to my girlfriends" (her emphasis made it sound more like GIRLfriends). Through further investigation I have discovered that there are 2 girlfriends who remain unnamed. At least we don't need to worry about Shea being bored or lonely next year when Meg goes to kindergarten—she'll just fabricate her own playmates!

One thing that I've never mentioned here because it's so normal to hear is one of Braeden's (10) favorite things to say. It occurred to me that it really is quite funny. Braeden is famous for getting distracted. If he has to walk past the television in order to complete a task, you can expect that the task will get overlooked or abandoned. As we often do, we hollered down the stairs for him to 'turn off the TV and do his job' (his room is downstairs, through the family room). He comes rushing up carrying an odd assortment of clothes that clearly won't work as an outfit for the next day. We asked what he was thinking . . . Braeden's reply, "My brain is soooo lazy! I can't control it!" Goofball!

When I Grow Up

Do you remember that question from your childhood—"what do you want to be when you grow up?"

Today was my brother-in-law's high school graduation. As each young adult was being handed their diploma, one of the teachers told us about their future plans. One was going to work, many had plans to travel, some were honest about their intentions to spend a year partying, others were going to college and/or university. I was struck by a few that clearly had BIG plans about what they wanted to be when they grew up. Medical school, dentistry, optometry, hair school, anthropology . . .

I remember answering the question any number of ways, depending on how I felt on that particular day. I'm sure I told more than one person I was going to be a doctor (I've definitely got the handwriting part down). I foolishly may have told one or two people that I'd like to be a teacher (me, with the patience and attention span of a two-year-old). If memory serves, when they read what I wrote for my graduation, it was something like this, "Tyler will take a year off to work, then attend Red Deer College where she will get her Bachelor of Arts in psychology."

I wonder how many of those nearly 400 graduates today will do what they said they would do. How many will completely change their minds. How many will change their life course due to a change in life circumstances.

I did get my BA in psych. Graduated in 2001. But during my first year at college (1997-1998, yes, after working for a year) my life course changed. Big time. I became a Mom. And the funny thing was, deep inside I knew that this was what I really wanted to be when I grew up. I finished university because, well, I guess I thought I should. But in my heart, all I really wanted was to be a Mom.

I remember walking around the neighbourhood with my childhood friend, Niki. We each had a stroller with a wrapped-up baby doll, and as we walked we talked. How many kids did we want? (I always wanted six.) How old did we want to be when we got married? (Me—no later than 24.) Would we work when we had children? (Of course not! We'd obviously be smart enough to marry guys who made good money.)

It amazes me how God can bring everything full-circle in our lives. Those lazy summer days playing Mommy came back to me today. And all I could do was thank God for giving me the desires of my heart. For bringing me back around—from 'ambition' to just living. Sometimes, just living is exactly what we're supposed to do.

Thank-you, Lord, for letting me grow up to be a Mommy. Help me to remember that this is a gift from You, that ***they*** *are a gift from You. Teach me to just live.*

A New Message

Ever read 2 Corinthians 12:7-10 from 2 Corinthians and been a bit confused? I know I have. I mean, what *exactly* is a thorn in my flesh? And how *exactly* is it that a thorn in my flesh will keep me from being conceited?

For the first time today, I encountered this passage of scripture as written in The Message.

Because of the extravagance of those revelations, and so I wouldn't get a big head, I was given the gift of a handicap to keep me in constant touch with my limitations. Satan's angel did his best to get me down; what he in fact did was push me to my knees. No danger then of walking around high and mighty! At first I didn't think of it as a gift, and begged God to remove it. Three times I did that, and then he told me,
"My grace is enough; it's all you need.
My strength comes into its own in your weakness."
Once I heard that, I was glad to let it happen. I quit focusing on the handicap and began appreciating the gift. It was a case of Christ's strength moving in on my weakness. Now I take limitations in stride, and with good cheer, these limitations that cut me down to size—abuse, accidents, opposition, bad breaks. I just let Christ take over! And so the weaker I get, the stronger I become.

Sometimes all it takes is another interpretation. I just love this, "what he in fact did was push me to my knees . . . no danger then of walking around high and mighty." Nope, if I'm on my knees the only way to look is UP to the One I'm serving. Thorn in the flesh, handicap, struggle, accident, bad break—whatever you call it—it's the gift that keeps us from trying to climb our wee little selves up into the throne belonging to the Almighty.

Got Faith?

If you have never done a Bible study by Beth Moore, I would encourage you to do so! She doesn't write 'frou-frou' studies with cheesy homework. Nu-uh. Beth is one tough cookie, and she is not satisfied unless she's got her women digging deep.

We just completed "Believing God: Experiencing a Fresh Explosion of Faith" in our women's study at our Church. Words can never accurately express the life-changing qualities of this study. My good friend Christine is currently working through the book, and she is telling me that I HAVE to read it this summer. We participated in the DVD and study guide version, and I've been telling Christine that she simply MUST watch the DVDs. I'm telling you people, this is powerful stuff!

Here are some truths I learned about faith through Beth's inspired teaching.

— Faith is more than just believing *in* God, faith is the decision to *believe* God—to trust His Word and His promises and His power in our lives, no matter what our circumstances. (I liken it to the concept of love in marriage—sometimes love is much more a decision than it is a feeling. Ditto for faith—believing God is a *choice* we make regardless of our emotions.)

— The #1 hindrance to our calling becoming our reality is unbelief. Belief is the only thing that will bring our theology into alignment with our reality (it is the thing that makes our *walk* match our *talk*).

— To be righteous (clean in the eyes of God), He requires our active belief. Romans 4:3 says *What does the Scripture say? "Abraham believed God, and it was credited to him as righteousness."* Believing can't just be something we say, it is something we do. Abraham believed through his actions, even when it didn't make sense. (Remember when God asked him to sacrifice his long-awaited for son, Isaac???)

This begs the question—how does a person *get* this kind of faith? Beth gives us 5 pointers:

1. Because faith is a fruit of the Spirit (Galatians 5:22-23 KJV), we are given the gift of faith when we allow ourselves to be filled with the Spirit. To be filled with the Holy Spirit, we must be yielded to His authority. In the NIV the term faithfulness is used, which can be described as serving and obeying God. So, to get faith, we should be yielded to the Spirit and obey the Lord.
2. Our faith is built by hearing the Word of God. This builds relationship with Him, thus making it 'easier' to trust Him. Come on, people, let's read it!
3. We can simply ask God to increase our faith (John 14:14).
4. Scripture (Mark 9:14-25) tells us that we need to confess our unbelief. If we can't be honest with God about those times we struggle in faith, who can we trust? Pour it out to Him, and ask Him to change it.
5. We can GROW in our faith. As with every ability, practice makes perfect (well, we'll never truly be perfect this side of Heaven, but you get what I mean). Psalm 37:3 tells us to feed on God's faithfulness. In other words, watch for those times where He's provided, record them, and read them to remind yourself (and your children) of who God is in your life. The more you see God's work in your life, the more you will believe Him—the greater your faith will grow.

R.E.S.P.E.C.T.—1

I'm one of those people who don't really learn a concept until I've taught it to someone else. Take math, for example. You know all of those 'solve for x' equations? Not to toot my own horn, but I'm awesome at them! The reason—I give all the credit to my grade 10 girlfriend, Chrissie. She didn't get it. Trying to find 'x' made her crazy and frustrated, and brought tears on more than one occasion. So we hung out in the back row of math class and I showed her how to do it. Now it's stuck in my brain. More years later than I will ever admit, I can solve algebraic equations (much to the amazement of my nephew, whom I helped home/cyber school when he was in grade 8-9).

There's a new concept I was introduced to a while back, and though I 'get it,' I'm just not getting it. Know what I mean? While it makes total sense, I cannot seem to master the concept. So if you'll humour me while I teach this concept to you, I will be eternally grateful. (As will my loving husband.)

Not long ago, Pat and I joined a group of couples at our Church and worked through the 'Love and Respect' conference on DVD by Dr. Emerson Eggerichs. Throughout the video sessions, Eggerichs kept returning to this scripture.

*However, each one of you also must **love** his wife as he loves himself, and the wife must **respect** her husband.* ~ Ephesians 5:33

It's interesting that (through Paul) God gave husbands the directive to LOVE and gave wives the directive to RESPECT. We all know that men and women speak totally different languages, right? So it makes sense that we would find our value through different means. We women understand the language of love: hugs, kisses, tender words, thoughtful gestures, small (or large) gifts. Feeling loved by our husbands makes us feel needed in our marriages. Because these acts of love speak to our hearts, we naturally try to communicate this same love to our husbands. But this does not make him feel needed! Nope. I guess that's why God figured He'd better put it right there in scripture for us. In order to communicate our love to our husbands, we need to use the language of *respect*.

Am I making sense so far? (I'm hoping that my synopsis of what Eggerichs spent 6 hours teaching is enough to do it justice.) I totally GET that my man needs respect, that when I show him that I respect him he will thrive. Honestly, it makes sense. If Pat showers me with little romantic gestures, I positively glow! But here is where I get all tangled up . . . what speaks unconditional respect to my man? I'm sure I could say "honey, I respect you" in the same way I warm up to hear him tell me he loves me. But really, could we find a way to communicate respect that is a little less, um, cheesy?!

R.E.S.P.E.C.T.—2

We're talking about how men and women are different (men really are from Mars, I'm sure of it), and how God created us with these amazing differences. Because He created us, He knows the desires of our hearts and tells us the secret to meeting those desires in our spouses.

However, each one of you also must ***love*** *his wife as he loves himself, and the wife must* ***respect*** *her husband.* ~Ephesians 5:33

In the same way that we need to feel loved *unconditionally*—that is, no matter how we look or what we do, but simply for who we are—our men need to feel respected unconditionally (yes, no matter how they look or what they do, or don't do) just **for who they are**. This is a tough one to wrap my mind around because I've always learned that 'you have to earn respect.' I just want to translate that concept into girl language for a moment . . .

Imagine being told that you had to earn love. If you do a good job, keep the house nice and clean, make healthy and hearty meals, dote on your children (who, by the way, are perfectly-behaved little gems), never lose your temper—if you do all of these things, then you are worthy of being loved. But if you are lazy, if you gain weight, if you lose your temper and say things you don't mean—well, you don't deserve to be loved. Imagine your husband saying to you, "Are you kidding?! I don't LOVE you. You don't do anything to deserve my love. After all, love is EARNED!"

Now, to save my fingers, re-read that portion (but imagine manly-type duties in there and pretend it's you speaking to him, and change the word love for respect). How many of us have ever told our husbands that they don't deserve our respect? Just read the part in quotation marks one more time—he's saying this to you—feel what that does to your heart. Anyone else falling under some heavy conviction for past hurtful words of disrespect we've dumped on our men? OUCH.

In addition to finding creative ways to show our husbands that we respect them, we also need to know what kinds of things (that we do or say) communicate disrespect to them—so that we can stop making those mistakes!

R.E.S.P.E.C.T.—3

What do you do or say that shows your man that he's the thang in your life?

How do you make him feel special, valued, necessary, even heroic?

What mistakes have you made that made your loved one feel crummy, unimportant, and disrespected?

So here's my contribution for ya . . .

In the book (mentioned previously), they coin the term 'The Crazy Cycle.' I'm sure I don't need to elaborate, but for the sake of completing this post . . . She (or I) feels unloved —> she reacts by acting disrespectful —> he feels disrespected —> he reacts by acting unloving —> and so on. We've all been there. The tricky part is getting out of the crazy cycle. Years ago, when our arguing could go on for hours, with each of us prepared to fight to the death in order to prove a point and be right, Pat and I came up with a silly idea (perhaps the idea really originated in some book somewhere, but whatever). Why not break up the moment with a humorous code word? We chose "pickle." Even now, if we're bickering and feel as if it's going nowhere but round and round, one of us will say (or holler) "PICKLE!" And bump—we're off the crazy cycle once again. Phew.

Undeserving . . .

I received an amazing gift today . . .

There are times when I'm struck with the dirty state of my heart, surprised by it. Today was one of those days. I received a blessing, only to realize how truly undeserving I am.

You may recall that I lead the women's ministry at our Church. Generally, I love it. Love the women. Love doing what I know God has called me to do. Love serving. Love being busy. LOVE IT!

But sometimes . . . Well, there are days when I heave a big sigh before answering the phone for a ministry related call. My plate got quite a bit fuller over the past few months and a part of me resented that. I grumbled about how much I was doing, and I wasn't serving joyfully. All I could think about was how I just needed a break.

Looking back, I can see that I've had a complaining attitude for quite a while. I was never really vocal about complaining, but the grumbling was lingering in my heart and my mind. *I'm too busy. No one sees how much I do—around the house, with the kids, at the Church. Why can't the kids just be good? I can't believe I need to be parent helper again. I'm so tired after the ministry meeting last night. All I want is to have a night out with my husband, is that too much to ask?* On and on it went round my head. I launched myself head-first into martyr mode.

At our women's Bible study, we all jot down our prayer needs each week, and our leader compiles them in an email sent to everyone. Last week I wrote, "pray that I will find rest for my soul." After all, I deserve a break (insert sarcasm). It's funny, because God spoke to me about that right away—literally. The DVD began and the lesson was entitled **Believing God When Victory Demands Your All**. In case I was thick-headed, though, God backed up the first message through a couple friends telling me that some people aren't called to rest, or sabbatical, or whatever term you'd like to insert—rather, certain people are called to persevere through the times when they feel overwhelmed. Hmmmm . . .

It has really only been within the past few days that I've softened my heart to God's ways and resisted this complaining spirit. My eyes were opened to the fact that I haven't been too busy at all. Sure, I've been busy. Yet somehow (praises to my Abba) everything is in order. My house is clean. The laundry is done (and almost all put away). Our planning meetings for Friendship Factor (our outreach to women) is flowing so smoothly—and with a record-breaking team of 11 women! We had the most amazing family day ever last weekend (I'll tell you about that later). God is so good! Even as I selfishly complained in my mind, He continued to fill my life with His provision. This is my first undeserved gift—His grace and mercy. It really is new every morning.

My second undeserved gift has humbled me. I am so blessed. I don't always deserve it, especially not lately, but I received the beautiful honour of appreciation.

Two pastors showed up at my door—my supervising pastor and our executive pastor (who is also a friend and mentor). They brought me a gift! One handed me a big bouquet of flowers. At that moment I was practically (not totally, you know me) speechless. I couldn't believe that they came out of their way to my home to say thanks. *Wow, that is so beautiful. I don't deserve this.*

I was in the process of inviting them in for an iced tea, when the other handed me a gift bag. I started rummaging through the pile of gift cards and big envelope with some sort of papers in it . . . then I realized I should be a good girl and read the card (smile). I read the card, looked again at the gift cards, re-read the papers in the envelope. *I don't understand. What is this? Why are they giving me this? Where did it come from?*

Finally, I look at my pastors and tell them that I'm confused. They tell me that they wanted to do something special to show me that they appreciate me, and that the hours I work do not go unnoticed. *But Lord, I've been so grouchy. I haven't been serving You with my whole heart.* They are sending Pat and me away for a weekend. This weekend. To Canmore, in the majestic Rocky Mountains. In a luxurious hotel. With gift cards for dinners and gas. And a gift card so my sitter can go to dinner after her exhausting weekend (thanks Mom—I can't believe you got suckered into two weekends with 5 kids, one only a few weeks after the last).

I am so undeserving. But isn't that just like God? He just looks for opportunities to be merciful to us! He could have punished me for my complaining attitude. He could have let me burn out, or allowed women's ministry to flop, or sent someone to tell me that I wasn't doing the job He called me to. He could have placed His conviction over me to humble me. To bring me back to my knees so that I would be in the proper position to look up at Him. Instead, He showered me with gifts. Beautiful, precious gifts. The very things I've been selfishly complaining that I couldn't find—rest for my soul, time with my husband, a break. *Father, forgive me. I have such a black heart! I deserve shame and guilt, condemnation. Thank-you, Lord, for being merciful to me. I accept Your gift, humble and undeserving, but oh so grateful.*

Thank-you, dear pastors, for being instruments of the Almighty. He used you to bless my heart. He also used you to show me, once again, how badly He wants to forgive me every time I mess up. Beth Moore says that God is so desperate to show us His love and mercy that He will go to any means. He went so far as to send His very own baby Son to die, so that we would understand His deep love and grace. *Wow, God. Wow. Thank-you, Jesus.*

Lessons from the Road

Here are a few things I've learned along the way . . .

— Unpacking every evening and packing every morning is not fun, but you get really good at it after a couple days.
— Washington is far more beautiful than I would have ever imagined.
— Day 3 on the road with kids is THE WORST!
— Oregon beaches are unbelievable—massive rock formations, crashing surf, live starfish sticking to the rocks when the tide's out. Wow! Lovin' it!
— Just when you finally think you're going to get a couple straight hours of driving in, someone has to pee.
— If you give your small children a roll of quarters and make them pay you for bad behaviour, it doesn't take long before they realize being good is a better idea.
— Just when you've walked down approximately 300 stairs to the beach, someone has to go poop. Doing 300 stairs—both ways—twice—is really good exercise.
— It is impossible to eat well camping. IMPOSSIBLE!
— If you want seven people to sleep in a cabin built for four, you must make sure everyone is super-super tired.
— No matter how late you keep them up, babies still like to rise at the crack of dawn.
— These are the moments life-long memories are made of.
— KOA (Kampgrounds of America) are everywhere. And they are great! Clean, clean, clean, and a pool in practically every location. What could be better?!

Pinching Those Pennies—Groceries

In our home, I am responsible for keeping track of the budget, paying the bills, grocery shopping, and the like. I take this responsibility seriously. If Pat is out there working his hiney off to provide, it's my job to use what he's providing wisely.

With gas prices these days (they really are the cause of all our woes, aren't they?), it can be tough to make ends meet some months. I've been blessed with a best friend who is VERY wise in managing money, and she took the time to teach me a few tricks. Thanks, Christine!

Here's how to grocery shop on a dime (even for a large family) . . .

#1—**Establish your budget. How much do you have to spend on food?** It's important to base this number on the reality of what you can *afford to spend*, not on how much you think you need/should spend, or on how much you've spent in the past. If you are on a particularly tight budget, it is realistic to spend $100-$150 per family member for the month. Really, you can do it!

#2—**Take that money out, in cash.** I am notorious for spending twice what I planned to spend at the grocery store. It's easy to do with debit and credit cards. If you have only cash, and leave the cards at home, you have a fool-proof method to prevent overspending.

#3—**Make a meal plan!** I know, the dreaded meal plan. I feel your pain. But without a plan, you are not in control of what you spend. (It may be helpful to do step five first, so you know what you've already got to work with when you plan.)

#4—**Create a detailed supply list from your meal plan.** If you're making baking powder biscuits with dinner one night, you better make sure you've got all those ingredients on the list. It simply wouldn't do to be out of eggs, for example! Don't forget to note how much you'll need (for example, if you plan to serve frozen mixed veggies a lot, you'll want to write down that you need 2 bags).

#5—**Go through your pantry.** Cross off items you've already got. That leaves you with your shopping list.

#6—**Price it out in advance.** Go through the shopping list item by item jotting down the approximate price (it's always better to estimate a bit high—it would be embarrassing to estimate too low and not have enough money once you get to the cashier . . . been there, done that). Calculate it all out. Does it fit your budget? If yes, well—go shopping! (see step 8.) If not, go for step 7.

#7—**Go through flyers and coupons.** Cut coupons for items you regularly buy (don't bother with those coupons that are 'a great deal' if they are for items you don't need—they'll just tempt you). Watch for sales. (Sometimes our stores will have 2-for-1 meat sales, where you can buy a pack of 3 pork roasts for $15-20 and you get the second pack of 3 for free. That's SIX roasts for $20—for us, 3-4 meals worth of meat.) Some stores have certain discount days, such as 15% off on the first Tuesday of the month. There have been times where I've driven to four or five different stores to get all that I need for the month.

#8—**Shop slowly and carefully.** Take your calculator and keep a running total. Shop ONLY from your list. Comparison shop—is the generic brand significantly cheaper? Maybe it's worth trying (though I don't recommend this for ketchup—Heinz really is better). I strongly suggest getting a sitter or leaving the kids home with hubs—children are distracting from this process and will cause you to make mistakes, and if they're anything like mine they'll be constantly badgering you to buy them items that are not on the list.

Have fun shopping on a budget! And take pride in it—rather than seeing it as a reflection of tight financial times, recognize that it is a skill and a talent and that you are giving a gift to your family (and your husband) by managing your resources wisely.

A wife of noble character who can find? She is worth far more than rubies . . . She is like the merchant ships, bringing her food from afar . . . She provides food for her family . . . She watches over the affairs of her household and does not eat the bread of idleness . . . Her children arise and call her blessed; her husband also, and he praises her: "Many women do noble things, but you surpass them all." ~Proverbs 31:1, 14, 15b, 27-29

A Rebel Without A Cause

Deep down in my heart, I love peace and order. I appreciate rules and like to follow them (most of the time). I am happy when things are in their assigned place. I live by lists. Any other Type As out there know what I'm talking about?

You'd think with this profile that I must have been an obedient child, a well-behaved teen, and a role-model as a young adult. But somewhere deep within lurks a nasty seed of rebellion . . .

Reflecting on my teen years is a dangerous thing, because I now see things through the eyes of a mother—with three daughters! It makes me love and appreciate my mom even more. It also makes me want to apologize to her.

While I was pregnant with my first, I became aware that I needed to grow up. I realized that I needed Jesus in my life—because there was no way I could do this motherhood thing without Him. Things like establishing a heritage of faith became very important to me. So I put aside my rebellious ways . . . Or so I thought.

Somewhere in my teen years I began a different pattern of rebellion. I rebelled against anything that was 'in' or 'cool' or 'trendy.' In many ways this was a natural response to the financial constraints that prevented me from achieving 'cool.' My mom was, for many years, single-parenting me. So there were some basic guidelines about shopping—she would buy what I needed, I had to take care of what I wanted. The one and only pair of Tommy Hilfiger jeans I owned took me months of saving! It didn't take me long to realize that no matter how hard I strove to fit in, I would not have the many trappings that were expected of the 'in' crowd. *(I tried to use the word "strived" here; apparently spellchecker thinks that word doesn't exist, but "strove" isn't much better, is it?)*

So what does one do when one realizes becoming popular is impossible? Well, one becomes bound and determined to avoid all things popular, to develop a strong disdain for all things trendy. Because the last thing one wants is for anyone to find out that one really does want nothing more than acceptance.

I chose to convert my desperate need to feel accepted by my peers into a passion for making choices that would make me different. Anyone else done this? I see so many teens heading through the mall in their 'goth' and 'emo' outfits (complete with makeup) and I think to myself, "I've got you figured . . ."

I just realized that that is still me. Even at 30-years-old, I mask my true desire to be accepted with a veneer of disdain for virtually anything considered trendy. Here are a few things I've been rebelling against . . .

Nice clothing. I continue to shop at Wal-Mart for clothing. Which would be fine (and it is nice financially, and given my frequent size changes), except that I choose casual over 'grown-up' every time. I was folding laundry yesterday and realized that 90% of my wardrobe is 100% cotton. I want to look nice, put-together, attractive, yet my heart of rebellion keeps me buying exercise gear and jeans—because I don't want people to think I all-of-a-sudden care about looking good and fitting in. *By the way, if 'What Not to Wear' comes to Canada, and anyone would like to nominate me, I'd gladly buy you a Timmy's coffee for your troubles!*

The environment. I barely recycle. I use disposable diapers and plastic bags at alarming rates. If I don't use way too much water and electricity it's simply because I'm trying to save money. People are forever talking about 'going green.' Everyone seems to be hopping on the 'environmentally friendly bandwagon.' But not me—nu-uh! I'm not going to start being all crazy about saving the environment . . . because we all know that nothing we do now can actually repair the damage that's been done, so ultimately it's just another one of those trendy things. *(*Being self-deprecating here . . . I really DO care, I just resist showing it.)*

Homeschooling. Before you get all excited—I WILL NOT be homeschooling my children anytime soon! I don't believe God is placing that call on me. But in the past I have made the same statement while in my head I thought, "I know, I know, all the cool moms are doing it. What is WITH this crazy trend, anyway? I will NEVER . . ." It really is a growing trend, and I do believe that there are a lot of moms doing it for the wrong reasons—such as fitting in, being admired, feeling like 'Super Mom.' But I realize, too, that there are a lot of women homeschooling because God has called them to—because that's what's best for them and their children, for this time in their lives.

Organic food. I've always said that I don't 'believe' in organic food. What I mean is that I don't buy all the hype that it's really better. I don't necessarily believe that all the kids who are being raised on organic have any less chance of developing cancer than we do. But largely, I've just been busy rebelling against the ever-growing popularity of eating organic. I'd rather just choose to be different. Every now and then I wonder, though, if what I'm feeding my kids does make a difference . . .

Lately, I have been praying against the spirit of rebellion in our family's history (there are many rebellious souls on both sides). I have been asking God to break that chain in our family, so that our children will be free from its hold. I am claiming His deliverance for my children, so that they will have hearts to walk in obedience to Him (and their parents) and not test Him (or us). I see the fruits of such rebellion in my nephew, who has turned far away from the Lord, and my heart breaks at the idea of my own children taking that same path.

I find it interesting that once I began praying against rebellion (which I thought I had 'grown out of'), God is showing me how rebellious my heart still is. God is a funny guy!

Disclaimer: This post is in no way intended to offend those who eat organic, homeschool their children, care about the environment, or dress nicely. I love you all very much and do not at all presume that your choices are based on the current trends. Once God deals with the rebellious nature of my heart, I may very well be doing some of those same things (with the exception of the homeschooling, though—really, I have my limits).

Reading Rainbow . . .

Anyone remember that show? I hear the tune playing in my head right now—it's all I can do to keep myself from singing it out "reading rainbowwwwwww!"

I love to read. If you come to my house you will find books on every handy surface—coffee table, toilet tank, bedside table, kitchen counter, odd little shelf by my front door. You get the picture. Even right now—there is literally a book on each of those surfaces.

Some are partially read and just sitting there waiting for me to return to them. (If a book doesn't grab me early on, I will often move on to another and come back to the original book in a week or two. The Type A in me won't allow me to leave a book unfinished (or a movie, for that matter) no matter how boring. So here's the rainbow of reading materials you would find scattered about my house this morning—if you were to stop over unannounced for a coffee. Which you should totally do, by the way!

Coffee table:
"No Other Gods: Confronting Our Modern-Day Idols" (The Living Room Series) by Kelly Minter. We've got a small group of us working through this together over the summer, on Wednesday nights. This is a LifeWay book, so my assumption from the beginning is that it wouldn't be a 'fluffy' study. The homework in week one left me disappointed, but let me tell you about week two—man, oh, man was it tough stuff! There were just four of us last night (three lucky girls were on holidays) and did we ever d.i.g. The book is designed for small-group in-home studies, offering recipes for dinner and dessert for each week. I baked last week. I'll say it again so you can grasp the importance of such a statement . . . I BAKED!

"The Busy Mom's Devotional: 10 Minutes a Week to a Life of Devotion" by ~~Lisa T. Bergren~~. This book is one of the first things I've won—ever! I am so thankful to Cindy for sending it to me, because it is good! I often find myself disappointed in devotional books. There are so many that you can just breeze through and never find the gems. But this book (and it really is only 10 minutes, once a week—no dates, it's divided by handy-dandy seasons) reaches in and touches my woman's heart. Lisa shares stories from her life and relates them to scripture, and she gets her readers into the Word, placing it in their hearts. My only complaint—I wish there were more, because I could do it every day!

"Believing God: Experiencing a Fresh Explosion of Faith" study guide by Beth Moore. I cannot say enough about this study. Because of this study (we did the DVD series with the study guide) my walk with God has been forever changed. I was challenged and stretched, pushed and pulled, and God's Word is more deeply embedded in my spirit. I wrote a post about it here, and eventually there will be more . . . I'm done working through it, but I'm keeping it handy because there is stuff in there that applies to every experience—it has become my second reference-guide.

Kitchen Counter:
"One Tuesday Morning" (book 1 of 2 in the September 11 series) by Karen Kingsbury. She is by far my favourite Christian fiction author! Every single book she's written has brought me tears and joy. Her stories are so true to life, real people with their real pain and heartache, a real God who brings reconciliation. I've always got to have one fiction book on the go (to take my mind off all the deep thought), and about 80% of the time it is by Kingsbury. I think I may have read just about everything she's ever written by now, though, so if you have another author to recommend I'd sure appreciate your suggestions!

Toilet Tank:
"The Explosive Child" (revised and updated) by Ross W. Greene, Ph.D. The caption of the book says "a new approach for understanding and parenting easily frustrated, chronically inflexible children."

I haven't gotten far, but I'm certain I'll finish this one in the next week or so, because I NEED SOME SUGGESTIONS! If it's good, and I try some of the ideas, I'll post about it. If you want me to. Well, it's my blog, I'll post about it whether you want me to or not, lol. **I just looked at the location of this book and its title—too funny! No pun intended.*

Bedside Table:
"The Prince" by Francine Rivers (book 3 of the Sons of Encouragement series). She's also my favourite author. Hey—I can have 2 faves if I want to! Rivers has a few novels that are totally fiction and will leave you sobbing (in particular "The Atonement Child" and "And The Shofar Blew"), but this series is special. Rivers does fiction based on scripture. This book is about Jonathan. I just finished the ones about Aaron and Caleb. Rivers has a gift for taking characters and scenes from scripture and elaborating on them (adding private thoughts, emotions, etc.) to make them come alive. This particular series tells the stories of "5 men who quietly changed eternity." She's also told the stories of some remarkable women of the Bible in "Lineage of Grace" and of Hadassah and her family in the Mark of the Lion series. Try reading one—the moment you put it down you will be rushing to your Bible to read the scriptural account!

Front Door Shelf:
"The Organic God" by Margaret Feinberg. This book was a gift from my Pastor. It is refreshing and insightful (and funny), but something hasn't grabbed at me quite enough to hold my interest. I have it dog-eared on page 140, chapter 8—"Unbelievably Stubborn" (yes, I dog-ear my pages all the time, forgive me, or not, whatever). I think when I do return to this book I will start over—I can see that I've made oodles of notes in the margins of the first 7 chapters, so it's obviously got some good stuff in there. I've got a serious case of book ADD.

I'll be honest with you here. There are more books in the piles in these locations. But I'm worried that you're getting bored with my sadly written book reviews (totally not my strong point). And really, it looks bad enough that I've got 7 books on the go (and of course my Bible—which is also on the coffee table—best book EVER written) and 5 children who are obviously being neglected and not properly fed while I pour through my many books. How terrible would it sound if I confessed that (including my Bible) there are actually 12 books that I am reading?!

How many books do you have on the go?

A Bunch of Handy Little Lists

Our pastor recently did a series on Song of Songs. I loved each sermon and learned a lot about marriage and sex, dating, and so on. So here are a couple notes I came across while cleaning out my purse.

7 Things Before You Say "I Do"—doing your homework to check out the other person's *character* (based on Song 2):

1. devotion—does he/she have eyes only for you?
2. desire—is it there? and are you both prepared to wait to fulfill it?
3. excitement—anticipation to be together, sacrifice, attention to detail
4. life and growth—are you inspired to be a better person? (rather than dragged down)
5. tenderness—affection, encouragement, builds you up
6. discovery/disclosure—it's better to reveal the baggage than to have deceit
7. covenant—total security in sickness, poverty, reality (a covenant says 'I will,' a contract says 'I'll try')

Why Relationships Go Bad:

— neglect to ask God for wisdom in evaluating your spouse's character *before* marrying
— neglect to build Godly friendships who will stand behind your marriage
— not enough time spent talking about expectations—before and during
— advancing the relationship too quickly (if you advance too soon physically, you skip past emotional connection)

And my personal favourite, taken from the refrigerator door of our pastor and his wife during their kids' teen years . . .

Rules of Dating:

1. Don't unzip anything.
2. Don't unbutton anything.
3. Do not lift anything up.
4. Do not pull anything down.
5. Keep your tongue in your own mouth.
6. Don't touch anything that sticks out.

Quote of the Day

Driving in the car today, belting out the VBS worship songs with the kids, Abbey tells me . . .

"The nails didn't hold Jesus to the cross. It was His love that held Him there."

I couldn't even speak for the ginormous lump in my throat.

My Anniversary Gift

I may have mentioned that today is my anniversary. Well, technically it's not MY anniversary—it's OUR anniversary. Pat and I, that is. Nine years married. I can hardly believe it's been so long—almost a decade. Yet it feels like the time flew by so quickly that I can't even comprehend how we've arrived here.

In honour of this special day, I want to tell you a bit about our marriage . . .

We did things in the wrong order, not the way God intended for them to be. We discovered we were expecting a baby, and a few months later moved in together. Those months during my pregnancy were tough. You know how I get a wee bit of PMS? Well, multiply the hormones coursing through my body exponentially . . . Oh, poor Pat. I was a wreck. This is one of the many reasons I love him beyond measure—Pat stuck with me through my crying, yelling, pouting hysterics. He is a good man.

When Braeden was a year-and-a-half old, we had our big day. The time preceding that big day was no walk in the park, though. That's how it can be when you don't do things God's way—rough, tough, and painful. We fought. A LOT. It wasn't nice. Here's another reason I love Pat—he was totally committed. No matter how rocky things got, he was definitely in this thing for life. (I've never felt more special and loved than the day I told him I thought we should just call it quits and he told me that 'divorce was not an option.')

Over the past nine years, I have discovered a million things I love about Pat, as we've grown and learned together. But the thing about Pat that I love the most is his deep commitment to me, our marriage, and our family. He is willing to do whatever it takes to show his love. He makes me feel absolutely precious. Honestly, there aren't words to describe what that does to a girl! Here's just a few highlights:

Our first year of marriage, 1999-2000: Pat took his job of providing for our family seriously, and made sure we were able to have the things we needed (and some nice little extras that we wanted).

2000-2001: Pat cheered me on and supported me while I finished my university degree. I was in school full-time, working Saturdays (for the experience), and volunteering about 10 hours per week—and he never complained. Not once!

2001-2002: Pat and I had the joyful experience of 'planning' a baby together. In spite of my 'issues' while pregnant with Braeden, Pat was willing to endure another nine months to make me happy.

2002-2003: We moved to Calgary for Pat's work. He knew it was hard for me, so he made sure I got to come back to Red Deer lots. And after the birth of Megan, when we realized I was struggling with post-partum depression, he didn't even hesitate—we moved back immediately. Pat has always made sure I know that I am a priority in his life.

2003-2004: My man again showed his commitment to our marriage by taking me on a 'Marriage Enrichment' weekend hosted by our Church. (We all know how much of stretch that must have been, but for me he did it. Absolute sweetheart—that's Pat. BTW, this was a life-changing experience, so if you've never gone to one—DO IT!)

2004-2005: Pat had a vasectomy after Megan was born, as we both thought we had our hands full enough. When I told him I was expecting baby #4, he reacted with joy. No questions, no doubts, no disappointment. What he didn't say told me that he loved me more than any words.

2005-2006: This year was a difficult one for me in ministry. I was worn out and feeling beaten down. But Pat wouldn't let me give up! He pushed me forward, he comforted me, and he prayed for me. He affirmed my role in ministry—even though it took my time away from him and the kids. When there was ministry stuff to do, Pat would take care of everything at home and send me away—guilt-free. What a blessing! (He still does that today. For our last women's retreat, he even insisted that I leave the 6-month-old baby at home with him.)

2006-2007: You may have heard that Pat only wanted one child . . . But he has embraced our big family wholeheartedly! I have never seen a Dad have so much loud, crazy fun as Pat when he's playing 'Tickle Monster' with his children. (I believe this insane game was invented in late 2006.)

2007-2008: One thing I've noticed this past year is that given the choice, Pat wants to hang out with me! (Don't get me wrong, he still does stuff with the guys—that's important, too.) He tells me I'm his best friend, and he really means it. And he's my best friend, too. Really, there's no one I'd rather spend my days with.

I love Pat's zany sense of humour, the way he can make me laugh when I'm feeling grouchy. I love his generosity to his friends and family. I love seeing how he adores his children and plays with them. I love his eyes, his smile, his laugh, his butt (heehee). But if I had to pick just one thing, I love his love. He pours out his love and commitment in everything he does. I feel it, know it, believe it. I am loved by my husband. And that is the best anniversary gift a girl could ever ask for!

Happy anniversary, honey. Thanks for loving me.

Keepin' It Real

I have a problem. I don't trust God. Well, that's not entirely true—in theory, I totally trust Him. But my actions speak differently. I like to plan and prepare and problem-solve. In short, I like to be in control. And trusting God requires that I relinquish my control.

One area that I've had particularly difficult time with is finances. Let's face it, there are times when I spend more than is coming in. And since I'm the one who takes care of our family's finances, this is my responsibility (read: under my control). At those times when there seems to be a bit less money than bills, it's easy to justify disobedience to God. *I'll just skip tithing for this paycheque, but I'll make up the amount in two weeks. Well, I can't pay all the bills and get all the food we need, so I guess I'll skip this bill and make it up next month. These are just tiny examples of my internal struggle.*

This week, though, there was a WAR going on in my heart and mind. Because of Braeden's disability, I receive some government funding to help in hiring skilled, adult, professional, trained people to do childcare (sometimes the teenager from down the street simply won't do). I was completing my paperwork, and realized that I have some unused hours for this contract year (my contract year begins July 1). Which means there was money available to me right now, but next week it would be gone forever. And I'm not talking a bit of extra pocket change—it was a BIG number.

God has been working on me in this area. He's promised me that He will provide for all our needs, if I just trust and obey Him. If I stick to the planned budget, if I meal plan and take my calculator grocery shopping, if I tithe first, pay bills second, and get groceries and gas last—He will ensure we have what we need. But I haven't been very careful with the budget, and I've spent some money foolishly on things we didn't need. So it's my responsibility to find more money, right? And then I discover this money that is practically sitting in my lap.

For some of you, you're thinking—*duh, stealing from the government is A BAD THING TO DO.* I know. I knew. Yet I wrestled this over in my heart for days. I prayed, I repented, then I coveted that money all over again. I prayed that the Lord would show me a way to turn away from this temptation, so that I wouldn't sin. Then I did the only thing left to do—I called my best friend who I knew I could trust to set my mind straight. Since I've been dying to use this phrase, and it perfectly fits this situation, indulge me . . . **I got a WORD, y'all!** Christine said to me, "a sin with your eyes wide open is a sin directly against God."

Having the matter firmly settled in my heart, I completed my paperwork for the hours I used and bid farewell to those I didn't. Signed, sealed, and delivered. I feel so free! And can I just tell you what God does with obedience, people? He blesses it!

Yesterday we returned some left-over supplies from the whole roofing project. There was enough money to buy all the household supplies I had run out of, plus a couple extras. Today, as I was pulling on my jeans, I found money in the back pocket. And not just five bucks. Enough money to pay for my Bible study book (which I need to pay for tonight), and to pay my Weight Watchers fee this morning, and even a bit extra above and beyond that.

I can't get over it! God is so good. I am faithless, like the Israelites wandering the desert. I am provided for and blessed, but the moment things seem a bit difficult I stop trusting and start complaining. I try to control my own destiny. Crazy and foolish. I've said it before, but I am so thankful that His mercies are new every morning. I deserve nothing less than death, yet He gives me life abundant.

Oh Canada, Our Home and Native Land

It's easy to complain. Gas prices are too high. It's too rainy. Too hot. Church was too long. Worship was too short. There's never enough money for this, that, and the other thing.

But today, I will not complain. We live in a country of great wealth and freedom. We are a blessed people. Why God chose for me to be born here I don't know, but I am so thankful.

Education is next to free, and is not only available for every child, but is mandated. Food is abundant, and if you are unable to afford food for your family there are many charitable organizations and food banks that will meet your needs. Everyone has a vehicle. Everyone has a cell phone. We are free to vote and free to choose not to vote—and whether we voted or not we are free to share our opinions on those in office. Churches rest on every corner, inviting all people. We can go to any Church we want, or (sadly) choose none. But there is no fear in either choice. Abundance flows, yet we are free to complain. And we do so, often.

This country is a land flowing with milk and honey. It is a refuge for the abused, battered, and endangered of other lands. This land is a place where freedom reigns for all. Today, I will not complain.

Happy Canada Day!

Thank-you, Lord, for placing our family in this blessed country. Thank-you for Your provision and Your freedom. I praise You for democracy and social services, for public education and freedom of religion. Lord God, bring revival in this land, for Your Name's sake.

Turn our eyes toward Your Son. Place Your hand of guidance on our political leaders. And Father, because of the wealth and freedoms that we enjoy, remind us to use our resources to bless the impoverished and abandoned people from around the world. Thank-you, Jesus. Amen.

Thankfulness

I was reminded today about the importance of having an attitude of gratitude.

It's so easy to be thankful for a list of good things in my life when my house is peaceful and my kids are being good. It's easy to sit down on Thanksgiving Day grateful for many things, then go home that night and be grouchy and miserable. What's difficult is being thankful for the blessings in life when things are not going smoothly. But I know that's what God expects of me, as His daughter. If I want others to see Jesus in me, the noticeable difference will be if I choose to be grateful during times of stress and struggle. If I choose to be joyful and thankful for the 'un'blessings in my life.

So I will praise the Lord for the tiredness I feel today, because I know there are many women with no children to keep them up at night. I will give thanks as I listen to my husband's snores at night, because there are wives whose husbands are away working, or fighting for freedom, or who have run away and left their families. I will smile and enjoy the constant commentary on 'families these days,' because I am one of the few who still has a strong, healthy, living Grandma. I will crank up the praise music over the bickering of my children in the van, because we are so blessed to have a vehicle (and one that fits our entire family, no less). I will scrub toilets and floors with a smile upon my face, for the Lord has provided us with a beautiful house that we can call home.

No more time to be wasted complaining and grumbling. Every little 'un'blessing that I might find to complain about exists only because of the abundance He has provided. Thanks be to God that my stomach is never empty, my clothes are not tattered, my house is heated, the biggest worry my children have is who's turn it is next. God is so good . . .

I Couldn't Have Said It Better . . .

There have been times in my life when I've found myself confused (surprise, surprise).

We're supposed to love and serve God first, then our husbands, then our children, and so on . . . But what happens when those things conflict? Then what do we do? Who do we follow?

Here's a practical example for you. Early in our marriage, I was attending Church and (tepidly) following the Lord. Pat wasn't there yet—he wasn't sure about all that 'religious' stuff. I sat in on a powerful sermon about tithing, and felt called to obedience by it. But the money in our account wasn't put there by me, and we had always agreed that expenses over a certain amount needed to be unanimous. To say that Pat wasn't particularly excited about my idea of giving a significant portion of his earnings to a Church he seldom attended is an understatement.

So what was a girl to do? For weeks I obsessed over this—obey God's Word and defy my husband? Honour my husband and disobey God? I did eventually work this out . . . I found other ways to tithe (of my time and talents) and waited for God to work out the money thing . . . which he has.

Every now and then, someone asks me about a similar situation. I can look up some handy scripture references for them (Ephesians 5:22-24, I Peter 3:1-5), but it can be so difficult to explain in a way that makes sense!

This Is Why I Do It

When I started out writing, I wasn't really sure what I was doing or why I was doing it.

There was a little resistant and rebellious part of me that didn't want to take up with this new fad. Only recently have I realized how this part of myself has been allowed to make far too many decisions on behalf of the whole me. Ultimately, I think the seeds of rebellion sprout up and take root in those of us who live under 'fear of rejection.' If we disqualify ourselves from the 'in crowd' by being opposite, they will have no opportunity to reject us, right?

Then there was the little competitive voice in my head telling me to do it, and do it better than everyone else. To be honest, this voice has always frightened me a bit, because it is the echo of 'fear of failure.' If being the best equals success, not being the best equals failure, right?

Deep with me, though, is another meaning. Something far greater than being out or fitting in, success or failure, rebellion or competition. This part of me, this deeper meaning, overrides my fears. This is the Holy Spirit within me, and He is my Counsellor. He leads me on the right path, tells me when to turn to the left or the right. For reasons I could not understand, I sensed the a nudging to go ahead and start a blog.

My mind tried to rationalize this heart nudge. *Maybe God will use my blog to grow an amazing and wonderful ministry!* (Whoa, back off competitive Tyler.) *What if no one ever reads it? Maybe I've been getting prideful and God wants to humble me.* (Ease up, insecure Tyler.)

Ultimately, my heart just told me to be me. Be real. Be open. Whether the Lord used what I wrote to bless and encourage others, or whether He used it to grow me. The end result isn't usually what matters with God. More often than not, He calls us to walk in obedience, and that's the **real** purpose. Not what will happen as a result, simply the fact that we are doing as He asks. So, I blogged.

Through this blogging thing, I have been blessed. No—I do not get 10,000 hits per day or 50 comments on every post. I'm not the best. The most beautiful thing about that is—I'm okay with it! A few people read what I write, they comment, I reply, and friendships are formed. I have emailed these new friends for advice on blogging, marriage, and child-raising. They have even emailed me for advice sometimes! (How crazy is that?!)

Children Aren't All That Different

We've been reading up on training our puppy, because we want to ensure that she is well-behaved now and as a large, adult dog. Our favourite source for information is "Dogs for Dummies" (2nd Edition)_by Gina Spadafori. I'm finding that many of the tips for puppy training can just as easily be applied to the children . . .

#1 - Resolve that you *must* train your dog, and that training is not a one-shot deal, but an intrinsic and ongoing part of the promise you make to your dog when you bring her into your life.

#2 - You should always be thinking of how you're molding this little baby into the confident, obedient dog of your dreams. It takes socialization, and it takes training. And most of all, it takes *time*.

#3 - Never let your puppy do anything you wouldn't want a grown dog to do.

#4 - Remember that *preventing* bad habits is easier than fixing them later.

#5 - If you want your puppy to learn, you need to be *consistent* about what's acceptable behavior and what's not. Follow through with the ground rules, every time. No letting things slide because you're tired [or] because he's cute.

#6 - Loosening the rules is easier than tightening them. Once your puppy is a well-mannered dog, you can invited him up on the couch or teach him to put his paws on your shoulder and give you a big slurpy kiss. The distinction between him doing what he wants and him doing what he wants *with your permission* is a big one.

#7 - If your puppy has been running around for a long time and just seems bratty, he may be tired. If that's the case, put him down for a nap in his crate. Ignore his fussing. Chances are he'll be asleep in a few minutes.

Some of the best parenting advice out there, wouldn't you agree?

Family Funnies

Megan (5) about the brand-new portable DVD player with 2 screens—"That is OFF THE HOOK!!!" *Seriously, where do they come up with this stuff?!*

Shea (3), broken-hearted that the girls in the row behind her wouldn't play with her, "They not be my buddy." *Aw, I would've even felt bad for her had it not been for the wailing that followed.*

Abbey (6) really bonded with one of her cousins, A. She may have a slight crush, as it seems she thinks he hung the moon. All we heard her say, for the whole three days driving home, "A says this . . . A says that." If anyone disagreed (including parents), she would grow quite insistent. We finally just gave up. If A says it's true, then it must be so . . . *I also noticed this phenomenon with the Kindergarten teacher. When did everyone else become the expert and I became the 'dumb mom?'*

And my personal favourite . . .

Braeden (10) discussing driving. Braeden asks Dad if he can have a Mustang when he's old enough to drive. A teasing debate ensues about whether Mustangs really are 'just for girls' as Dad insists, or the 'coolest cars ever' in Braeden's humble opinion. When the goofiness settled down, Dad (referring to an old rusty Ford pick-up parked behind our garage) tells Braeden he can have his truck when he turns 16. Braeden responds with more excitement than we could have imagined, shrieking and 'woohoo'ing and bouncing up and down. He says, "Dad, you rock! Can I have your job, too?!" *About an hour later, once Pat and I had wiped the tears from our eyes and caught our breath, he explained to Braeden that he wasn't referring to* ***that*** *truck (his work truck).* Braeden's disappointment was palpable, "Bummer, dude."

Big Bang?

Have you ever heard of the "Big Bang Theory?" I'm certain I won't do it justice, but my understanding is that; basically, the earth and all things on it came into existence at one moment in time. This moment was a massive, cataclysmic explosion in outer space. One moment there is nothing but empty space. The next . . . Crash, boom, bang—earth exists, plant life exists, animals exist, people exist.

The interesting thing about this theory (for me, at least) is that proponents of it claim that it is the only logical scientific way of explaining things. Many people (at least those I've met) who believe in the "Big Bang" are those you would consider scientists—well educated, logical, analytical.

Now, I don't want to get into an argument of intellect. I haven't done all the research and can't back my beliefs with "cold, hard evidence." But then, neither can the scientists! I may have lost a lot of my book learning in my years of mothering, but I'm certain I recall one basic principal along the lines of *it takes matter to create matter*. Don't quote me on that, though. You get my drift, I'm sure. The big bang doesn't seem particularly scientific.

Personally, I believe in creation. There is a God—ONE God—who is mighty and powerful, all-knowing and omnipresent. He created the earth, the creatures, the plants, and the people. He created it all for His own enjoyment. He enjoys relationship, desires relationship, and created the earth and all things on it so that they can be in relationship with Him.

I don't have scientific proof (though I have heard some good solid evidence that seems to support creation), but I do have this . . . .

The desert. Wide open spaces filled with deep, dry heat. Winds gusting over the lands. Stark, yet beautiful.

The ocean. Water on the earth meets water on the sky. Crashing waves pummel giant cliffs, shaping them into jutting rock formations. Tides moving back and forth, changing the shoreline moment by moment.

The forest. Towering trees dance and cast their shadows on the inhabitants below. Leaves reach for the skies, roots dig to the springs hidden within the earth. Ever growing and changing.

The mountains. Giants, pressing heavenward, pushed up from the earth below. Snow-capped peaks on top, lush valleys and beaches below. Majestic. Incomparable. Unfathomable.

In my heart, in my spirit, there is no other explanation. All this indescribable beauty could only have been placed here by a Divine Creator's loving hands.

Not at all scientific, but plain, simple truth nonetheless. Big bang? I think not.

My Prerogative

Last night Kai started fussing just before 11pm.

We were in already in bed (getting old, I know), chatting about our days. I looked at Pat and said, "Your son is crying. You should go take him a bottle." *Yes, he's still waking in the night. I'm just too tired to tough out the crying required to get him sleeping through. Sigh.*

Pat laughed and challenged me to a game of Paper-Rock-Scissors for the duty. One, two, three—rock, rock. Again—scissors (Pat), paper (me).

I insisted that PRS is always best of three.
One, two, three—rock, rock. Again—paper (Pat), rock (me).

He smirks and rolls over, making some smart comment about how I should bring him a drink of water when I come back. So I did what any self-respecting woman would do—I whined (with a flirtatious smile on my face, of course)! "But honeeeeeey, I always have to get up with him in the middle of the niiiiiight. The least you can do is take him a bottle when you're still up." (insert the batting of eyelashes)

So my sweet, darling husband rolled out of bed and took his baby a bottle. When he came back to bed I was giggling. He gave me a long-suffering patience kinda look. I decided it wise to keep my smart mouth shut. But honey, here's what I was giggling about . . .

The moral of the story is—even when I'm wrong, I'm right; even when I lose, I win. From now on you should just do what I want right from the start and save yourself the humiliation.

LOL!

Beauty

I'm not generally one who finds lovely little analogies in everyday moments. But today, I saw something that simply begged for me to tell it.

A little girl and her grandma sat down in Tim Horton's for an afternoon treat. One must have been about seven and-a half (my guess based on the two-tooth sized gap at the bottom of her smile). The other, sixty years older or so. The little one was a tow-head with straight, fine hair past her shoulders. The older one, gracefully coloured hair in a beautiful shade of auburn. The young one had pale, unblemished skin; the older had dark spots of age smattering across her hands. The contrast was so striking.

Grandma opened a bag containing two long johns covered in chocolate, each with a dash of sprinkles on one end. In typical zest-of-youth style, the girl dove into her long john sprinkled end first. Grandma started at the other end, apparently saving the best for last. I watched them enjoying one another's company, chit-chatting about their weeks, nibbling away until their doughnuts were less than half their original size.

Then the grandma reached out to her grand-daughter, and offered to trade doughnuts with her. The girl seemed a bit confused, but quickly accepted the trade once she realized that she would have the pleasure of eating BOTH of the sprinkled ends.

Their exchange reminded me of the Christian walk.

When we are "young" we tend to dive in to "the good stuff" as quickly as possible. We don't want to wait even one moment for those delicious sprinkles. We don't hesitate or waste any time.

As we get "older" we take things more slowly. We tend to wait, hoping to save the best for last. We savour every single bit that takes us closer to the sprinkled end.

Neither approach is wrong, nor right—just different. Sometimes it's wisest to go slowly and methodically, waiting for the good things God has in store. Other times we should hurry and do what He asks quickly, with all our hearts and energy.

The true beauty, though, is what happens if we do the "wrong" thing. Perhaps sometimes we jump in, full of fervour, not thinking of the consequences. We rush ahead of God's plan and push our way through. We eat the sprinkles first, when we should have saved them for later. But God, in His ever-patient and understanding way, seldom lets us end that way. He doesn't like to leave us empty and disappointed, having gobbled down the sweet sprinkles too quickly. Rather, He extends His hand of grace and trades doughnuts with us. He lets us have the delicious reward at the end of the journey, in spite of our own impulsiveness.

We sit there, confused. Knowing that we did nothing to deserve such a sweet reward. That's the perfection of God's grace—He is ready to hand us the end with the sprinkles on it, even before we ask.

My Heart for Women

A question I was asked: Although all those ministry things are great and bring glory to the Lord, do you still feel the Lord leading you to serve there, or are you just doing because you've simply always done it? I hope that's not offensive to you . . . cause I know I can do that at times . . . I just keep serving somewhere even though I feel the Lord moving me somewhere else but I don't want to hurt feelings by moving on. Ya know what I mean?

Yes, my secret friend, I do know what you mean! There have been many times where I've realized that I am doing this.

For years, I helped in the nursery at our Church. I felt I should—after all, I've put a lot of strain on the system! LOL! Every time I helped in the nursery I would head home after Church feeling exhausted and cranky, and every little sound my own children made grated like nails on a chalkboard. Someone very wise told me two key things . . . First, if the experience of serving leaves you drained rather than pumped up, you're probably serving in the wrong area (God designed us each with our unique gifts for a purpose—He wants us to serve using those gifts, and that experience should leave us feeling fulfilled, purposeful, and satisfied). And second, if you serve in a particular ministry area simply because "someone needs to do it," or "if I don't do it, who will?" you may actually be interfering with God's plan. Often, people do not hear or believe God's call on them to ministry, and if they feel a call but don't see a need, they may ignore that calling. Sometimes the best thing we can do is leave a gap wide open, for the right person to walk in and fill it.

Even within women's ministry, I've experienced this. We have a number of ministry areas for women, and my job is to oversee each of them, and encourage/equip the leaders. The difficult part of my job comes down to what to do when there isn't a leader for a particular area. Do we leave that position vacant and let that ministry area fall away? Or am I to step in and fill the vacancy until someone comes forward or is found? I am so thankful that I work with a team of women who can help me discern such things.

So, in answer to your **real** question, do I still feel the Lord leading me to serve there [women's ministry] or am I just doing it because I've simply always done it? (Oh, and don't you worry about offending me—I'm not, it's a GREAT question!)

Women are the heart of the home. They set the tone for the entire family. But so many women today are hurting, broken, insecure, isolated. My heart burns with passion to reach these women, and to share life with them, to speak love to them, to help them see how amazing they are—so that ultimately they can embrace Jesus Christ and pour His love out in their homes!

Though I had accepted Christ as my Lord and Saviour, I spent years believing that my worth as a woman was tied up in the love of a man. If I wasn't loved, I was nothing. When I found the love of a good man, though, I wasn't satisfied. Perhaps I really wouldn't be a valuable contributor to society until I was a mother? Unfortunately, the main feeling that motherhood brought me was—loneliness . . . isolation. I was aching and empty, and my marriage and children were suffering because of my emotional void.

One day, way out of my comfort zone, I decided to attend a women's group. (I think, hoping the void could be filled by developing friendships with other women.) Little connections were made, and I felt myself emerging from the "new mommy fog." I went to a women's retreat . . . Things were changing in my heart. At first I thought it was the friendships—they were what I needed all along! But it didn't take long for me to realize that the filling of my soul was coming from the Only Source with the ability to fill. The other women were simply the tool He used to reach me!

I knew, in one simple moment, without a doubt, that I ***needed*** to bring other women out of their dark loneliness. That somehow, way beyond my personal abilities, God could use the work of my hands to touch the lives of other women—if I simply did what He said to do. So I did it. Because how could I not?!

For now, and for as many days as I feel the certainty of this call on my heart, I will pour myself into women's ministry.

Of course, marriage-family-home must be priority number one. It would be impossible for me to show one other woman how Christ can change her life—making her strong and beautiful and satisfied, in spite of all the crap the world tells her about how to "find herself"—if I am not living the satisfied (and balanced) life in my own home. If I have learned one thing, though, it's that you can't *teach* such things. In order to truly experience them, we must **live them together** as women.

So until the day God tells me "STOP" or "GO HERE NOW" and the team of wise and discerning women I am blessed to call friends back up what He's saying, I stay. I stay, not because I'm simply doing what I've always done. I stay because He is doing the great thing that He does, and I get to be a part of it!

Likewise, teach the older women to be reverent in the way they live, not to be slanderers or addicted to much wine, but to teach what is good. Then they can train the younger women to love their husbands and children, to be self-controlled and pure, to be busy at home, to be kind, and to be subject to their husbands, so that no one will malign the Word of God. ~Titus 2:3-5

Family Funnies

Shea had her first day of playschool this week. Meg, Kai and I dropped her off and headed back home. Meg (5) asked me if it would be just her and Kai at home for the morning.

Thinking the prospect of some 'Mommy time' would be pleasing to her, I respond "Yes! And we'll put Kai down for a nap, so it will be just you and Mom!"

Meg's response was an unenthused, "Oh, that will be sooooooo boooooooring."

One of the signs you were born into a large family.

Abbey (6) has started grade 1 this year. Last year, with full-day Kindergarten two days per week (and a third day on alternate weeks), she was a very tired and emotional girl until mid-October. So I haven't been expecting anything different this year . . .

The other morning she was quite certain that she needed to stay home from school because she was sick. I shared my theory that she was simply tired and needed to go to bed a bit earlier until she got used to being in school full time. But she insisted—she was really sick!

Long story short, after some rest, some debate about television (and how it's not allowed if you're sick, because you should be resting), and some Q & A . . . "Mom, why can't you just let me sleep in bed longer in the mornings?!" Which brought us back to the whole tired and needing to go to bed earlier conversation. Resulting in a tearful and heartfelt, "BUT I'M NOT TIRED!!!!"

Sure kid, whatever you say.

We had guests for dinner this weekend (which was really fun, by the way). The girls nibbled from their plates and asked to be excused from the table. Braeden (10) ate 3 generous helpings as quickly as humanly possible. But he decided to stay at the table with the grown-ups.

Our guests asked him a few questions about school and racing . . . Twenty minutes later, after none of us were able to get a word in edgewise, Pat and I were giggling about the tougher aspects of a large family—some kids obviously don't get to talk (and listened to) nearly enough.

Shea (3), telling me about how much fun her first day of playschool was. "And we did a painting, and I played with babies, and I like my teachers, and I rode a car, and I ate all my snack, and I made a friend." Breath. I jumped in to ask her friend's name. "Ummmm, I 'get. But I played with blocks, and I did a puzzle, and I singed a song, and I . . . ."

For a couple months, Kai (almost 1) has been making certain sounds in certain situations that make me think he's talking. But I don't want to be one of those moms who acts like her kids is the most brilliant. *I know, I know.*

Anyway, I have now decided that he is DEFINITELY saying "hi." Anytime anyone enters a room, he says "eye!"

Other things I suspect he is saying (though few of these words sound quite like the **actual** words) . . .

Braeden—Baaaaaa!
Daisy—Day
Dad—DA!
Mom—Mamama
Off (command we say to the dog, loudly and often)—Ah

And a two-word phrase that he's been saying for a couple months—"eye DA!" Every day at about 5:15pm . . .

Doing Life Together

For a while now, Pat and I have been looking for ways to connect on a spiritual level. We're both growing, but it's more of an individual experience—I grow and serve, he grows and serves, sometimes we talk about how we're each growing and serving . . . We don't' think that's what God intended when He thought it would be good for Adam to have a wife. In fact, we're pretty darn certain that He's got a bigger, better, and more exciting plan for mixing up marriage, love, and spiritual growth!

Last night we tried something new. *(Get your mind out of the gutters, people!)* We joined a life group. Your Church might call it something different, but basically it's a group of people that meet together weekly. Our Church has a fairly loose definition of a small group . . . Some do in-depth Bible studies together, some just hang out, and lots do something in-between. It doesn't really matter what 'material' is covered. The point is to 'do life' together.

Pat and I left with the knowledge that this is the group for us! It was so comfortable, and everyone was really ***real***. You know? The guys hung out on the deck while they flipped burgers, and they cut right through the niceties—they were talking about their spiritual walks, how much they read their Bibles, their biggest struggles. The women didn't get quite so deep and personal (I think, by nature, we're more guarded—read: insecure), but we had a wonderful time getting to know one another.

We have debated about trying to find a group for this past year. It's hard to figure out how we can fit yet another weekly commitment into our family schedule. But we are no longer satisfied with living separate spiritual lives. So other sacrifices may need to be made. I might have to bid farewell to the women's Bible study I attend weekly. Maybe we'll have to take less "date nights." (That doesn't mean we won't still have date nights—we'll just need to be creative about making it a special and fun time together at home. Even our budget would appreciate that change.)

If you are not a part of a small group, think about why not . . . Can you imagine anything better than having a group of friends who are intentional about their spiritual walks? A group that will challenge each other to keep growing, and lift one another up in the areas where they're struggling? I think if we're all honest about it, we don't have nearly enough friendships like that. Most of us sit on the surface of life with our friends—things are "goooood"—and never cut through the b.s. to say what's really in our hearts.

Good-Bye Plan B

I don't know about you, but I'm big on having a 'Plan B.' You know, just in case 'Plan A' doesn't go quite as expected.

In some cases, having a back-up plan is a good idea. For example, life insurance. I think that's a 'Plan B' we can all agree on. Just in case 'Plan A'—staying alive for a long, long time—doesn't work out, carrying life insurance to provide for our loved ones is solid planning.

Other times, though, I find I hang onto a 'Plan B' that is more sentimental than practical. One example I can think of is from my teen years. (Please note: I do not adhere to the following policy any more.) Boyfriends used to be disposable in my life. We'd hang out for 3-4 months, then I'd find myself getting bored . . . or too attached . . . or distracted. Occasionally he'd be the one who'd move on. Either way, it was never a big worry for me. Nope. Because I had a 'Plan B.' There was always another guy—one who liked me, or who I liked, just enough to know that it wasn't a far stretch to becoming a couple. I cannot think of many guys I dated in high school that weren't my back-up plans. *If I break-up with so-and-so, then I can just go out with such-and-such. I'll never need to be alone (or lonely) if I've always got a backup plan.*

This morning I was reading in Kings, and it occurred to me that we often hang onto a 'Plan B' when it comes to God. We're ready to be obedient and go where He calls us, but we keep a safety net below us . . . just in case God lets us fall down. Maybe He's asking us to make a drastic change—like give up TV—so we do, eventually, but we keep the old televisions in the garage . . . just in case. Or He calls us to tithe to His Church, but we wait. Just a few months to be sure there's some money in savings first. It's too risky to give all that money away every month without having some put aside for an emergency.

I can't count how many times I've gone forward with God, but still hanging onto my backup plan.

Elisha (in Kings) sets an example I think we should all strive for. Elijah came to him and put his cloak over Elisha's shoulders—this was his way of telling Elisha God was calling him to join Elijah in his work, prophesying to the Israelites. Elisha didn't doubt, question, wait, or create backup plans. When Elijah came to him, Elisha was plowing his fields (with the help of many oxen). You know what Elisha did? "He took his yoke of oxen and slaughtered them. He burned the plowing equipment to cook the meat and gave it to the people, and they ate. Then he set out to follow Elijah and became his attendant." ~I Kings 19:19-21

Can you believe that? The thought of it makes me a little bit queasy! Here's what I wrote in the margin of my Bible, "Elisha didn't just go where God said, he destroyed anything that might lure him to turn back." Isn't that what we're doing when we hang onto our 'Plan B?' We're just leaving something lingering, something to tempt us to turn back as soon as things get tough. God never promised that things would be easy when we follow Him, in fact He warns us that they will be difficult (James 1:2, Philippians 3:10, and many more). But we're to persist, persevere, keep on following Him. How much easier would it be to do that if we didn't have something to go back to? If we didn't have that safety net to fall into? If the only thing that remained was HIM?!

So, the next time God calls you to do something, I challenge you to do it wholeheartedly. Drop everything, and follow. Wait—don't just drop everything—burn it all! (Figuratively.) Don't make a 'Plan B,' let nothing hold you back. Leave yourself nothing to turn back to, so that your only option is to move ahead and follow Him. I'll try it, too . . . We can go together, hand-in-hand with Jesus, with nothing but 'Plan A.'

This Settles It!

I've always said that girls are way tougher than boys.

For example, child-bearing. Need I say more? Well, for those who seem to think this isn't evidence enough—here's further proof.

This week our family was stuck by a stomach virus. Pat went down first, Tuesday night around midnight. Braeden was calling for me by 2:30am. Kai was next in the wee hours of the morning. Pat and Braeden spent the entire day sleeping it off; Kai wanted to be held constantly. It was a long day . . .

Today, Braeden is still home, whining and moaning as in the throes of death. Pat headed off to work, clearly in a weakened state with some achy bones. Kai—well, he's a baby—so he's just running and playing, then collapsing into tears.

Last night at bedtime (Wednesday), Abbey informed me she was beginning to feel sick. I gave her a bucket for 'just in case.' This morning, she comes upstairs and informs me that she "threw up" in the night. She brings me the bucket full of evidence (ick!) and I ask her how she's feeling now (thinking she'd be needing some rest and probably stay home from school).

Abbey says, "Well, I think I'll go to school. I'm done throwing up now." She proceeded to get ready and headed off for the bus, smile upon her face with a spring in her step. (Okay, okay, she never actually leaves the house *that* cheerfully.)

Lest there be any further debate about who is tougher—six-year-old girl versus thirty-year-old man. 'Nough said.

Spiritual Warfare —1

When it comes to struggles of the spiritual nature, people tend to sway from one extreme to the next . . . Some believe all things have spiritual "roots" (that is, their causes are good or evil, blessing or attack). Others simply refuse to acknowledge the existence of any type of supernatural powers. I'd like to suggest that somewhere in the middle is probably closest to correct.

I believe that spiritual warfare does happen. *For our struggle is not against flesh and blood, but against the rulers, against the authorities, against the powers of this dark world and against the spiritual forces of evil in the heavenly realms.* ~Ephesians 6:12

But I do not believe that every "bad thing" in our lives is caused by Satan. Sometimes, bad things occur as a result of our choices (Deuteronomy 8:5, Job 5:17). Sometimes bad things are allowed in our lives so that God can refine us (Psalm 66:10). Sometimes, though, bad things are from the enemy. I think this is especially true of those areas we struggle in, where we're weak—these are the places that it is easiest for him to come against us (and come against Christ in us).

For example, one of my greatest struggles is my desire to be accepted. (According to my personality profile, this is typical of us highly-organized, be-the-boss, OCD types.) Put simply, I want people to like me. But as a leader in ministry, there are times I need to do or say things and make certain decisions that will result in others being unhappy. And some people (particularly women, and especially during certain times of the month) can get quite bent out of shape, often questioning my leadership and attacking my character. (Don't get me wrong here, I am soooooo not perfect, and there have been times where I've done or said the WRONG thing—but I'm not talking about those times.)

In these situations, I am plagued with doubts. Am I really supposed to be leading women's ministry? This person is so hurt/angry—did I really do the right thing? If I'm really called by God to do this, shouldn't others affirm that? Maybe I'm not hearing God at all . . .

Over time and with experience, I have come to discover that the desire to be accepted is one of my big fleshly struggles. The enemy has picked up on this, and he tries to use it to his advantage whenever possible. He stirs up dissension, which causes me to feel like someone doesn't like me, and feelings of self-pity keep me too busy to do anything useful for God's Kingdom . . .

Do you have any areas of struggle like that? Ones that seem to keep cropping up, going round and round, that you never seem to be able to get out of? Chances are that the enemy is messing around; doing his darndest to keep you from the works God is calling you to.

Now, what to do when the enemy is picking and prodding at you?

Spiritual Warfare—2

Now that we've set the groundwork, let's talk about doing battle.

God is omniscient (all-knowing), omnipresent (everywhere at once), and omnipotent (all-powerful). Satan is NOT.

We can pray to God in our minds and hearts and He hears us; He knows our every thought. Satan, on the other hand, only knows what he learns through our words and actions. Therefore, if you feel like the enemy of our souls is attempting to wreak havoc in your life, you cannot simply "think him away." In order to get rid of the enemy, you need to tell him to leave in an audible voice. This is one of the reasons we should invest our time in memorizing Scripture—nothing holds more power than the Word of God spoken aloud. On a side note, all the words we speak hold great power—the power to build up or the power to destroy—so be careful what you say! (Proverbs 18:21)

God is with us—each one of us—wherever we are, all the time. Satan can only be in one place at a time. So if you're feeling attacked, and I'm feeling attacked, at least one of us is being harangued by a being that "works for" the enemy—a demon. Okay, I can sense some of my friends cringing right now. But think about it—God has angels that He sends to deliver messages of hope and peace, and sometimes He asks them to step in and intervene in situations. Don't you think the one who wishes to be like God would copy His model and get servants of his own? So, when renouncing evil, it is important to tell both Satan and demon powers to "get behind me!" (Matthew 16:23)

God has all the power of the world (and more) in His hands! We have His Spirit living in us, which means we also have this power. We are NOT powerless against the schemes of the enemy! If we speak in the Name of Jesus (which is, in essence, putting His signature at the bottom of our page), we can have victory over evil. In fact, God has assured us that the battle has already been won—all we need to do is believe it (and speak up about it). (I Corinthians 15:57)

The Neighbours from Heck

Anyone have one of ***those*** neighbours?

When we moved in almost three years ago, we found our older neighbours to be very friendly. Warning bells should have gone off in my head when, only a couple weeks later, they spent a good half hour telling us about their neighbours on the other side—and every activity said neighbours had participated in that contributed to "bringing down the entire block." No, not warning bells about their other neighbours—about them!

In my entire life of renting and owning, never have I encountered so many complaints.

Here is the short list of what we have done so far to ruin their living experience for them (in no particular order):

— allow our children to drive their Power Wheels vehicles on the road (we live in a close, with a large green space in the middle, and no one drives around it if they don't live here . . . and we never let the kids do this at "busy" times like after work on weekdays)
— take too long to mow the lawn (we've been known to let it go a whole week in the summer)
— have visitors over who, ever so rudely, park their vehicles—*on the public street*—in front of their house
— spray the weeds in our yard with products that are safe for children and dogs, but according the odour they send into the neighbours window they are clearly toxic
— park our old pickup truck in front
— park our old pickup truck in back
— sit around our firepit with our kids

— have exterminators in to deal with our problem with carpenter ants
— have a particularly loud gathering in our yard, around that dratted fire pit, until (*gasp) midnight (the one and only of these types of gatherings we've ever had at this house) — the story of how their adult son "retaliated" for our noise is a whole post on its own!
— and many, many other small but irritating/ annoying/ dangerous/ discourteous things we do over the course of just being alive

Most recently, though, is the problem with our puppy. When we got her, we worked hard to train Daisy to relieve herself only in one section of the yard—it's a little patch of grass at the side of the house that the kids don't play on. I have been told that "the smell is just horrible!" and informed, under no uncertain terms, that I "just have to train her to go somewhere else. I have a big yard, and the dog just CANNOT 'go' near the fence right next to [their] yard anymore!" (I really should mention that our dining room window overlooks this patch of grass, and we have never noticed an unpleasant odour while dining.) Being the good neighbour that I am, I apologized for not cleaning up as often as I should. Since then, I have made an effort to ensure all is cleaned up every second day or so. Unfortunately, this is not good enough. I received a letter from the City, informing that we have seven days to get it cleaned up or we will be subject to a $200 fine. Next time, $400.

I am thinking that it is best for me to just bite my tongue and comply. So **in exactly seven day**s I will go out and clean up all the dog poop. Ha! (Totally kidding, we're now trying to clean it up daily.)

And I thought the party-ers we lived next to a few years back were bad . . .

Called?

Do nothing out of selfish ambition or vain conceit, but in humility consider others better than yourselves. ~Philippians 2:3

How do I know that I am moving ahead in the right direction? Am I following the plans God has for me? What if I heard things wrong?

We all ask ourselves (and others) these questions at times. We feel that God has given us a vision, a dream for the future. But then we wonder and doubt and second-guess. Perhaps we are actually allowing our dreams to be guided by our own desires.

Paul gives us a foolproof "check stop" for us to assess our motivations with in Philippians 2.

Imagine for a moment the fulfillment of the dream in your heart—maybe you envision being an author, a mother, a missionary—let the entirety of that dream take over your imagination. Now, where are you? How do you feel? What are others around you doing?

Are you at the front of the crowd, admired and praised by all? Do you feel like a super-hero? If so, chances are that what's on your heart is not where God is calling you to go.

We are commanded to *do nothing out of selfish ambition or vain conceit*. These are tough words. No one wants to admit to selfishness. But pride is one of the enemy's greatest tricks. The evil one whispers lies in our ears, convincing us that we need to be (deserve to be) recognized for the work that we do. But first Peter 5:5 tells us that *God opposes the proud*. Ouch! If we move forward with our own agendas and wrong motivations, GOD WILL OPPOSE US.

If, on the other hand, when you envision the pursuit of your dream, the picture you see has less to do with you personally, and more to do with Christ, His Kingdom, and lives changed . . . you're probably headed on the right track. Don't get me wrong here, this is not to say that God calls us to anonymity and ambiguity, forever serving without joy.

Simply because something excites us, stirs up our passion, and fulfills a life-long dream does not mean it can't be from God. This is another one of those lies fed to us by the enemy of our souls—he tells us that "if it's fun and brings us pleasure, it must be based in selfishness. Serving God should be a sacrifice." The truth of the matter can be found in Psalm 37:4, *delight yourself in the LORD, and He will give you the desires of your heart*. We have His blessing to be passionate and completely fulfilled in our service!

If you are unsure whether your dream is of God or not, ask Him to reveal to you the motivations behind that vision.

Is the song of your heart to adopt dozens of children from all across the globe? Ask the Holy Spirit to show you your motives. Supermom = wrong motives. Pouring out Christ's love and raising Christ-followers = His motivations. Do you have a passion for speaking and teaching in front of large groups? Be like Beth = wrong motives. Be a part of something beautiful in changing lives for Christ = His motives.

Do not allow yourselves to be confused! Saturate your minds with God's Truth, and the enemy will not be able to trip you up. Don't go to others to find out if your desire comes from self or God—go to Him! God already knows the vision He has placed in our hearts. We don't need to "figure it out." He created us, He predestined us, and He will reveal Himself to us through His Word.

In Him we were also chosen, having been predestined according to the plan of Him who works out everything in conformity with the purpose of His will. ~Ephesians 1:11

The Earth is Square

It must be, because I have definitely fallen over the edge!

A group had booked our Church facility for their large women's conference. Twenty (or so) volunteers were needed to keep things clean and running smoothly. Those volunteers needed someone to coordinate what to do, when to do it, and the like. That was me. ☺

It was a great blessing to serve, and the team of volunteers connected and had a lot of fun together. But man, my legs and feet ache. I am currently propping my eyelids open with toothpicks.

While I was gone, my man did dishes, made meals, and (drumroll, please) did laundry! (He even put it all away.) His homemaking skills totally trumped mine, and I'd like to offer him a new job with a much lower pay scale than he's used to. Thanks, honey! You rule!

The Heart of Worship

I don't know about you, but I like to crank out the worship music while I drive.

It's the one time I can sing all the love and joy that's in my heart without risk of anyone hearing when I hit a wrong note.

I often raise up one hand to the roof, getting caught up in the moment. But as I pull up to a light, especially a red light with other vehicles stopped, I often drop my arm back into my lap. Every now and then, though, I throw caution to the wind.

Filling of the Spirit

In Church this morning, I wrote copious notes! It was just one of those sermons. Mostly to help cement the Truth in my own heart, I am going to record the highlights here.

Five marks of a Spirit-filled Church:

1. The people are **fully committed** to:
   —teaching—hunger to learn God's Word;
   —fellowship—hunger to be with other believers;
   —breaking of bread (celebrating communion)—Christ's death and resurrection are at the centre;
   —prayer—devoted to pray together for all things (set aside a 'place of prayer').

2. Spiritual power—AMAZING things happen when the Spirit is working. (Some examples in the book of Acts are 300 new believers in a day, dead raised to life, healings, evil spirits cast out.) In order to have the power of the Spirit working within you, you must have a personal relationship with Christ (does He talk to you? is the Bible personal for you, speaking into your specific life circumstances?), you must obey the Lord with all your heart, and you need to ask Him to fill you with His Spirit.

3. Sacrificial love for one another (see Acts 2 and Deuteronomy 15). The people give to one another as they see a need—generously. Quote of the day, "what we do (or don't do) with our material possessions is an indication of the Spirit's presence."
4. Unquenchable joy, in all life's circumstances.

5. External focus—desire to bring others to the Lord, and He adds to their numbers because of their obedience in this.

The basic instruction for growing into a body of believers that is filled with the Spirit is for each person of the body to seek that filling up. Believe God. Obey the promptings of the Spirit. And give all the glory and credit to God.

So there's my summary. Now for my thoughts. Three things I feel God spoke into my heart during the service.

First, I need to find my special place for prayer. A place where the distractions of my world don't interrupt, a place where my sole purpose of being there is to commune with the Holy One. I remember my Tante (German for Auntie) disappearing into her en suite bathroom for long periods of time . . . one day I dared to go ask what she was doing in there (surely no single person needed to spend that much time in the bathroom) and she told me that was where she went to have uninterrupted prayer time. Cool, eh! Do you have a place of prayer?

Second, I need to be willing. Willing to give, even if it's my last $20, at the moment I feel the Holy Spirit prompting. Willing to speak, even if it's with people who intimidate me, every time He opens the conversational doors. Willing to not take the credit, even if I offered my time and talents sacrificially, for all the good things He does through me. I think my biggest struggle in this is that willingness to speak up about Jesus and what He's done for me. Are there any areas of willingness that trip you up?

Third, I need to be joyful. The true mark of the Spirit within . . . the thing that gets the attention of other people . . . the source that keeps us enduring our life's walk—this is the indescribable, incomparable, unquenchable joy of the Lord. Joy because (no matter how we mess up) our rotten stinking sin has been washed away. Joy because (no matter the circumstances—even great loss and pain) God is with us every step of the way. Joy because He has poured out His goodness, mercy, and love on us for no other reason than this—He wanted to! I do believe that this kind of joy is possible, but grasping hold of it in the midst of a bad day where I can't balance the budget, the kids are misbehaving, and my sweetheart is far away is something I know I cannot do in my own strength. Have you ever glimpsed this joy?

Just imagine it for a moment. A Church where all the people in it are filled with joy—true joy, not just fake "I'm okay" ness, where there is not one single needy person among them because everyone is taking care of one another, where every Sunday hundreds of new people pour through the doors . . . Who wouldn't want to be a part of that?!

Come, Holy Spirit, come . . .

Christmas Appreciation

Do you ever wonder, "what the heck should I be giving all those teachers for Christmas?"

Maybe you don't bother with this—I understand. There's a part of me that cries out against the senseless guilt-driven tradition of gifting the bus driver, Sunday school teacher, et al. But there's this other part of me—the part that has learned that people do better when encouraged—that tells me I must. Not because I'm obligated, but because I'm called. If I don't take the time to let all these people know how much I value the time and effort they put into building up my children, who will? And truly, there are many who invest much more in my children than what they are paid to! (Have a special needs child—you know what I'm talking about. These people are *gifted*!)

The difficult thing of giving to a whole bunch of people I really don't know is, well, figuring out what to give! Sometimes, the season gets ahead of me and I'm left on December 15 madly rushing through Wal-Mart to purchase a bunch of chocolates. But when I'm thinking ahead, it's nice to offer something that requires a little more effort (maybe even some kid participation).

This year, our offering will be homemade Saskatoon berry jam, a la Grandma! I'm not really sure the kids helped her at all along the way, but who doesn't love homemade jam?! For next year, though, I just may have found the perfect project—not too difficult for mom AND good for kiddo participation.

But for this year, we'll rely on Grandma (aka Suzie Homemaker) and her homemade jam. Yummy! At least she's related to the kids . . . that makes it better than buying chocolates, right?!

P.S. I just want to give a shout out to any of you who are employed or volunteer in a position that impacts the lives of kids. Words simply cannot express how precious your work is. Just in case you don't hear it from anyone else this Christmas—THANK-YOU!!!

Accountable for His Flock

Ezekiel 34: 1-10 (emphases mine)

The word of the LORD came to me: "Son of man, prophesy against the shepherds of Israel; prophesy and say to them: 'This is what the Sovereign LORD says: Woe to the shepherds of Israel who only take care of themselves! **Should not shepherds take care of the flock?** You eat the curds, clothe yourselves with the wool and slaughter the choice animals, but you do not take care of the flock. **You have not strengthened the weak or healed the sick or bound up the injured. You have not brought back the strays or searched for the lost.** You have ruled them harshly and brutally. So they were scattered because there was no shepherd, and when they were scattered they became food for all the wild animals. My sheep wandered over all the mountains and on every high hill. They were scattered over the whole earth, and no one searched or looked for them."

'Therefore, you shepherds, hear the word of the LORD : As surely as I live, declares the Sovereign LORD, because my flock lacks a shepherd and so has been plundered and has become food for all the wild animals, and because my shepherds did not search for my flock but cared for themselves rather than for my flock, therefore, O shepherds, hear the word of the LORD : This is what the Sovereign LORD says: I am against the shepherds and **will hold them accountable for my flock**. I will remove them from tending the flock so that the shepherds can no longer feed themselves. I will rescue my flock from their mouths, and it will no longer be food for them.

As I read this passage this morning, I reflected on the "flocks" God has called me to be shepherd to. First, to my children. Next, to other women. I had to ask myself these questions:

- Have I strengthened anyone lately?
- Have I offered words or prayers of healing?
- Will anyone say of me, "I was injured and she bound me up."?
- Do I diligently search for those who have lost their way?

The answer was not "yes" as often as it should have been.

I recall times when my children have acted badly . . . but instead of encouraging and strengthening I became frustrated and impatient. I think of women who have shared health concerns, and I simply told them, "I'll be praying for you," but didn't pray with them right then. But then the Father reminds me of the many times my little ones have been sick in the night, where I comforted and cared for them, prayed over them. He brings to mind a couple women I know who have wandered away from His love, and the way that I pray for them and keep connected with them.

He tells me that I'm doing all right in some areas, but lets me know that I can still do better . . . Ever so gently through His Word, He speaks.

Who are you shepherd to in your life?

Do As I Say, Not As I Do

I don't know if you've experienced this, but I've noticed an interesting phenomenon . . . the more babies I have, the more certain I become about the "right" way of doing things.

- Scheduled feedings versus feeding on demand—my philosophy has become "if a boob in the mouth keeps the babe quiet—do it!"
- Night waking . . . Be tough. They can sleep through the night at about six months old if you just make them learn how. Get earplugs and let 'em go hard at it for a couple nights, then welcome to bliss!
- Spit up. Use bibs, don't waste time changing clothes. In fact, why bother with actual clothes?! Sleepers are so much easier. The baby doesn't care what he/she is wearing.
- Solids, whole milk, etc.—when should we start? Basically, tell the health nurses what you know they want to hear, and do what works for you.
- To those who prefer to heat up the bottles under hot running water—use the microwave, people! It's sooooo much easier.

I am (gasp) becoming like my mother! (No offence, Mom—it's really a statement about all mothers in general. *smile*) It is less and less likely that I will keep my opinions to myself—after all, with all this experience I'm most certainly "right." Right?

Last week I buckled down. I had had enough of being bleary-eyed and just plain exhausted. NO MORE NIGHT BOTTLES! *Go ahead and scroll up to the top of the post so you can double-check my opinions . . . Uh-huh, that's right, six months. Yes, yes, now you can scroll through old posts until you're certain—Malakai is, in fact, fourteen months old. And until last week he was waking up (count 'em) AT LEAST three times per night.*

Anyway, you can now let out a cheer for me. We have slept through the night for a week! Yay! Well, not totally through the night, I do have to take him a bottle around 5am to get another hour or so out of him . . . But hey, it's much better than two weeks ago.

At Wal-Mart last weekend, though, I made an interesting purchase. One that runs completely contrary to my baby-raising philosophy. Do you ever get to the point where the bottle nipples are sticky-ish and icky? Gross, eh? Most of Kai's bottles have achieved this state of loveliness. Fitting with my philosophy of "off the bottle at a year," the plan was to toss each bottle once the nipple had bit the dust.

Yeah, um, so I picked up a new six-pack of bottle nipples. Because we can only conquer so many key issues at a time, and mastery of the whole sleep thing took about as much energy as I could muster up for the next few months.

So, I'm not Super-Mommy after all. Sorry to disappoint. (But I do give totally great advice about how to do things right. Seriously.)

How Do Your Pages Read?

Some things I read this morning (thank-you Shannon Ethridge) that struck me . . .

"So many people will never read a Bible to discover God themselves. Instead, **they read the believer**. (emphasis mine) If someone were to read your life, what would they learn about God? about the Christian faith? Would they want to become like you? Would they want to get to know God better because of what they see in you? . . . How can we show others how much God's love changes a person for the better if others don't see us as the recipients of His lavish love? Does a woman who knows she is deeply loved by God continuously walk around moping, stressed, depressed, and complaining about life? Not if the love of God has entered her heart and penetrated her soul."

So I am asking myself these questions, and I'm disappointed in my pathetic reflection of God. How will anyone know I have the love of Jesus in my heart when they hear me complain about fighting children, or grumble about doing housework? Would other women really look at me and say "wow, I want what she's got" if they walked by my house and heard me hollering at the children about their bad behaviour?

God has called us (me) to do a big thing for Him—to reconcile His children to Him. It doesn't matter where we work or play or attend services, as long as in each of those places we are fulfilling (or at least doing our best) this purpose. He has called us to bring others to know Him—His peace, His joy, His love. This calling is impossible to fulfill unless those qualities are a permeating aspect of my countenance. Is it evident to others that I know Jesus personally? Do I reflect His peace, joy, and love in my own life? Even in tough circumstances?

These are good questions to return to nearly a year later. I will resist the urge to get down on myself for the ways I have failed to change, and am still failing to show other who Christ is through my actions. The mantle of condemnation is not from the Lord, and I will refuse to wear it! Rather, I will try to focus on the improvements I have made since the original writing—and I will praise God for His life-changing work in me. As for those stumbling blocks, once again I'm giving them over. (Maybe I'll come back in a year from now and assess the progress.)

So, if the people around you are reading you to see who Christ is, what kind of story are you telling?

On Earth, As It Is In Heaven

Do you hear it?

God is speaking . . .

We're learning our way through the book of Acts on Sunday mornings. Our family has been profoundly blessed in an unexpected way. Everywhere I turn there is a message about "radical obedience."

God is speaking to me . . .

God is speaking to me, and I'm a little bit scared of what he might be saying . . .

My New Year's Resolution

Show me your ways, O LORD,
teach me your paths;

guide me in your truth and teach me,
for you are God my Savior,
and my hope is in you all day *long.*

~Psalm 25:4-5

Selfish

A lot of my prayer life is spent asking God about me. You know the prayers: What is your plan for me? Help me be a better wife/ mother. Financial provision. Direction for the family.

I have spent ~~months~~ years praying that God show me clearly how many children we should have. (Not specifically, as in—how many?—but when was the right time to stop.) Then, when it seemed He gave some direction, I spent many more months asking Him to help me feel "settled" with it.

Over the years, I cannot count the times that we have found ourselves with time left in the month and no money left in the account. Each of those times, my prayer life launched into all-day conversations with the Lord.

Basically, my prayers tend to be quite selfish in nature. *Me, me, me. Answer my prayer. Show me. Tell me. Guide me. Help me. Speak to ME!*

I wonder what would happen if I became selfish for God? If I asked Him what He needs, what He wants, what He's passionate about . . . And then I allowed His desires to be the driving force behind my prayers?

The only thing I can imagine the Holy God being "selfish" for, is us. (Another way I've heard it said is that He is jealous for us, for our affections and devotion.) He wants His people to know Him and love Him, to be in a relationship with Him. God's desire for US is so strong that He allowed the murder of His Son to make an easier way for us to know Him.

Just think on that for a moment—God is jealous for YOU.

If I look at each person I encounter in my day as someone that He is jealous for, how would that change me? Would I be cranky on the phone with the telemarketer if I were cognizant of the fact that God WANTS her? If I were reflecting on how God DESIRES him, would I step back in shame/fear/disgust/sadness at the sight of the disheveled man, smelling of alcohol, on the sidewalk downtown?

But what if I take it even deeper into my heart? What would happen if I allowed God's Spirit to fill me with His passion for people? I would WANT them to know Him. My heart's DESIRE would be for them to discover His love. Our prayers are filled with the stuff of our hearts, so it stands to reason that my prayer life would take a dramatic turn. No more *me, me, me*.

Lord, hear and answer the telemarketer's prayer, so that she will know You.

Father, show the homeless man Your plan for his life, so that he will find hope in You.

Holy One, tell them about Your Son.

Majesty, guide them in Your ways.

Saviour, help them live for You.

I wonder . . . In the grand scheme of eternity, which of my prayers would really matter?

My To Do List

I have this crazy bad habit of giving myself reams of projects to work on whenever the kids are on school holidays. I realize that this makes no sense. It would be much more sensible to work while at least a couple of them are at school—less kids means less distraction. So, I'm going to blame it all on Pat and tell you that when it's vacation time *he* gets motivated. I'm just going with the flow . . .

For the last few years, we have invited friends with kids over for New Year's Eve. This way, no one needs to get a sitter, kids can be put to bed if needed, and the basement is totally kiddo friendly. It's always a fun evening filled with board games, food, and noise. I would like to point out that NYE is *Wednesday* and today is ~~Sunday~~ *Monday*. The deadline for project completion looms dangerously close!

Pat suggested that we should finally refinish the kitchen cabinets. After all, we have lived here nearly three years now. And they are especially ugly. Since I am not willing to get in the way of my husband's motivation, we went for it. Pat is making the doors beautiful for me, by stapling a "frame" around the outside edges of the front. He has also (bless his heart) taken care of all the sanding. I am the painter of the house.

We would be right on track to completion before ~~D-Day~~ NYE, except for this pesky little thing called work. That Pat has to go to. *All day* today and tomorrow. Maybe even Wednesday. So here I am, major project on hand, five kids home from school, and a large social gathering in my home in just three days.

And you know what large gatherings mean, right? Cleaning, creating food trays, putting away Christmas decorations, organizing the kids' space, more cleaning, and um—of course—not having your entire kitchen cupboards strewn across the kitchen table and counters.

Holiday Randomness

First, a few questions . . .

How can it be possible, that no matter what time the children go to bed—whether 7:30pm or 10pm or somewhere in-between—they are fully capable of waking up just after 6am?

When did the word "holidays" become synonymous with the phrase "completely pig out until you're so full that you might throw up"?

No matter how simple I attempt to make the gift-giving aspect of Christmas for the kids, why do we end up needed to completely rearrange the house to fit their new haul?

Who knew that a completely gluten-free Christmas day could taste so good that I would "holidays"?

And now, a brief statement on my character . . .

For a girl who prides herself on being quite practical, I was surprised to realize that the thought of my husband buying me a brand new vacuum for Christmas wasn't all that exciting. I was relieved, overjoyed (and a bit embarrassed at seeing my true, completely non-practical side take over) when I opened my gift to find a gorgeous new family ring. Seven stones, two of them glimmery diamonds for our April babies. It's very "blingy"—I love it! *Just a brief note to any men—this is a very important lesson—never. ever. buy your wife a vacuum as a gift. Seriously, don't do it! She really isn't nearly as practical as she thinks she is.*

Another surprising bit of self-discovery: my vain side also made an appearance when I was holding out my hand to show off my gift (yes, if you're counting, it seems there are at least three sides to my personality). #1—I need to get acrylic nails; my hands are ugly! #2—It is really not attractive for a nearly 31-year-old woman to bite her nails down to the quick.

Merry Christmas, happy holidays, try to sleep in a bit, and enjoy your gifts (even if there are far too many of them kicking around your house). The most important thing, though, is that you teach your kids to sleep in. Geeeeesh!

God in the Flesh

Our family has been on a new adventure lately. Together, we are trying to listen to the nudges of the Holy Spirit and act on what we hear. It all started a while back with one (of an awesome series) on Acts . . .

A few weeks ago at church, our pastor told a story about a pastor friend of his. This friend was going to be preaching a message that very morning where he would ask his congregation to leave their coats on their seats when the service was over; they would be given to the large homeless population in their area.

You could sense our congregation squirming in their seats. Much to our relief, no such request was made. Much to my chagrin, before the service ended Pat told me that he felt God calling our family to leave our coats.

Pat talked to all the kids about it, prayed with them, and coats were unzipped. Shea freely and willingly passed her winter coat to Daddy. Abbey was a bit reluctant (she was wearing a special coat that she didn't want to part with). As Meg removed her fantastically puffy winter coat, she reassured Abbey, "don't worry, Abs, God will give us new coats." Together, they tossed their parkas onto the stage (the sanctuary was empty by this time). I reluctantly put my one and only ski jacket on top of theirs, and even more reluctantly unzipped Kai's red Baby Gap coat (a treasured hand-me-down from cousins). Braeden wasn't sure about all this business, and he's the kinda guy who needs to think things over, so he wore his coat home and offered it up just moments following his baptism.

During the following service, an additional 32 coats were left. All were donated to the homeless in our town.

Pat and I talked about buying them new coats, to help them see how God (sometimes) rewards us tangibly when we obey him. But we just didn't feel settled about it. God did provide, though, because when we came home and checked our closet of extra winter gear we found a coat in the right size for each of the girls and Kai. They were last year's hand-me-downs, so not the best quality as far as warmth, but they would do . . .

Today, our children received brand new winter coats—good, thick, puffy, top quality parkas (in matching colours, teehee)! A gift from our church, inspired by the Executive Assistant. We talked with them about their obedience a few weeks ago . . . how God saw that and used our church family to return what they had freely offered.

As we were walking out the doors of the church, Pat overheard Shea tell some children, "God gave me this new coat!" Yes. He sure did.

Oh, the Anticipation!

For unto us a Child is born,
Unto us a Son is given;
And the government will be upon His shoulder.
And His name will be called
Wonderful, Counselor, Mighty God,
Everlasting Father, Prince of Peace.

Isaiah 9:6 (NKJV)

Think Generous

Phew. I am all done doing housework. Three hours of scouring and scrubbing, spraying and wiping. Worked my buns off, and it looks great! I won't be enjoying the freshness, though, because it wasn't my house.

There's a woman in our church family struggling with post-partum depression. She and her hubby have six kids. She's maxed out. It's hard to think of how to help someone in her shoes.

Because I've been there, as have some of my friends, we knew right away. The hardest parts of coping with the day-to-day are cooking and cleaning. When you're emotionally drained, the last thing you can muster up the energy for is housekeeping.

So we rallied up a small group of gals (thanks for joining in Frieda, Lynne, and Lindsey), brought our cleaning supplies, gave the family some coupons for swimming and McDonald's, and set to work.

I don't tell you this story to "toot my own horn." I assure you, there are many opportunities I've had to bless others that I have not taken. Many friends and family whom I haven't helped in their time of need. This is just one small thing.

I tell you because it's such a small thing to make someone's life feel cope-able (I made that one up, do you like it?). As women, we see other women who are stressed out and overwhelmed all the time (sure, we often try to hide it from one another, but there comes a point when the truth starts to peek through). What do we do? How do we respond to the needs of our sisters? A ready-to-cook meal, a couple hours of babysitting, a few bags of groceries, a gift card for a meal out, a bouquet of flowers, an invitation for coffee or a play date, help with folding laundry, a big hug, a cleaning bee . . . just a few of the small things that hold BIG meaning.

I remember after Shea was born, Braeden came home on the school bus and his bus driver waves me over. He handed me two huge boxes. Unpacking them on my kitchen table, I found a freezer meal from each of his teachers and aides (total of five in that class) with recipes included, an adorable baby girl outfit, a stuffed toy for Braeden, and fancy hairbands for the girls. I had never before received the gift of food, and I was amazed. The way that blessed me and made life easier for me in those first weeks after a new baby—words cannot describe.

I want to be more in touch with the needs of the women around me. I want to really listen, so that I don't miss any more opportunities to make someone's day-to-day a bit easier. A little bit of my time can change the landscape of someone else's week (or month). How about you? I encourage you to try it—just once—and you'll be hooked. Come on, think generous!

Keep Keepin' On

My heart is burdened . . .

In the past several months, I personally know at least six couples who are divorcing. In all of these couples, at least one partner is a believer; in most of them, both are Christians (a couple of them missionaries).

I feel so helpless to support and encourage them. All I want to do (and have done) is cry and pray.

I know that God's heart absolutely breaks at the very thought of divorce. I also know that sometimes a marriage is abusive in many ways and is not a safe place to be.

I only know one side of the story in most of these cases, but my understanding is that emotional and verbal abuse were rife in several of these marriages . . . there have been some hints of physical abuse as well . . . infidelity, lies, and betrayal.

The enemy is at work here. He is insidiously and systematically destroying what God has brought together. Why? Your guess is as good as mine—havoc, chaos, destruction . . . anything to get in the way of God's Kingdom coming here on earth (Matthew 6:10). Among the shock and sorrow that echo in my mind, one question resounds—how has the evil one infiltrated our churches? What have we done, as a Church (not my church, specifically, but the Church that is the Bride of Christ), to allow the darkness and destruction to enter?

I don't know what to do, besides weep and pray . . . pray and weep.

Here are some random Scriptures that I've been rolling over in my heart and mind . . .

Luke 21:5-36—Yay! All this mess means Jesus is ever closer to coming back to earth.

James 1:27—We—other women, families, the Church—need to be caring for those who are broken and bruised among us.

Ephesians 6:10-20—The key to stopping the destruction of marriages in the Church really is prayer!

If you are in a strong, committed, Godly marriage, please take a moment to thank the Lord for that blessing. Don't take it for granted. And ask God's protection over it daily.

If you are in the broken place, where life as you've known it has fallen apart, please don't turn away from the One who loves you. He will always love you. He can restore what has been broken in your soul. He can give you so much more than what you have lost. He can restore the years that the locusts have eaten (Joel 2:24-26). And please, don't give up on us—your friends. Sometimes we don't know what to say or how to help—don't take that to mean that we don't care. In reality, we care so much that your hurt becomes our own.

I have been in that broken place, so please know that my words are not spoken casually. Someday, with Pat's permission, I will share what God has done in our marriage . . . the wicked that He has redeemed and now uses for His purposes.

In the words of a very wise song from the Seeker play:

I'm gonna keep on prayin'. (x4)
Pray, pray, every day,
And my prayers will accomplish much!

Look out dragons 'cause you're gonna go down;
We're gonna stomp you into the ground.

Look out dragons, can't you hear that sound?
I don't think you better stick around.

Put on your running shoes,
We're here with the Good News.
Light is pushing darkness away!

The prayer of the righteous is a powerful thing.
You are fighting evil forces that you can and cannot see.
But there's strength and there's help when you call upon the King.
So be strong, ***keep keepin' on****!*

Keep on praying and don't give up.
Resist the dragons and they will run.
Shout out praises to the King of Kings.
Keep believing and keep. on. prayin'.

But Have Not Love . . .

My mom sent me this email today . . .

1 Corinthians 13 Christmas Style

If I decorate my house perfectly with lovely plaid bows, strands of twinkling lights, and shiny glass balls, but do not show love to my family—I'm just another decorator.

If I slave away in the kitchen, baking dozens of Christmas cookies, preparing gourmet meals, and arranging a beautifully adorned table at mealtime, but do not show love to my family—I'm just another cook.

If I work at the soup kitchen, carol in the nursing home, and give all that I have to charity, but do not show love to my family—It profits me nothing.

If I trim the spruce with shimmering angels and crocheted snowflakes, attend a myriad of holiday parties, and sing in the choir's cantata but do not focus on Christ, I have missed the point.

Love stops the cooking to hug the child.

Love sets aside the decorating to kiss the husband.

Love is kind, though harried and tired.

Love doesn't envy another home that has coordinated Christmas china and table linens.

Love doesn't yell at the kids to get out of the way.

Love doesn't give only to those who are able to give in return, but rejoices in giving to those who can't.

Love bears all things, believes all things, hopes all things, and endures all things.

Love never fails.

Video games will break; pearl necklaces will be lost; golf clubs will rust. But giving the gift of love will endure

Excuse Me, I Seem to Have a Little Something in My Eye

You know what I love about Christmas? The craziness.

Yep, you heard me. I LOVE CRAZY!!! (Like you didn't already know that.)

That first weekend of December, when Pat drags out the boxes of decorations and the tree so I can "deck the halls" around this place—that is just about my favourite day of the year (it's definitely in the running, right after Christmas day, my birthday, the last day of school, and the first day of school).

There is something so deeply satisfying in taking a day (or six) of shopping and reaching the point of being able to say, "I'm done!"

I especially enjoy the anticipation in the children's eyes as they admire the wrapped gifts under the tree.

The busy-ness of running from Christmas concerts to work parties to friend's houses is a joyful kind of insane. It's even worth the tired and cranky little ones who've been allowed to stay up a wee bit late a time or two.

The best part of the craziness, though, is the family. For a couple weeks of the year I can count on everyone available to make an appearance. Weddings, funerals, and Christmas—those special times that really bring people together. If only for a couple days . . .

You see, my brother and sister are technically my "step" siblings. Our families merged when I was about 12 years old. This often leaves me as "odd man out" when it comes to sibling stuff. It doesn't help that I have a pack of five kids, and they are both child-free at this time in their lives. (Not only does it mean that we don't have a lot in common as far as what we do in our free time, who we hang with, etc.; I am, quite frankly, not very available for just hanging out kinda stuff.)

This divide is often just what I accept as life. Embrace what time we do get together, but try not to get hung up on the loss of my dream (you know, the Cleavers . . . laughter, love, connection, being the best of friends). Every now and then, though, it makes me a little sad. But this season—this month—for just a short bit of time, wipes that divide away. We're all together, crammed into small loud places, celebrating as a family. It's crazy, it's busy, but it is oh-so-beautiful.

There's a Party in Heaven

We have had the privilege of celebrating a couple of exciting milestones in our family this week.

#1—Meg sang in the chorus for a play called "Seeker: The Armor of Light." The plays (and books that they're based on, and songs) are a great ministry that share the Truth of God's Love through allegory. Seeker and his friends live in the Kingdom with the King, and they are part of His army. They fight off dragons (the dragons in this particular story were Anger and Abuse) and bring people out of the darkness and into the Light, where the King gives each of them a new name.

I can't say enough great things about the plays and the songs. They minister to me, bringing home God's Truths in a new way. As their "creator," Dian Layton says, they are most definitely "divine downloads!"

Anyway, at the end of each performance, the audience is told that there is a Real King who loves them. The Good News is shared and an invitation is offered. On Saturday, while watching the play with my parents (I was backstage helping), Shea decided that she wanted to go pray and ask Jesus into her heart! Yay, King Jesus!

#2—Sunday afternoon was a special occasion in our Church, called the "Big Birthday Bash." The reason—celebrating new life for 16 children. Two of mine were included in the sixteen children who chose to be baptized!

Unfortunately, Braeden was intimidated by the crowds of people (there were at least 150 in attendance), and he decided not to be baptized right then. Apparently, he wants to be baptized in the bathtub tonight. If so, we'll put on some trunks and take pictures to document the special moment.

Abbey, though, pushed through her fears and acted in obedience to what God had called her to do! Double yay, King Jesus! (I should mention that all the kids being baptized were given invitations to hand out. Abbey's teacher and principal came. Man, do I ever love our school!)

After the baptism, while we were enjoying our birthday cake, I was telling Abbey how very proud I was of her. She was giggling and grinning and bouncing up and down. She said to me, "I'm so happy, Mommy!" I told her that maybe she felt so happy because Jesus was smiling. With the confidence of a child, she replied, "Of course He is! There's a party in Heaven right now!"

Precious.

I ask that you pray for protection over our family during the next couple of weeks, that the children's faith decisions will settle deep within their spirits, and that the enemy will not be able to mess with God's work in them (or in our family). As a family, we have been strapping on our Armor of Light at bedtime and in the morning . . .

Update, More Heavenly Partying

Relating to my prior message_earlier today . . .

I planned to just leave it alone, let Braeden come to me. I didn't want to push or pressure him in any way. Baptism needs to be a decision made of your own will, with no convincing or cajoling.

I believed that God had put it on Braeden's heart to be baptized, but fear overcame obedience. Regardless of that belief, I still wasn't about to "suggest" anything.

Before climbing in the tub tonight, he told me again, "Mom, I want to get baptized. Tonight. In the bathtub." (If you know Braeden, it really sounded more like, "Mom, Ina get 'tised. 'Night. Buhtub.") I told him to get clean while Pat and I talked.

The conversation went a little like this . . .

In the bathtub? Really? Can we *do* that?

Um, well, I don't know if it's *technically* how it's *typically* done. But should we really say no?

Hmmm. Yeah. Okay. Let me look in my Bible.

Okay. Let me go scrub the tub for pictures.

Braeden's earthly Abba shared some words from the heart of his Heavenly Daddy and then baptized our son in the bathtub.

Triple yay, King Jesus!

A couple notes:

— I do not believe you need to have someone "official" to make a baptism real, true, or meaningful. (It's nice, but not necessary. I also can't find anywhere in the Bible that says it must be a Pastor/Reverend.)

— I do believe that when God tells us to act we need to do so immediately. But for those times when we let fear get in the way of our obedience (like Braeden did yesterday), He is faithful to give us another chance. Braeden told me that God TOLD him last night, "Braeden, you need to get baptized TOMORROW." Who am I to question what the Almighty Lord commanded my son to do.

— I could not be more proud of both Braeden and Abbey for taking a bold step of faith, moving forward in their walk with the Lord.

Jude 17-23 (Msg)

But remember, dear friends, that the apostles of our Master, Jesus Christ, told us this would happen: "In the last days there will be people who don't take these things seriously anymore. They'll treat them like a joke, and make a religion of their own whims and lusts." These are the ones who split churches, thinking only of themselves. There's nothing to them, no sign of the Spirit!

But you, dear friends, carefully build yourselves up in this most holy faith by praying in the Holy Spirit, staying right at the center of God's love, keeping your arms open and outstretched, ready for the mercy of our Master, Jesus Christ. This is the unending life, the real life!

Go easy on those who hesitate in the faith. Go after those who take the wrong way. Be tender with sinners, but not soft on sin. The sin itself stinks to high heaven.

Pondering in my Heart

In my quiet time this morning, I felt the Lord leading me to the book of James. There is so much wise counsel on those six pages, I had a difficult time deciding what to underline. I decided to pick a couple small sections to ponder throughout my day.

Trials and Temptations
Consider it pure joy, my brothers, whenever you face trials of many kinds, because you know that the testing of your faith develops perseverance. Perseverance must finish its work so that you may be mature and complete, not lacking in anything. ~James 1:2-4

Right from the beginning of his letter, James packs a punch. I know I want to be mature in my faith, not lacking. I even accept that oftentimes maturity is only developed through adversity. But to consider it pure joy? Whew.

Listening and Doing
My dear brothers, take note of this: Everyone should be quick to listen, slow to speak and slow to become angry, for man's anger does not bring about the righteous life that God desires . . . If anyone considers himself religious and yet does not keep a tight rein on his tongue, he deceives himself and his religion is worthless. ~James 1:19-20, 26 (also read all of chapter 3).

It seems straightforward—watch your mouth. But how? God needs to remind me of this command often. You know, "thou shalt not gossip/yell/complain/nag." That one. It seems I'm a bit slow in learning, or forgetful. I think the tongue is an area that a lot of women stumble in. Isn't it? Please tell me I'm not the only one!

Are there any passages that God has laid on your heart lately, that you are taking the time to ponder?

The Daily

Because I'm still feeling slightly frazzled/frantic/crazy/nutso, I am going to share my morning gymnastics routine with you in point form. Imagine me talking really, really fast, and breathing too loud.

— Abbey is sick—joy
— Kai is grouchy (and naughty)—excellent
— Shea is home today—is kindergarten really still two whole years away?
— getting Meg out the door for school without her sister—fun; chasing after her halfway down the block to put her lunch in her backpack—even more fun
— having tummy troubles that keep me running—wonderful
— seeing Braeden's bus pull up, when I have not yet seen the boy—fantabulous
— going out in sub-sub-sub zero weather to start the beast—great
— putting grouchy boy to bed for morning nap, in spite of the fact that I know he will not give me an afternoon nap—totally worth it
— plugging in a movie for sick girl and little girl and letting them munch granola bars in my bed—even more worth it

In spite of what my "self" wants to feel, I will have joy. These are things that could break my day, if I choose to allow them. I won't. I will laugh at the silly crazy morning. I will enjoy a few minutes of slow-breathing and sipping my steaming coffee. Then I will throw the peed on sheets in the wash (from two beds) and set to my daily work. This work that God has called me to do—no matter how mundane.

This is the day the LORD has made; let us rejoice and be glad in it. ~Psalm 118:24

Nothing

Ah LORD God!
Behold. You have made
the heavens and the earth
by Your great power and
by Your outstretched arm!
***Nothing** is too difficult for You.*

~ Jeremiah 32:17 (NASB)

Questions on the State of Our Hearts

This is love for God: to obey His commands . . . for everyone born of God overcomes the world. ~ 1 John 5:2b,4a

In our lives, do we show others that we love God? Are we really God's children? Do we obey His commands? Are we overcoming the world? Or do we simply pay lip service to the Holy One of Heaven?

God is light: in Him there is no darkness at all. If we claim to have fellowship with Him yet walk in the darkness, we lie and do not live by the truth. ~ 1 John 1:5b-6

Are we walking in the light, or are we lying to ourselves?

Anyone who claims to be in the light but hates his brother is still in the darkness. ~ 1 John 1:9

Are we in the light?
Do not love the world or anything in the world. If anyone loves the world, the love of the Father is not in him. ~ 1 John 2:15

Do we allow our hearts and spirits to be so full of love for the things of this world, that there is no room for the love of the Father?

If anyone has material possessions and sees his brother in need but has no pity on him, how can the love of God be in him? ~ 1 John 3:17

Do we view those in need with concern, or have we allowed our hearts to grow hard? Does the love of God reside in us?

Whoever does not love does not know God, because God is love. ~ 1 John 4:8

Are our lives a reflection of God's love to those around us? Do we **really** know Him?

Be You

The fellowship of other women is one of society's most undervalued blessings.

We fool ourselves into believing that we don't need it. *I'm too busy to make new friends. We don't have anything in common. She won't like me. I prefer to be alone.* Sound familiar?

I think we can all agree that women (generally) tend to be more emotional and expressive than men. We have an innate need to "talk things through." Men, on the other hand, want to "fix" things, and as such are not particularly good at listening while we talk it through. Only another woman can truly understand the need to talk about one subject until all possible avenues of discussion have been exhausted.

Women are also fairly detail-oriented. We like to be certain that all the pieces of the puzzle will fit together—before we even click those first two pieces together. Men tend to be more global in their thinking (that's my polite way of saying they're vague and/or lazy). You will never find a man who wants to hear how you have planned out your entire day in half-hour time slots. A girlfriend is the only one you can freely share stories of "poo and puke" without fear.

The best thing about other women, though, is their wisdom. Women live and they learn. Then they share what they've learned. If one woman has found something that works well for training up her children, or if she's discovered the secret to her hubby's happiness, or she knows where to find toilet paper for really, really cheap—she will tell other women!

It is through that exchange of wisdom that mentoring is born. It's not mentoring in the traditional sense, but a reciprocal relationship of teaching and gleaning, leaning and lifting, breaking down and building up. There is no relationship quite like the one formed on the foundation of fellowship—just being together.

Is it really even possible to be too busy to make new friends?! All you have to be is you. All you have to do is what comes naturally. The simplicity of *just being* removes any complexity.

Do not let your adorning be external—the braiding of hair and the putting on of gold jewelry, or the clothing you wear— but let your adorning be the hidden person of the heart with the imperishable beauty of a gentle and quiet spirit, which in God's sight is very precious. ~ 1 Peter 3:3-4

A Time to Weep . . .

I am experiencing near-meltdown today. My emotions are running amok.

I am aware that there is a slim chance I'm being hyper-sensitive and mildly irrational. I realize that factors such as too little sleep, PMS, and hunger are likely conspiring together against my mental health.

None of this self-awareness changes the fact that I am teetering on the brink of tears.

I was cranky, harsh, unreasonable, and any number of similar adjectives toward my husband. He is not at fault for how I'm feeling. Yet I blamed him.

Sometimes, though, a girl just wants to be hugged. She needs to be reassured that she is lovable and loved, in spite of her "issues." She wants to be told that everything will be all right, and have her hair smoothed back from her teary eyes.

Given some time to think, and some worship music cranked in the house, I am reminded of some things I know to be true . . .

- — a fool gives full vent to his anger
- — the fruit of the spirit is love, joy, peace, patience, kindness, goodness, faithfulness, gentleness and self-control
- — be slow to speak and slower to anger
- — a contentious wife is like a constant dripping

Feeling emotional is not an excuse for behaving like a child—selfish and pouty. I still feel weepy (and obviously need to go to bed early tonight), but because of the One who lives in me, the One whose glory I want to reflect, I need to act in the Spirit. Not because I have any ability on my own to change my attitude and actions, but only with His strength.

Honey, I'm sorry.

Sometimes, I kinda wish I was the me before I knew Him . . . just for a brief moment in time . . . so I wouldn't feel convicted of my wrongness so quickly. I kinda miss getting mad and staying mad—there was an emotional release to it.

Then again, that release can't even compare to the freedom that comes with life with Him. Nothing compares to that.

Now the Lord is the Spirit, and where the Spirit of the Lord is, there is freedom. ~2 Corinthians 3:17

Refreshment

I believe that taking time away from the everyday grind is an important aspect of our spiritual walk. Through the fray of life, it can be difficult to hear God's voice and feel His gentle touch. Too much busy-ness can easily overtake us, leaving us feeling parched.

I like to plan for the odd weekend away to counteract the dry times. For me, nothing refreshes quite like corporate worship, inspired teaching, and not having to cook or clean (grin). It reconnects me to the Source of Living Water.

Pat and I, along with another couple, are heading off this weekend for a conference.

If we come to your mind this weekend, please pray that the four of us will be refreshed. That we will feel His presence and hear His voice. That this time will be full of learning, growing, and joy. Please pray that none of us will have any worries while we're away, that our kiddos will be safe (and have lots of fun) at home with their caregivers. Thank-you.

May you find time for refreshment, too, as He calls you to come away with Him.

Come to me, all who labor and are heavy laden, and I will give you rest. ~Matthew 11:28

Time is in His Hands

First—It is waaaaay harder than I thought it would be to pause after each activity and ask God what to do next! I'm in the habit of running my own days, so when I complete one task I keep catching myself just flowing into the next logical thing. It is taking a conscious effort to take that minute and seek God.

Second—I sometimes like my own plan better than God's! He keeps telling me, "no, today is not the day to plan out your trip." I really just want to sit here for a couple hours, plot out my map on MapQuest, find hotels/cabins/vacation rentals, book, and have all the details settled. But it wasn't on God's list either yesterday or today.

Third—It is totally amazing to me how God can ensure I get all the important and urgent stuff taken care of in one short day! Amazing . . .

Here is yesterday's list . . .

~~—pick up fresh produce~~ - *not today*
~~—go to bank~~ - *not today*
~~—write for book~~ - *not today*
—exercise - *yes*
—meet with ministry co-worker - *yes*
—sort out ministry binder - *yes*
~~—mail out e-News~~ - *delegate*
—put away laundry - *yes*
~~—vacuum~~, sweep & wash - *just kitchen*
~~—plan out Disney trip~~ - *not today*
—retreat meeting - *yes*
—send out reference letter - *yes*
—Bible time - *of course, first*

* Of course, a few things not on my list of "to dos" came up throughout the day—dealing with emails, phone calls, feeding people, etc. I tried to take a moment each time another task popped into my head to ask the Lord about it.

It was neat, because during my quiet morning time, I really felt I needed to go exercise before the kids needed to get ready for school, but God told me to just stay and hang out with Him a while longer. He assured me He'd provide time to exercise later. Once two kids were off, the other three settled in for a movie and I was able to go for a good 20 minutes on my new (to me) recumbent bike. If you can believe it, there was time for me to do all of the "yeses" **plus** do lunch, play "Guess Who" with kiddos, do supper, receive and reply to more than 50 emails, and I even read a novel for 15 minutes!

I am a bit frustrated and confused that He has told me for two days in a row NOT to write, as I have also felt nudged that I'm supposed to be spending some dedicated time writing. When?! I know He can make enough time, and give me the words so the writing goes quickly, but I'd just like to have it all mapped out a little more clearly. Ha! I guess He'll tell me when to write.

Now, as much as I would like to surf the net and plot out my map, I just took a moment to seek guidance and it's time to get something ready for supper. Then I'm interviewing 2 potentials for childcare providers, and God did tell me to vacuum today . . .

Fourth—Now I know why the Lord commanded us to take the Sabbath day and rest! After six days like this, I am going to savour a day of rest!

And on the seventh day God finished his work that he had done, and he rested on the seventh day from all his work that he had done. ~Genesis 2:2

All the Growing Up

We have entered into a new phase in our family—one where mom no longer has to do everything.

Today, I was able to send Abbey to the downstairs fridge to bring up a jug of milk.

Braeden's new daily job is to take out the garbage and recycling.

All four of the bigger kids are taking their plates to the counter after a meal. Whoever is done last takes Kai's plate (that's usually Meg, she's a good eater).

Shea likes to help me with the Windex.

Meg loves to dust with the little electro-static Swiffer duster.

Every job I do has become less mine, and I love it! To be honest, I don't completely love the help all the time—let's be real, kids helping is often more like "teaching hour" than anything resembling productive. What I do love is seeing the pride on their faces at a job well done. Each child is developing a sense of ownership over his or her chores. And seeing a sibling working hard at a task inspires the others to do likewise. What's not to love? Well, except for that nasty part of step-by-step training them in the tasks . . .

I also discovered another great idea today! It's very crazy to try to do three kids completely different homework at once. With Meg just learning to read, she needs my full attention as she reads her book. But I really needed Braeden and Abbey to practice their spelling words. So, I handed Braeden Abbey's list and Abbey Braeden's list. I told them to take turns reading each other a word that they could spell out on their paper.

Not only did this ingenious idea save me time and energy, it was amazing for Braeden's speech! He had to concentrate so hard on pronouncing each word clearly enough that Abbey would know what it was, and if she couldn't understand she just asked again and again until he said it in a way that she got it. Never again will I do spelling practice with my children.

I must say, the mourning period over the "I'm never again going to have another wee, tiny, beautiful baby" might just be coming to an end. This growing up, it is neat stuff!

Train up a child in the way he should go; even when he is old he will not depart from it. ~Proverbs 22:6

MIA

Yes, that's me. Missing. In. Action. Suddenly, life just tipped slightly to the far side of chaos. So, here's a quick blurb to update . . .

Weight loss—I've been trying to eat well, but not starve myself. And the exercise routine has been pretty slow in developing. BUT, at least 10 women commented that I was looking thinner on Wed, so I'll take that as an affirmative weigh-in

Family—My husband has been away for work more than expected, which just throws a loop into life in general. The routine is all out-of-whack, resulting in the kids' behavior getting a little whacky, too. I'm trying to be a not-too-loud and cranky Mommy, but so far I'm averaging about 1 for 5. Boo!

Ministry—I've inadvertently taken on the job of leading our Wed AM women's group. At first, VERY reluctantly (as it's busy enough taking care of the administrative details and relational stuff of leading women's ministry, let alone adding the leading of a weekly event). But God has been working on me, softening me up, and I'm really growing excited about that, too! A few women have approached me with interest in being part of the leadership team for next year—so it seems Friendship Factor may actually have a TEAM next year rather than a couple women. Phew. (But I'll let you in on a secret and a prayer request—I'm kinda beginning to sense that I'll be in the lead position for that ministry area for at least the next year. In addition to my regular 'job' of overseeing *Women of Worth* (WOW) as a whole.) Fun. Exciting. Slightly crazy. Busy. But so blessed.

Also, our women's retreat is fast approaching, and the busy factor is rising exponentially! I'm so very excited about what God will do at this retreat. This, my friends, is the kind of excitement/stress I live for. And I am so thankful that God provided a beautiful woman to lead this year—I get to enjoy doing the work and getting my hands dirty, with none of the heavy responsibility (or the constant last minute phone calls, lol).

So, that's it in a nutshell. Better get back to the housework—this place is a pigsty!

And he said to them, "The harvest is plentiful, but the laborers are few. Therefore pray earnestly to the Lord of the harvest to send out laborers into his harvest. ~Luke 10:2

* * *

Family Funnies

My kids are pretty darn funny sometimes
Heard early this morning, as I called Abbey upstairs to get ready for school . . .
Megan (4 1/2): Abbey! Mom is calling you to get dressed for school. NOW GO!
Abbey (6), very tired and whiney today: I wannna watch the moooovieeeee . . . .
Meg: Abbey—obey your mother!

The 3 girls (A & M mentioned above and Shea—2 1/2) were playing out in our green, hauling all kinds of kiddie-sized lawn chairs out there. I watched them set them in a circle, sit in them for a while, then haul them all back to our yard. I asked what they were doing out there with the chairs.

Abbey: We were having a meeting, Mom!
Braeden (almost 10): Mom, you're pretty.
Mom: Thanks, sweetheart. You just made me feel so good!
Braeden, blushing: Awwww, Mo-om!

Behold, children are a heritage from the Lord, the fruit of the womb a reward. ~Psalm 127:3

Happy B'Day to the B-Boy

Recently, I turned 30. No trauma, no big deal. Yesterday (March 16), my big boy turned 10! I cannot believe how he's growing up . . . and I really can't believe how old that makes me—I have a child in the double-digits!

I remember the day he was born. My husband and I were just barely adults. We had a crazy love/hate relationship going on—high drama every day. But we were committed to making our family 'stick' for our baby.

Braeden arrived at 6:21pm, squishy and purple and totally beautiful. They whisked him away for x-rays of his left arm, as it hung limp and flaccid at his side. Determining that nothing was broken or dislocated, the doctors brought him back to me for some bonding. Specialists galore took a look at Braeden's shoulder, arm, wrist, and hand, offering a variety of diagnoses. An MRI revealed a number of brain abnormalities. The doctors offered a bleak picture—a boy who would likely never walk, never be 'normal.' At age 2 we noticed a distinctive in-turn of his left eye and visited an ophthalmologist—you've never seen such thick bi-focals (but they do the trick). At 2 1/2 Braeden had his first complex partial seizure—thankfully, they are well under control now with medication. On Christmas Eve, nearly 3 months before his 3rd birthday, our big boy took his first independent steps! Woohoo!

At age 5, after extensive research, Pat and I suggested that all of Braeden's symptoms stacked together formed a pretty clear picture of cerebral palsy . . . doctors agreed and we finally had a diagnosis—left hemiparesis cerebral palsy with epilepsy.

There have been many occasions for grieving the differences I see in my boy compared to typical children his age—school, sports, aborted attempts at vacation Bible school, the day they told me he would have more success in a special education classroom, when other children ask him why he drools/drips/slobbers (or whatever descriptive word they choose), hearing the question 'what's wrong with your arm?' and so on.

But the joys are so much greater. The sweet success of toilet training. Hearing a stranger in the store talk to him and realizing that stranger was able to understand Braeden's words. Listening to Braeden answer questions with, "I have palsy. I was born with it. God made me this way," with pride and self-confidence. Seeing typical children include him in their play out of love. Listening to his contagious giggle as he makes a joke—Braeden is the FUNNIEST kid ever! Listening to him read an entire 'Franklin' book without help. Seeing him play with his long-awaited baby brother. Watching him ride his adapted bike around, listening to other kids telling him how cool his 4-wheel drive is. Seeing how his tender heart breaks when someone is sad. Hearing him tell me, "you're pretty, Mom."

This child of mine is a gift from Almighty God. He brings me both joy and pain, love and heartache. He is mine . . . for a time. He is beautiful, precious, and perfect just the way he is. I love him and he loves me. And it is his special day. Thank-you, Lord, for the gift of my boy . . .

Before I formed you in the womb I knew you, before you were born I set you apart; I appointed you as a prophet to the nations. ~Jeremiah 1:5

A Bridal Love Story

Have you ever been a bride or a bridesmaid? Or even attended a wedding? Take yourself there for a moment. Imagine the night before the wedding, neither the bride nor the groom is getting any sleep. Each of them is restless, excited, anxiously anticipating that moment when they will see each other at opposite ends of the Church aisle tomorrow. She is reviewing each detail of her special day, from getting her hair done to being walked down the aisle, from the processional song to the toasts and first dance. Hoping and praying for each detail to fall into place as perfectly as she's planned. He is nearly giddy with the anticipation of seeing her glide down the aisle toward him, both nervous and thrilled for their wedding night.

Let yourself be transported for a moment—you are the bride. You wake up ready to be forever united to the one and only man you'll ever love. Visions of cherubic children and endless laughter fill your future. You stand among your dearest girlfriends and family while they primp your hair and dress. You are about to become the eternal partner of your best friend. Someone slips a note under your door (you know it's from him—your adoring groom) and you eagerly scoop it up. Suddenly shy, you look around the room at all your loved ones. As only your best friend can, she realizes you want to be alone to savour your love letter in private, and she shoos the girls away. You settle into a comfy chair in the corner, careful not to wrinkle your gown, and delicately open the envelope. Your eyes devour the words of your lover, and you bury his promises deep into your heart, reading them over and again. Your heart is ready to burst, your eyes are welling with tears, there's a catch in your throat, and your blood is thrumming through your veins. You are going to be MARRIED!!!

You giggle a bit imagining his excitement as he anticipates the moment you arrive. Can't you just see him? Pacing up and down, back and forth, pulling at his bow tie. His face is flushed and there's a lump in his throat. His buddies are gathered around him, cracking jokes trying to lighten the moment. But he doesn't really hear them. All he can think about is YOU. He checks the clock obsessively and asks over and over if you're limo has arrived yet. Finally, it's time. He and his groomsmen make their way to the front of the Church. There's a sea of faces watching him, but he notices no one and nothing—his eyes are fixed on the door that you will come through. The music begins . . . he shifts from one foot to the other . . . the bridesmaids make their way slowly down the aisle. Next come the flower girl and ring bearer—he runs ahead of her, and she cries and forgets to toss any rose petals on the floor. Your groom doesn't notice, he's still staring at that door. The music changes, the guests rise, and you step into the room on your Daddy's arm. Your eyes seek out his—he drinks in the full scope of your beauty. The whole world stands still.

This, my friend, is the love relationship your God desires with you! He has eyes only for you. He is wild about you, madly in love with you. He thinks you are the most beautiful creature on the face of the earth! Look up the aisle at Him. Do you see Him, willing you with His eyes to come to Him? You are the bride, Jesus is your Groom, and He longs to feel your spirit married to His for all eternity. Think back . . . He has written you a precious letter of love. Do you take His Words into your secret place? Do you bury them deep within your heart and soul? Do you let His love wash over you through those words every single day?

For your Maker is your Husband—the LORD Almighty is His name. ~ Isaiah 54:5a

God's Word is filled with images of His lavish love for His bride, His Church. In our humanness, though, we can be so unfaithful in our love to Him. We give our hearts away daily to our families, our jobs, our ministries. We love the things of this world (like our homes, our cars, our free time) so much that we begin to simply forget how God desires us. Much like an earthly marriage, we begin to take our Groom for granted. We forget to revel in His love letters, we don't make time to bask in His presence, we just expect that He'll be there waiting patiently when we finally have the time. Just as neglect can cause our earthly marriages to grow cold, so it can with our relationship to Christ. But we can be thankful that when we seek His forgiveness for our adulterous hearts, He never needs time to think about it. He simply opens His arms up wide and says "I've missed you, my darling!"

It may stretch your understanding of God to accept this view of Him as your Heavenly Bridegroom. The Bible is rich with wedding and marriage imagery, but it's easy to gloss over those parts as if they are not intended for us personally. But if you are willing to let go of your pre-conceived notions of who God is, and open your heart to His lavish love, you can be assured that your life will NEVER be the same again! No more 'looking for love in all the wrong places.' You won't need your spouse, your friends, your children, or your Pastor to fill you up. Their love is just icing on the cake, because your heart and soul will be overflowing from the love of Christ in you!

This is one of the many deep truths we learned on our weekend retreat with Shannon Ethridge (hosted by Women of Worth).

Jesus wants to pour out His love over you—will you let Him?

The LORD your God will rejoice over you with gladness, He will quiet you with His love, He will rejoice over you with singing. ~ Zephaniah 3:17

Understanding Jesus

Blessed are the merciful . . .

It's pretty easy to show mercy and compassion to some people. It takes little effort to give a homeless man a few coins or a sandwich. It's easy to send money to a global organization for the purpose of feeding an adorable little child. It makes sense to give of our time and money to charities and clubs that have programs for helping those who are less fortunate. Somehow, though, I suspect that Jesus is asking for something deeper, something that's not so easy to give, when He calls us to be merciful. I suspect that this has a lot more to do with loving our enemies that it does with loving those in need. For me, I can sense Him asking me to show love to people who irritate me . . . well, one person in particular. Someone who (in my mind) seems very self-centred and finds a way to make every circumstance a major dramatic and traumatic event. Someone who gets my blood boiling whenever I am asked about that person or that particular situation. This person needs my mercy, my forgiveness, and my love . . .

Blessed are the pure in heart . . .

To be sure I really 'got' this, the concordance in my Bible defines the heart as the centre of one's being, including mind, will, and emotions. My thesaurus gives all sorts of great descriptive words for pure, too: uncontaminated, wholesome, chaste, uncorrupted, and authentic. To not allow my mind or emotions to be contaminated or corrupted, to keep my thoughts, desires, and actions wholesome—this is purity of heart. Not simply good intentions, but chasteness in my spirit.

Blessed are the peacemakers . . .

I am sensing a theme here! Again, the first thing that comes to mind is loving our enemies. Making peace the priority, at all costs. Sacrificing the desire to 'be right' in the name of keeping harmony. Not only submitting my own will in order to show Christ's love to those who don't know Him, but submitting in disagreements with other believers. Building unity and trust within the body of Christ . . . To again quote my concordance, "In so doing, they reflect the character of their Heavenly Father and so are called **[daughters] of God**." It just struck me that, if I am the opposite of a peacemaker (so basically, I act in any way that does not promote peace), I will also be the opposite of a daughter of God (an enemy of God). Ouch!

That's a lot to digest in one morning . . . I'm going to go spend some time with my Daddy now, because I know I can't make these changes on my own strength!

Therefore, if anyone is in Christ, he is a new creation. The old has passed away; behold, the new has come. ~2 Corinthians 5:17

The Setting of the Sun

Don't let the sun go down on your anger.
~Ephesians 4:26b (HCSB)

My perspective on these words was changed last night.

I had always assumed that the Lord was instructing us to "make up" before the day ended. So anytime I needed more time to process and cool off, anytime the other person was unwilling to talk, anytime the problem was not fixed before bedtime brought guilt and shame. I felt like a failure as a Christian.

But what if that is NOT what this verse means? God knows that it is unlikely for selfish and flawed humans to resolve their issues in a day. Especially where great hurt has been inflicted. What if He is really just telling us that, before this day ends, we need to bring our anger (and hurt, resentment, frustration, etc.) to Him?

If we go to Him and pour out our hearts, "Lord, I'm so angry! I need you to take my pain and my rage—bear it for me—because if I hang onto it I will surely collapse," isn't He faithful to take our deepest emotions and heal our brokenness?

Don't go to bed angry. Turn it over to God and let Him work.

**credit goes to Beth Moore and "It's Tough Being a Woman" for my new revelation*

My God Chronicles

For a number of years, we struggled financially. Many of our struggles could be attributed to living beyond our means. I was beginning to feel hopeless and helpless, that creditors would never stop calling.

I had prayed about our finances before, but it was always more of a "rescue me" prayer filled with hope that God would provide through a surprise source of funding. And many, many times He did. But this time, my prayer was one of repentance. I was desperate for God to change our financial situation in a permanent way, and I knew that would require sacrifice.

God provided me with a friend who had experienced "being broke" in a way I could never understand. She was (and is) incredibly wise in money management and budgeting. She took many hours of her time to build me a budget that worked—within our means—and had me paying off the debt we had accrued over the years. Though I felt we couldn't "afford" it, I had her build in a section for tithing in that budget.

Some of the rules of this new budget included making a meal plan, NEVER eating out, praying over every purchase, shopping several stores, paying bills first and groceries last, using cash only for things like entertainment and beauty. It wasn't easy, but it was what I knew God had called me to do, and I was finally ready to obey. Thanks to frugal living and following the rules, we dug ourselves out of the hole. And because of God's miraculous provision for months on end, even though our budget showed a red $800 at the bottom of the "estimated" column, with all bills paid the "actual" column each month showed a beautiful black $0!

We decided this financial obedience thing had something behind it. So when God called us to pay for a friend to have a sitter once a week for a few hours, we created a new budget line for that expense. The red number grew bigger, yet the black number held steady at $0.

Next step—move from "giving" to the church when there was extra to "tithing" to the church and considering the rest our extra. The red number grew. I kept on with the crazy grocery shopping in four stores and saving money for three months to get my hair coloured. The black number remained.

Then, the most unusual thing happened . . . A man who we barely knew took my husband to a quiet corner of the church one Sunday and handed him a card. It was a fuel card. No—NOT a gift card for fuel, but a credit card for fuel. He and his wife had been praying about whom to bless, and God brought us (near strangers) to their minds. The credit card, he said, was ours to use for the next year. *Wow, God, you are wild!* Given the vehicle we have, changing our fuel costs to zero brought that red number waaaaaay down. I am not even surprised that the bottom of the page still reads $0 at the end of the month. So humbled, thankful, and blessed, but not surprised.

God's love is so extravagant. He provided a blessing to help us out of a nasty situation that we deserved to be in. The definition of grace.

Let me just say, when we feel that gentle nudging to provide for someone else's needs, whether it be money, a meal, coats, childcare, prayer . . . we have learned to stop and listen. Not everything we do is rewarded in turn. Not every dollar we put out is replaced. In fact, sometimes we sacrifice what we want and what we think we need in order to obey. But never, ever have we suffered, because it's impossible to suffer when you have the joy and peace of being in the centre of God's will.

God has trusted us with His money, and nothing gives Him greater pleasure than watching us give it away. Just try it, and bask in the warmth of His delighted smile.

Give, and it will be given to you. Good measure, pressed down, shaken together, running over, will be put into your lap. For with the measure you use it will be measured back to you." ~Luke 6:38

Time Management Works for Me (Usually)

Have you ever wondered, "how will I ever get it all done?"

We have so much to do in each day, so many activities and obligations packed into our weeks. It's a symptom of our ADD, over-stimulated, immediate gratification society. Some would argue that we need to remove ourselves from society's mindset, but I'm not sure that would solve the problem. In fact, if we aren't keeping up (in our work, ministry, family life) with the rest of society, we're likely to encounter other problems.

So how can we live IN this world (and function at the level required to do so), without becoming OF this world?

I believe the first distinction is how we establish our priorities. I have found, by trial and error that setting my heart on God and His ways first thing each morning has the power to alter my entire day. If I start out taking time with Him, the many other things that require my time that day tend to get done. If I start out my day on my own strength, though, I spend the next fifteen hours feeling as though I am one step behind.

Romans 12:2 says, *Do not conform any longer to the pattern of this world, but be transformed by the renewing of your mind. Then you will be able to test and approve what God's will is—His good, pleasing and perfect will.* Taking time each morning to renew my mind helps establish His priorities for my day, rather than my own.

This week I am taking an experiment in life. Each morning, after my coffee time with Jesus, I am going to make a list of all the things

I think I need to accomplish for the day. Then I'm going to ask the Lord to show me what to keep, what to move to another day, what to toss altogether, and what to add. Once I have turned over my list into His (much more) capable hands, I am going to ask Him, "Lord, what do you want me to do now?" At the conclusion of each activity, I'll ask that question again. I can't wait to see how He uses my time!

The heart of man plans his way, but the Lord establishes his steps. ~Proverbs 16:9

Grandma

(By my mother, Frieda).
Not too long ago I had the pleasure of having my 83 year old mother come for a visit. One of the things that challenges me each time she visits is wondering how I can gain some assurance about her faith. I want to know that she'll be waiting to greet me in heaven if she dies before me. *You see, we all* ***think*** *that Grandma believes, but it's just not something she really talks about. Maybe it's a generational thing . . .*

On the last day of our visit, as she and I were leaving a grocery store, mom tripped on a speed bump in the parking lot. Before I could even react, she was down. Truly, one moment she was walking beside me and the next she was laying on the ground with blood pouring out of her nose and mouth. Now—you have to know my mom. No mention of any pain, just striving instantly to get up because she was embarrassed. *She is a tough cookie!* I convinced mom to lie still until we were sure nothing was broken and with the help of several bystanders, helped her to the car and took her home. Mom was battered, bruised and swollen. Her lip was cracked and puffy, she had a scrape on her forehead and cheek and her hand was swelling up as we applied ice. Over and over she kept saying how glad she was she hadn't broken her dentures (that happened in a previous fall), and I kept saying how glad I was she hadn't broken her hip or anything more serious.

Anyway, after a couple of hours, because of her age and because she was flying home the next day, I decided we really should take her to the emergency department. Long and short of it, it truly could have been much more serious. She had no concussion but she did have a break in the knuckle of her small finger. The doctor told her she'd require surgery and a pin because it was an 'unstable' break. They gave us a CD of her x-rays to take home with her and sent us on her way. *I just have to interject here—I think it's worthwhile to note that the doctor didn't say "it looks like it might be a hairline fracture, but the x-rays aren't too clear" or something like that, he* ***clearly*** *saw a* ***serious*** *break on the finger and was certain it would require surgery.*

The next day we were at the airport sharing the events of this story to family when a man standing close to us heard mom needed surgery and said he was a surgeon. The man was obviously Jewish, a long flowing beard and a black skull cap (forgive me if that's not what it's called). I jokingly said, hey, we need a surgeon. He then grabbed my mom's hand and for whatever reason, asked mom if she understood German (she does—Low German) and proceeded to pray over her hand. He then told us that he was also a chiropractor but that God was the Great Physician. When he was done praying, he told her it 'is finished.' Trust me—family reactions were mixed. I thought it was cool, my niece looked like she thought a kook had just prayed over her grandma, my sister in law (a nurse) looked sort of indulgent but unbelieving, and my mom—the woman who's faith we sometimes worry about—thanked the man for his prayer and told me she thought she was healed.

A few days later after a visit to her own family doctor and more x-rays . . . . her doctor told her she was fine and nothing further was required. *When my mom shared this part with me, my doubting self had to ask, "well, did he take more x-rays? did he show her the x-rays? what does he mean nothing further is required?" I wanted some sort of earthly explanation.*

You know, there are times that I really try to rationalize God. I want it to make sense. But today, I want to say thank you to a man who overheard a conversation in an airport and had the boldness to take my mother's hand and pray over it. And the biggest thank you to God—the Great Physician. He absolutely showed me where my mother's faith is—Praise God. And He heals, He really heals! *Cool, eh?! Whenever I think of it I just shake my head and grin. God is so good!*

Is anyone among you sick? Let him call for the elders of the church, and let them pray over him, anointing him with oil in the name of the Lord. ~James 5:14

Lead Your Heart

"Follow your heart." We've all heard it before. But the effects I've seen of this "heart following" are all too often negative—divorce, broken families, adultery, broken trust.

The heart (the emotions) is a fickle thing. We tend to be motivated by what feels good, what makes us happy, by what we believe we deserve. I am so guilty of this! I frequently decide that I am not feeling loved enough by my husband. Maybe I even feel taken for granted. My heart begins to ache a little bit, and I follow it. I follow it right down the path of blame and accusation, dissatisfaction and criticism. Very soon, neither of us is "happy" in our marriage.

So where would we be if I kept on following my heart down that path? Probably in a state so miserable that divorcing and breaking our family apart would seem to be the only path back to happiness.

I believe it is healthier, wiser, and better for the heart if we choose to "lead our hearts." Like I said, emotions can change on a dime (they are not the best compass to follow). How much wiser would it be for us to direct our hearts (our emotions) in the way they ***should*** go?

What do I mean? I mean this—regardless of the feelings, we choose to act in ways that reflect what we want to be feeling. We choose to show love regardless of how loving (or not) we are feeling. Come back with me to the place where I'm feeling unloved or taken for granted. I don't have to follow my heart to the pit of despair. No way! I can make a choice, in that very moment, to lead my heart.

For me, leading my heart might look like doing something to show my husband that I love him (even though I am feeling unloved)—even better, doing something to show Pat that I respect him. It might be forgiving that my work has been taken for granted, and picking up the strewn laundry because I love him. It might look like clamping my mouth shut when all I really want to do is spew and vent how horrible I feel, and praying that God changes my heart (rather than praying that God changes my husband).

The funny thing I've noticed is that when I lead my heart, it doesn't take long before my emotions follow where I want them to go. The feelings of hurt and discontentment ease away. Loving thoughts and feelings work their way back in. I begin to feel "happier" and my actions reflect it. And more often than not, a chain reaction begins. Rather than ending up unhappy and divorced, we end up stronger and more committed.

In *The Love Dare* it says this: *The world says to follow your heart, but if you are not leading it, then someone or something else is. The Bible says that 'the heart is more deceitful than all else' (Jeremiah 17:9), and it will always pursue that which feels right at the moment . . . The Love Dare journey is not a process of trying to change your spouse into the person you want them to be . . . The truth is, love is a decision and not just a feeling.*

We each have a choice to make. Follow the heart and hope to heaven we find love and that we feel loved. Or **lead** the heart and choose to be love and show love.

A soft answer turns away wrath, but a harsh word stirs up anger. ~Proverbs 15:1

The Hard Work

You know the expression, "good things come to those who wait?" There are few things in my life that have just happened as I sat back on my heels and waited for them. With the exception of (finally) going into labour after a long wait, most things require effort on my part.

This losing weight thing is one of those effort-full experiences.

I'm not a stranger to weight loss. In fact, I've done it four times over with relative success. *As much as success can be measured by maintaining the loss until the next pregnancy, that is.* But something about this time is different—more difficult—than the other times.

I have been pondering my struggle, and come up with a couple reasons why this time is tougher:

— I am over 30 and my metabolism has changed (it hates me now),
— I had a boy, and boys make that weight stick in a way that girls don't (it took me a good 2 1/2 years to lose after the first boy),
— I am subconsciously clinging to this baby weight because it is my very last baby weight—ever,
— I just can't get down to where I was before and I need to accept it, along with a myriad of other great justifications.

If I get real with myself, though, about the reason I am simply not losing this weight, I have no choice but to accept full responsibility for it. I am not losing weight because I am not doing the work. I am not fully committed. I follow Weight Watchers for a few weeks, experience some success, and decide to take a little "break" from all the points-counting. I talk myself out of exercising regularly (*I'm too busy, it's too expensive, I really don't* ***need*** *to*).

Losing weight, not yelling at the children, being a good wife, saving money, spiritual growth—all these things require work. None of them just happens based on my good intentions.

And now I sit here with no good ending for this post. Because this is as far as I've come. I need to do the work. The question that lingers in the back of my mind is this—how do I keep motivated to keep up the work as time goes on? What's to prevent me from losing and re-gaining the same dumb 10 pounds I've lost and gained four times already in the past year?!

Or do you not know that your body is a temple of the Holy Spirit within you, whom you have from God? You are not your own, for you were bought with a price. So glorify God in your body. ~1 Corinthians 6:19-20

On the Horizon

I find myself looking ahead to this summer with a mix of anticipation and sadness.

Summer is my favourite! I love the warmth (even if we really do only get a month of it). I enjoy the freedom. I adore the beach. And if I'm honest, there is a (very tiny itty bitty wee small) part of me that basks in the lack of structure and routine.

This summer, though, is our last summer before a year of changes.

At the end of this summer, Braeden (11) will be going into middle school (grade six)—new school, new teachers, new friends, new bus, longer hours. Transitions such as this are particularly difficult for him, so our summer is really the calm before a stormy year.

As this summer comes to a close, Malakai (1) will be turning two. I will no longer have a baby, and will not have a baby ever again. He will move into a toddler bed, start potty training (maybe?), speak in sentences such as "I do it!"

The girls will be growing up, too. Abbey's (7) change from first to second grade should be a fairly smooth transition. On the other hand, Meg's (6) move up from kindergarten to grade one is likely to put a few bumps in our road. Five full days a week is hard work! Last year Abbey came home tired and cranky until December. If anything, I expect Meg to be a little more so (she's just got a bit more *personality* going on).

Shea (4) will move on up to the four-year-old class in preschool. It's still only two mornings per week, but so much new learning will take place—the alphabet, printing, numbers, colours, patterns . . . All the stuff that will give her a head start for kindergarten.

I am standing on a wide expanse of beach. The shoreline is nearby—free, easy, relaxed, fun. But off on the barely-visible horizon I see the hint of things unknown, and I feel the need to brace myself, and remember:

Jesus Christ is the same yesterday and today and forever. ~Hebrews 13:8

Read the WHOLE Book!

Have you ever decided, "I'm going to read my WHOLE Bible," gotten started in Genesis, and three months later been stuck somewhere around Numbers of Leviticus? I have *started* reading my Bible countless times, only to give up at this stage.

About two years ago, I decided to try something different. I picked a book from the Old Testament to read, and when I finished that I moved to a book in the New Testament. I put a check beside each book's name in the Table of Contents as I completed it.

It was out-of-order, and sometimes I needed to go review something from somewhere else in the Bible to make sense of what I was reading, but about a year and a half later I had marked off every. single. book! I'm now on my second time through using my random Old/New method, turning my check marks into "x's."

Our Pastor recently suggested that we do this, but he added a new twist—he said we should read one book from each testament at the same time. So during our morning quiet time, read a chapter from Proverbs and a chapter from John, for example.

Those long and sometimes difficult OT books are so much easier to work through when you know you've got something completely different to read (in the NT) once you're done there!

(Just a note: there are more books in the OT than the NT, so when they belong together—such as 1 and 2 Chronicles—read them as if they were one book. This should help keep you from running out of NT books too soon.)

But he answered, "It is written, "'Man shall not live by bread alone, but by every word that comes from the mouth of God.'" ~Matthew 4:4

Giving IS Frugal

One of the things I've learned over the years, quite by accident, is the art of trading services.

Actually, "trading" is not quite the correct term! Really, it began as me trying to think of things I could do to be a blessing to the people around me.

You see, I am not a very talented person. I don't say that to be self-deprecating; I'm just bein' honest. For example, I can't offer friends in need delicious baked goods, because I can't bake! But I am pretty darn good at administrative things: schedules, organizing, and budgets. At some point I decided to stop feeling guilty because I wasn't signing up to bring casseroles to the new mom, and instead began to listen for people needing help with things I could do. A couple friends were talking about over-spending, so I offered to help them create a customized budget. One friend was feeling over-run in her kitchen, so I came over and helped her purge and organize. Someone's toilet was plugged, so I sent my sweet hubby over to help (he apprenticed as a plumber, and is quite gifted with the "handy" skills).

You may be wondering how in the world this has saved me money. Here's the how . . . Its kind-of a "pay it forward" concept. Be a blessing, and chances are you will be blessed. It's not really a trade, because often those we help out aren't able to help us in return (which is fine, because we also usually have little to offer to those who help us).

I believe that if we are good steward of the money and gifts we have been given—and that includes giving them away without reservation or hesitation when we feel God calling us to do so—we will be blessed for it. That is, if the heart is right. We should not be motivated to give in order to get back. Our motivation needs to be both obedience to Christ and a desire to be a blessing.

To those who use well what they are given, even more will be given, and they will have an abundance. But from those who do nothing, even what little they have will be taken away.

~Matthew 25:29

There are so many times I walk away from a situation, feeling as though I should do something, and yet do nothing. It's not an easy thing to be generous with my money or my abilities when finances and time are tight. But little by little, I am learning to listen to God's gentle nudging's to give. And often, at times I least expect it (but most need it), I find myself being blessed and encouraged by the love and generosity of someone else.

Give, and it will be given to you. Good measure, pressed down, shaken together, running over, will be put into your lap. For with the measure you use it will be measured back to you. ~Luke 6:38

God's Small Stories

I often try to find a "big story" to write about. But because I see God's work in my day-to-day life, too, I wanted to share some of those "smaller stories."

Throughout my day, people I know just come to my mind. For example, I could be cooking tacos—which are one of my nephew's favourite things to chow down on at my house—and suddenly I'm thinking of him and wondering how he's doing. When this happens, I try to take a minute to pray for that person. Not always, but sometimes this happens at just the right moment when someone was really in need of a little prayer. Periodically, I'll even wake up in the middle of the night with someone on my mind and pray for them.

Have you ever had a time where it seems like the same message is being repeated, over and over again? I once had a friend who said to me, "I don't know what God's trying to tell me, but the parable of the Prodigal son has appeared at least six times in the past week!" I get that. I think God must know my hard-hearted nature, and the way I assume every message I hear is just perfect for someone else. In order for me to get it through my thick head that He's speaking to me, He needs to get that message to me repeatedly—through devotionals, sermons, books I'm reading, movies I'm watching, stories friends tell, and so on.

Delays and interruptions can be so annoying. I am a "schedule person." I thrive on order, organization, and time-tables. I can sometimes get so structured that I miss out on God's still small voice in my day. There are days, though, when nothing goes as planned. (Like the two days I lost internet a couple months back. Argh!) It's funny, though, that in the midst of days filled with frustration and schedule glitches; I begin to seek God a little more. It often starts with me praying, "Lord, nothing is going as planned. Please help put my day back on track." And then I sense Him telling me, *you needed to be a little off-track today, because otherwise you would not have come to Me.* Ah-ha.

God is just as present in the everyday things as He is in the parting-the-sea style miracles. Sometimes it just takes me a little bit before I catch on . . .

One who is faithful in a very little is also faithful in much . . . Luke 16:10

The Crazy Mom

Last night, we had a slightly spontaneous girls' night out. By "slightly" I mean that some of us (yes, me) needed a little more than one hour's notice, but were able to pull it off with a day's notice.

I was positively giddy as I bid my family good-night and headed out the door! I think I even made my husband giggle. It has been a while . . .

We enjoyed far too much food, a bit of shoe shopping, and a very girly movie. By "very" I mean that the entire theatre echoed with the sounds of women sniffling, nose blowing, and giggling at themselves through their tears.

We saw My Sister's Keeper. I would give it two thumbs up for story line and emotional satisfaction, but one thumb down (if I had three thumbs, that is) for using the Lord's name in vain repeatedly (even the children in the movie) and a bit of teenage sexuality. If you haven't heard of it, the story is that of a girl who was conceived with the purpose of being a donor to save her older sister from cancer.

The ethical ramifications of genetically engineering a baby in order to help save your other child are huge. Regardless of whether or not I would take those same measures, though, I understood that mother's heart.

Throughout the movie, this mother was depicted as a little crazed and highly controlling. When her children or husband tried to express a view that did not match hers, you could feel the tension in the theatre as we all waited for the explosion. I know there were people watching the movie thinking to themselves, "That woman is nuts! I can't believe she's doing this! She is going to destroy her family and ruin her children forever." I know it because those same thoughts crossed my mind.

But at this one moment where she lost all control, I had a revelation. She wasn't a crazy woman out to control everyone's lives. She was afraid. Terrified. This was a mother whose greatest fear—losing a child—was playing out in front of her eyes. And she was doing everything she could to not let her child slip away.

My heart moved from judgement to a deep compassion. I understood that fear . . . those reactions. On a much smaller scale, I became her only a few short weeks ago when faced with Braeden's school change.

We women are so hard on one another, so quick to judge. Yet the things we criticise in other women are so often things we ourselves think, say, or do—and we hate them (and ourselves for them).

How much more willing would I be to come alongside another woman if I viewed her actions from a heart of compassion instead of my pedestal of judgement? How much lighter would her burden feel if I encouraged her rather than looked down on her?

Next time I see a mother parenting in a way that I don't understand or agree with, I hope I will remember that I could be just one tiny life change away from being in her shoes. In fact, I've been the crazy mom before; it just depends on the day.

Be kind to one another, tender-hearted, forgiving one another, as God in Christ forgave you. ~Ephesians 4:32

Gold Nuggets

I've decided to share my nuggets of learning from Sunday's sermon (in point form, because I am not so much in good writing mode this early morn), based in Deuteronomy 4-6:

—refusing to trust God results in us forfeiting our claim to the Promised Land

—there is an unending chain of influence through the generations

—we each have a responsibility to invest spiritually in succeeding generations to ensure continuation of Biblical faith in the One True God and the fulfillment of His mission on earth

—one of the biggest hindrances in people's pursuit of bold faith is their parents ("You can't go to Africa, it's too dangerous!" "Maybe you should have a back-up plan in case this ministry thing doesn't work out." etc.)

—four things we can do to mentor the next generation: share God's stories (past and present); model the blessing of obedience; let our love for God show; encourage bold faith; mentor young leaders (um, that's five—the last one is a freebie)

1. I need to be telling my children about those tough things we do to walk in obedience.
2. I should stop being such a wuss when it comes to sharing my faith and stepping out in faith. I am so easily swayed by "what will s/he think," "so-and-so won't agree with this," "I don't want to stir things up," etc. Bold faith is not being afraid to give Jesus the credit, even when I'm around others who won't 'get it.' Bold faith is about doing what God tells me to do, when He tells me to do it, and not hesitating

because I'm afraid that friends/family will think I'm crazy. (I mean, look what happened to all those people who thought Noah was crazy! I'm just sayin'.)

Great is the Lord, and greatly to be praised, and his greatness is unsearchable. One generation shall commend your works to another, and shall declare your mighty acts. ~Psalm 145:3-4

God is in the Quiet Whispers

We were out camping earlier this week. I had good intentions of taking my morning quiet times to seek God, to read my Bible, to pray, to journal, to write for my book proposal. But the reality of camping with five children, two of them still small and needy, altered those plans.

My heart was not okay with spending four days and three nights starved for His Word and His voice. I had to find a way to spend time in His Presence that was different from my usual way.

As I lay in my bed in the early morning, awakened by the cawing of crows, I asked Him to be with me that day. He whispered, *I am with you always.*

While sitting on a park bench watching the children climb and slide and climb again, I recited His Word (my memory verses) in my head. He whispered, *take the bread of life and eat.*

Standing on the beach, turning slow circles and counting heads 1-2-3-4-5, I begged him to inspire me. He whispered pages of words for me to write to glorify Him.

This morning, as I savoured my still quiet, I praised and thanked Him for the way He stays close to me. He whispered, *when you call on Me I will answer you; seek Me with all of your heart and you will find Me.*

What has He been whispering to your heart lately?

But he answered, "It is written, "'Man shall not live by bread alone, but by every word that comes from the mouth of God.'" ~Matthew 4:4

Getting Ready (Pre-Prayered)

Right now, there are about 500 women in North America frantically getting prepared for the *She Speaks Conference.* I am one of them. Because of God's great provision, four women from our women's ministry team are able to attend and learn from the experiences and teaching of the team.

For many of us, preparations include getting our hair cut and coloured, trying on countless outfits, and the like. I don't know what it is, but us women usually do more to get ready for a date with other women than we do for dates with our men! This is me. Tonight is chalk full of 'primping' appointments.

Others are also clicking away on their computers in efforts to complete book proposals or practice talks. For many hopefuls, this is our 'one shot' at getting our ideas and our abilities reviewed (and maybe even accepted). Again, this is me. These last few days are packed with plans to write and re-write, making last-minute revisions and memorizing talks.

Virtually all of us are trying to get our homes ready for our absence. Cleaning to be done, meals to be planned (maybe even prepared and frozen), schedules to be written out, notes to be left. Yes, this too, is me. Maybe. If I find time. Otherwise, they are on their own and I expect that McDonald's and Pizza 73 will be getting a lot of business over the next weekend.

I find myself stopping, though, in the midst of all these preparations. I hear a still, small voice whisper to my soul, *Spend time with Me. No matter what you do to prepare, you will never be ready for all I have for you at* She Speaks *if you are not with Me.* And oh, how I need Him by my side! Each time I hear that whisper I stop, and in the words of Moses I tell Him, *I cannot go without Your Presence, Lord! I will not move from this spot unless I know You are with me!* ~Exodus 33:15

I believe that, in so many ways, this conference will be life-changing, ministry-reviving, heart-refining, utterly amazing. But without Him, it will merely be a good experience. I've had too many God experiences to be willing to settle for a good experience. And God experiences don't happen by accident, they happen with intentionality—by seeking HIM (and not being focused on things like good hair, meetings with influential people, etc.).

Lord, help me to keep my eyes focused on You. Still my excited mind, so that it will pay attention to You. Though my hands are busy with getting pre-pared, may my heart stay attuned to being pre-prayered.

Show me Your ways, O LORD, teach me Your paths. Guide me in Your truth and teach me. For You are God my Saviour and my hope is in You all day long. ~Psalm 25:4-5

Is there something you are getting ready for, working on, or hopeful about that is taking up space in your heart and mind? Are you doing what you *really* need to be doing to be prepared—are you pre-prayered?

(Now, if you're wondering whether I will be cancelling my hair appointment this evening, the answer is no! Are you kidding? I cannot go to a conference with 500 other women with bad roots! BUT, I have promised God and myself, and I promise you—I will spend the same amount of time in communion with Him that I spend in conversation with my stylist. Fair enough?)

The Anticipation is THICK in the Air

I awoke this morning with a Scripture pressing on my heart . . .

However, as it is written: "No eye has seen, no ear has heard, no mind has conceived what God has prepared for those who love him" ~1 Corinthians 2:9 (NIV)

No one's ever seen or heard anything like this, Never so much as imagined anything quite like it — What God has arranged for those who love him. But you've seen and heard it because God by his Spirit has brought it all out into the open before you. (Msg)

As I pondered this verse in multiple versions on biblegateway, I saw that it referenced back to Isaiah 64:4 . . .

Since before time began no one has ever imagined, no ear heard, no eye seen, a God like you who works for those who wait for him. You meet those who happily do what is right, who keep a good memory of the way you work. ~Isaiah 64:4 (Msg)

Today is going to be a really good day! Today is going to be a GOD day!

Questions that Keep me up at Night

Why is the divorce rate in churches the same (and in some cases higher) than the divorce rate of the general population?

When faced with devastation (financial, loss of a child, etc.) how come some people fall to pieces and others endure? What's the difference between those two types of people?

How do some people truly manage to live completely free of debt?

How in the world do "mega families" afford to feed everyone? How much money does Jim Bob Dugger actually earn????

What makes some people seem at peace no matter what, while others always seem stressed out? Are their circumstances *that* different, or is it something else?

What would it be like to walk with God so faithfully that one eventually just walks right up to Heaven? How *hard* would that be?!

How come some children seem to be born with rebellion in their spirit?

Why, when I'm tired, do I stay up until midnight pondering unanswerable questions?

And can someone please teach me the technique to back-combing hair so that I can get a little volume near the top?! Seriously—how does one learn to do that???

Oh, the depth of the riches and wisdom and knowledge of God! How unsearchable are his judgments and how inscrutable his ways! ~Romans 11:33

Ragged Beauty

We had just finished our tea and a visit, were ready to leave the coffee shop. Both of us stood to use the facilities before heading our separate ways. My black bag, heavy laden with laptop and all the accessories remained on the chair.

At the same moment in time, we noticed a man at the table behind us. Long, grey, unkempt beard; wrinkles sagging a face worn out by time; blue eyes, crinkled and watery. On his head he wore a dirty blue ball cap, his burgundy coat faded, dirty, and well-used.

We paused on our trek to the washroom, looked at the man then at one another. She said, "I'll wait here. You go ahead." And she sat back down. I peered again at the man, turned to her, and nodded my head.

In my few quiet moments, I pondered my reaction to this man. Did I truly believe this man, possibly homeless, would grab my laptop and run? I did not. Yet some would, so how do I discern who is trustworthy?

I returned to the table, ready to grab my bag and go on my way. She headed to the washroom. And he focused his watery eyes on me. It was as though he could read my thoughts, and I felt the heat of shame climb up my neck. He twitched his dry, cracked lips and opened into a smile. The most beautiful, bright white smile! I wondered if they were veneers or dentures, so gleaming was their surface. Not the teeth of a man with no home.

And he spoke to me. "Are you a writer?" he asked with genuine interest.

"I am," I replied. "Well, I'm trying to be."

"What do you write? Short stories, magazine articles, or are you a student?"

"I am writing a book, actually. Hopefully." His curiosity made me uncomfortable, less confident, unsure, and ashamed.

We continued for several minutes, him drawing more and more information from me, with painstaking patience. He offered praise and encouragement. He suggested a writer's group. He smiled and smiled. And he was so beautiful.

As we bid farewell and I heaved my briefcase onto my shoulder, I noticed his companion. A man in a suit—younger, maybe his son. The younger man chewed thoughtfully on his sandwich, absorbing our dialogue, as though it were a familiar scene. My scraggly-bearded friend had no food, only a lone cup of coffee. He did not appear to be hungry. Not what you'd expect from a homeless man.

As I drove home, I allowed my imagination to drift . . . Who was this kind character in the coffee shop? Why did I misjudge him? What is God trying to teach me though that old man?

Perhaps he was just there to encourage me. Maybe to teach me not to judge what I see but to discern with my heart. Or was he demonstrating for me how I ought to love and encourage others?

All I know for sure is that the old, ragged, worn-out man I met in the coffee shop was there for **me**. The charm of his personality and the mystery of his smile remain with me—in my head, in my heart.

Do not neglect to show hospitality to strangers, for thereby some have entertained angels unawares. ~Hebrews 13:2

Parchedwithout Prayer

Why am I ignoring His call?

Morning by morning, 5:30 a.m. the alarm clock sings out country music, and I hear Him invite me.

Yet I roll over, hitting snooze again and again, telling Him, "Later, Jesus. Soon. Just a few more minutes of sleep."

Yesterday Shea (4) came to me with tears in her eyes. No one would play with her, would I? The temptation to put her off was strong—laundry, dinner prep, budgeting, and a million other household tasks called my name. But in my mind's eye I saw her face crumpling as she received another rejection. So I turned my eyes from the mess and sat at the table in front of the Yahtzee board.

Her face lit up, glowing with joy and excitement. Once she knew she had my attention she chattered and giggled, taking deep gasping breaths between word-full sentences.

If I were to heed that early morning call to communion, would it light His face? Would He grab the opportunity and pour out His Words into my heart?

When I put Him off, does His face fall like a child who's been turned away?

When I say "not now," I am telling Him that filling my body with sleep is more important than filling my soul with Him. Oh, how wrong that is! Sleep—my body can live with less. But Jesus—my soul cannot live without.

Without Him, my soul dries out, parches, it cries out in thirst. The longer I leave my soul in such a state, the more withered it becomes. Eventually, the dryness will feel normal and the thirst will be dulled. Until the lack of moisture leaves gaping cracks—broken places.

Lord, forgive me for thinking so much of myself that I begin to believe I can afford to postpone my time in Your Presence. Tomorrow morning, and each morning after, give me an unquenchable thirst for Jesus when that alarm clock sounds. I don't want to become a withered old soul! Abba Daddy, I love you. YOU are more important than anything—including sleep. Draw me closer . . .

As a deer pants for flowing streams, so pants my soul for you, O God.
~Psalm 42:1

Steps of Fear FAITH

Our church is a missional church. In recent years, we launched two big mission-focused programs. *Give Life* is all about being a blessing to those around us, and is primarily focused on what we do in our communities and neighbourhoods. To reach the world in a tangible way, we developed the *Global Compassion Campaign*. The GCC chose three organizations that we will work closely with over the next five years—they will receive significant financial support and numerous short-term missions' teams over these years.

Now, why in the world would you want to know what's going on in our church?

Christmas Eve, 2008 . . . Our congregation was introduced to one of the projects that we will be supporting—*Haiti Arise*. Here's the short-version of Haiti's story: the people in political authority back in 1804 made a pact with the devil, and turned the country over to him for 200 years; for 200 years, voodoo has been the religion of choice, selling children as slaves the economy of choice; the curse was broken in 2004 and the people are receptive to the gospel of Jesus Christ. *Haiti Arise* has a vision to educate the people so that they can bring about economic change, with a Christ-centred approach.

After viewing the video about *Haiti Arise* last Christmas, my husband turned to me and said, "We're going to Haiti. I don't know when or how, but we'll be there." I attempted to swallow the massive ball of fear in my throat unsuccessfully, so I just nodded. I knew it, too.

This Sunday, the couple that runs the mission was at our church. Marc preached a message, and then Marc and Lisa invited interested people to join them in a luncheon. There was no doubt that we would be staying for the lunch. There was also no doubt that my husband would be joining the team heading to Haiti in October. (A little God-incidence for you: My husband talked to the team lead, and he shared that they had been praying for one more man to join the team. Ha!)

I don't believe this first step in obedience will be the last of our story with Haiti. But rather than guess what God has planned for our future, we've decided to take one step at a time. My husband signed up, then we asked God, what is the next step you want us to take? One hairy scary step at a time, we will walk in faith, trust, and obedience.

But as it is written: "Eye has not seen, nor ear heard, nor have entered into the heart of man the things which God has prepared for those who love Him." ~1Corinthians 2:9

How to Pray Your way Through Temptation

As I work on my book about *mother anger*, one surprising discovery I have made is that anger itself is not the problem. In fact, anger often rears its ugly head due to irritation, annoyance, interruption (not situations that should elicit a true angry response).

The problem with mother anger has much more to do with the emotional release that comes from venting (also known as exploding). The release is cathartic—it gives a rush, a high. And we become seekers of that high. We become addicted to that sensation of the release from tension. And every annoying/irritating/interrupting situation tempts us into seeking that release.

As I begin to see my struggle for what it truly is—me being unable to resist sin and caving into temptation, the path to freedom becomes less cluttered.

In point-form, some steps to help you pray your way through temptation:

1. Pray about your issue constantly—even at times when you don't feel as though you're struggling. When you wake up, before moving from your bed, remind God (and yourself) that you are prone to being tempted (whether it be yelling at your children, smoking, using foul words, gossiping—just sharing a nasty laundry list with y'all, though God and I kicked the smoking one many, many years ago), and ask Him to help you. Keep on reminding Him all day. It's not that He needs reminding, but we need to remember that He is the only help for our struggles.

pray continually ~1 Thessalonians 5:17

2. Pray the Word of God the very moment you find yourself staring temptation in the face. It helps to write out Scriptures that speak to your struggle on index cards, so you have God's specific Words handy. Try using a concordance and writing out verses on: temptation, sin, perseverance, faith, holiness, trials, struggle, submission, and so on. If you believe the Bible addresses your issue specifically (such as immorality or anger), look for verses on those topics as well.

In Matthew 4, Jesus spent 40 days in the desert and the devil tried to tempt Him into sinning against His Father. Jesus' reply to each suggestion of the devil was,

It is written . . .

3. Seek trusted people to pray for you. We are not in the battle against evil on our own—we have brothers and sisters who can stand beside us.

Confess your sins to each other and pray for each other so that you may be healed. The prayer of a righteous man is powerful and effective. ~James 5:16

4. Remember that at each juncture, you have a choice. You can choose to submit yourself to temptation (and thus to sin), or you can submit yourself to Christ.

Submit yourselves, then, to God. Resist the devil and he will flee from you. ~James 4:7

. . . God is faithful; He will not let you be tempted beyond what you can bear. But when you are tempted, He will also provide a way out so that you can stand up under it. ~1 Corinthians 10:13

Day 24

I have completed 23 days of my fast food/junk food/processed food fast. More than halfway!

The prospect that I have only 17 days left is exciting. On September 13th I get to weigh myself and see if there have been physical results of my spiritual discipline. (If I'm totally honest, I fear that there won't be, and I'll be discouraged. Even though I *know* that this hasn't really been about losing weight at all.) On September 13th I am free to enjoy a slurpee or potato chips, maybe a chocolate bar or some french fries. Or how about anything that I don't need to make from scratch?!

I wonder if these remaining 17 days will be enough . . . Will I have grown closer to God? Will I be more willing to obey Him because of this? Will I have the strength to continue in seeking Him about what I eat? Or will I fall back into what is comfortable? These questions are troubling . . .

I so badly want to be changed! I know that I've grown complacent. And eating habits are really an outward symbol of my inner state. If I lack discipline in my eating, in my homemaking, in my parenting, in my marriage, finances, etc.—these are all indicators that I am lacking in spiritual discipline as well. I don't know if this is true for everyone, but I know that when my spiritual life is in order the rest of my life follows suit. Because a spirit that is yielded to the Spirit is not satisfied with complacency or laziness in any area.

I believe that God called me to 40 days of submitting to Him in my eating habits in order to draw me into His will in other areas. And I am so afraid that I am just missing the point! Missing the blessing.

Oh Lord, that I would seek You with all my heart, in all things I do! Show me where I am walking outside of Your will for my life. Lay before me all the areas I am lacking in discipline and self-control. I no longer want to walk in disobedience and disregard, Father. Change my heart through this purifying of my body. Teach me, Jesus. Change me. ***Unsettle me . . .***

I appeal to you therefore, brothers, by the mercies of God, to present your bodies as a living sacrifice, holy and acceptable to God, which is your spiritual worship. ~Romans 12:1

Unsettle Me

For this one, I am going to need to take you back a ways. Right to the beginning of this year, when I prayed that the Lord would unsettle me. I knew it was a dangerous prayer, but I was wildly ready for anything He might toss my way.

And somewhere in that first part of this year my husband shared with me that he was sensing a change on the horizon. We attended the *BreakForth* conference together and came home expecting BIG things.

Then we went about our lives as usual.

I remembered my prayer for the new year when it was convenient, but mostly I let myself forget about it. You see, I don't actually do well with change. I like consistency, stability, predictability.

A few short weeks ago, God reminded me of my desire to be unsettled. He said, "You don't want to have all this normalcy, do you? It's so . . . . boring. Why not come on an adventure with Me? Why don't you show people that your faith isn't just something you say, it's something you do."

I replied, "Um, no thanks God. I'm good. I'm not bored at all. Life is so perfectly *settled* right now; I'd rather not change."

The moment those words came out, I head the phrase "unsettle me" echoing in my soul.

Our family will be moving soon. Not just to a new house, but to a new city with new schools and a new church. We are brought there by a new job, one that promises a whole new life for our family. At this new job, Daddy will be home every.single.night for supper. He will have a long weekend to spend with us every.second.week. He will not be called to work out of town for weeks on end—in fact, he will not be called to work out of town EVER.

Today we are in the midst of the sloppy business of moving forward, with the excitement and adventure of the new ahead, and the sorrow of leaving so much good behind. Man, does it ever hurt to let go of GOOD things! The only thing that helps is to know that when God asks us to do that, He already has even BETTER things on the horizon. And there is comfort in knowing that rather than just leaving all this love behind, we will actually end up with two homes where we are loved. A new one and the old one. A double-blessing.

In this process, God's handiwork has been evident in a million small and large ways:

- — the peace we had with making a very fast decision; the encouragement and words of affirmation from other believers
- — the fact that I asked God to show confirmation for this decision by making it possible to keep our house here and rent it out, and He did
- — the first house we looked at was not only good for our family, but it had a whole bunch of features that my husband and I had only dreamed of (three living rooms, a den/office, a large attached garage, a veranda, an eat-in kitchen and a dining room, a fireplace, oodles of bathrooms, a jet tub); honestly, at first I felt that we should not even consider this house because it was so much of what we wanted, that I was certain we didn't deserve it—funny thing about God, though, is that He likes to give good gifts to His children just because
- — we closed the deal on that house tonight, and though the steps along the way were not bump-free, they were relatively quick and easy
- — finding a Christian program within the public schools that is totally FREE

— knowing that the ministry I love—my baby—is in the best hands of the most amazing, competent, Godly, visionary team of women
— and many more.

I don't know why God is moving us. But I do know that He is answering a decade-long prayer of ours for my husband to have a job that provides well but doesn't have him away. And I am certain that He has a plan for friends, schools, a church family, a home (not just a house), and more. I believe that sometimes God calls us to do really difficult things so that we are stretched and moved closer to Him, and so that our faith in His goodness and His provision can grow. I fully trust Him to take care of us, our friends, our family, and our ministries—and I believe that He even has a BETTER thing in store for each of them.

It won't be easy. Change is difficult, scary even. We will be like foreigners in a new country. It could end up feeling a bit like a desert for a while. So as we walk I will tilt my head to the sky, and I will follow the Pillar of Cloud that goes ahead of me, showing the way.

And the Lord went before them by day in a pillar of cloud to lead them along the way, and by night in a pillar of fire to give them light, that they might travel by day and by night. The pillar of cloud by day and the pillar of fire by night did not depart from before the people. ~Exodus 13:21-22

The LORD is There

This morning I was talking to God about my sadness at leaving so many special people. I love my sisters here so much, and when they shared news of our move to the group of women at *Friendship Factor* (our women's coffee break) yesterday, we all got a little choked-up. For a moment, the excitement of things to come took a back burner to the sadness of letting go and saying good-bye.

So this morning, I thanked God for those sisters of mine, I lifted up their families to Him, I asked Him to bless them, and I told Him how I was counting on Him to fill the empty space in my heart that belongs to them.

He reminded me of a special gift I received in the prayer room at *She Speaks*. The conference organizers spent time praying over each of the names of the attendees, and with the guidance of the Holy Spirit placed our names next to one of the Names of God. My name was beside Jehovah-Shammah: the LORD is there.

He whispered to my spirit this morning:

When you are in a new land, I AM THERE.

When you feel sad and are praying for a friend, I AM THERE.

When your heart longs for the familiar of what was before, I AM THERE.

When tears of loneliness pour from your eyes, I AM THERE.

Wherever you go, when you go in My Name, you go with My Blessing, you bring with you My Presence, and I AM THERE.

And with His promises held tightly in my heart, I will go with Him. But my sisters, I sure will miss you.

Behold, I am doing a new thing; now it springs forth, do you not perceive it? I will make a way in the wilderness and rivers in the desert. ~Isaiah 43:19

A Special Day for a Special Gal

Today is my Mom's birthday. She's at the tippy-top of the hill now, just about to go over—but not quite!

In honor of her birthday, here are 50 reasons I love my Mommy . . .

1. She never gave up on me, even during my rebellious phase.
2. She sings my kids the same lullabies she sang to me.
3. We share a love for reading.
4. I enjoy hanging out with her.
5. She cleans my bathrooms almost every time she comes over.
6. She's my best friend.
7. She is fiercely loyal to her family.
8. She's a super Bible study leader.
9. She's the bestest, most full of energy Grandma in the whole world.
10. She makes us dinner every Sunday night.
11. She doesn't mind that I call her 14 times a day at work just to visit.
12. She puts up with my husband's wise-cracks.
13. She mows my grass almost every time she comes over in the summer.
14. She loves to babysit.
15. She will say "no" to babysitting when she needs to.
16. She's not afraid to look foolish in the name of fun.
17. She likes to dance.
18. She's a good singer.
19. She's pretty.
20. She's smart.

21. She's patient (have I mentioned that I have some hormone issues?).
22. She's forgiving.
23. She's generous.
24. She will sacrifice her own desires for the people she loves.
25. She helps me prevent drowning incidents at the beach and pool.
26. She is brave enough to take my kids camping.
27. The kids get to learn about gardening because of her.
28. The kids' faith is supported and cemented in her home.
29. Even if she doesn't like it, she always supports what I do.
30. She has painted in every house I've ever owned.
31. Its fun to watch her drive her new "sporty" car with a big grin on her face.
32. The kids are allowed to play and be kids at her house.
33. The kids are disciplined if they misbehave at her house.
34. She jokes back with her smart-alec son-in-laws.
35. She loves all of her kids with her whole heart, regardless of who gave birth to them.
36. She raised her grandson for 13 years.
37. Even though she dislikes it, she bums around home improvement stores with her husband.
38. She honours her marriage.
39. She honours God.
40. Family is everything to her.
41. She drags me out in the cold of winter to take the kids sledding.
42. Her dragging makes me do things I am too lazy to do on my own.
43. Her dragging makes me have fun!
44. She never got mad when I borrowed her clothes without asking.
45. My friends went to her for help and counsel.
46. Some of my friends still go to her for help and counsel.
47. She is wise.
48. I love her freckles.
49. She is an overcomer.
50. She doesn't want a big deal made about her big birthday.

Rest is Good for the Heart

A season in life when hands are full, days are busy.

In Chinese, the symbols used to describe the word busy are heart and dead.

Busy = heart dead.

Too busy to stop and enjoy. Too busy to go slow and savour. Too busy to listen. Too busy to seek. Too busy to pray. The result—a dry, aching, empty heart.

This fall has come crashing in on me. A move, with all of its headaches and details to tend to—buy a house, find new schools, move utilities, switch this, research that . . . A big party to plan and carry out, with friends and family to entertain. A blessing, yet a busy time. A women's event. A ministry fair. A course in Biblical exegesis. A slightly incomplete renovation. Children to tend, love, and feed. A house to keep. A husband working 15 hour days. A million and one ministry details to wrap up and leave in good order for someone new.

And somewhere in the busy, the heart's lifebeat slows.

I have considered hiring a housekeeper, putting the little ones in a dayhome, going back on anti-depressants after five years without, getting help with anything that can be done by someone else. Yet I know that none of that will revive this heart of mine.

The One who brings hearts back to life, who removes the busy and replaces it with peace and joy—He is the solution this heart needs.

Busy = heart dead.

Rest in Him = true life, full life.

Find rest, o my soul, in God alone; my hope comes from Him. ~Psalm 62:5

What is Joy?

Reflecting on the inverse relationship between joy and anger . . . Digging through the Scriptures to better understand joy . . . Today my heart settled on this:

Be joyful always.~ 1 Thessalonians 5:16

In dictionary.com I find joyful defined as "full of joy, as a person or one's heart; showing or expressing joy, as looks, actions, or speech."

I consider my looks, my actions, my words. Do they express joy?

Sure. Usually. Sometimes. Well, occasionally. Definitely not *always*.

For the next two weeks, as I commit this short passage to memory, I will recite it in my head before I speak. Daily, hundreds of times (I do talk a lot), I will allow God's Word to remind me, and pray that joy overtakes anger, peace overtakes strife, love overtakes irritability.

Rejoice in the Lord always; again I will say, Rejoice. ~Philippians 4:4

God In-cidences

When we move next month, our plan has always been to rent this house out.

Renter #1—A girl who used to work with my husband, bringing her boyfriend and her brother. She said she wanted it, my husband said she could have it. I felt unsettled, but was prepared to stand behind his word to her. But I really felt like this house is a *family* home. When we got to serious talking about leases and such, she changed her mind. Coincidence?

Renter #2—A couple . . . a blended family . . . just starting fresh. There were no red flags with them, but numerous yellow flags. For example, he was employed, but just started at this new job a week earlier due to a layoff. We were uncertain if we needed to heed these yellow flags or if we were supposed to be compassionate and give them a chance. We prayed about it. We asked them to come for an interview. They declined. Chance?

Renter #3—An African family with 5 very young children. Very friendly and appreciative. They kept talking about where there things would fit in this house. We both felt really good about them. They wanted to stay and fill out a rental application on the spot.

Renter #4—Came to look on the heels of #3. A young couple with 3 kids. Friendly, social, very interested in the house. We both really liked them. They also wanted to stay and fill out an application.

We were unsure, but decided to go with our gut feeling on the first family. It was a risk, because they could change their minds in the meantime (before we got damage deposit). And then the second couple could have found something else. We'd be back at square one . . . But we prayed about it and felt that "this house is home for the African family."

When we told them we wanted them to be in our house, the husband exclaimed, "praise the Lord!" When we told the other couple (#4) that we were renting it to someone else, they seemed relieved.

The wife later told me that they had been looking at a few places to rent, but none of them felt right to her. They were about to pay the deposit on a house and she asked her husband to wait another couple days. For some reason, he decided to search the internet for other rentals. She told me that he never searches the internet, and that before this day they had never even heard of a website called kijiji. On just that very day, renter #2 didn't pan out, and I decided to re-post my ad on kijiji. When the husband googled "houses to rent in Red Deer" the very first link that came up was our ad.

She tells me that she believes God has provided this house for them, just for their family. She said she can feel that the Holy Spirit dwells here. She says it already feels like home. I told her that we have been praying for just the right renters, and that we believe God has provided them for this house. Good luck?

I don't believe in luck, chance, or coincidence. Nothing is done by accident, without the foreknowledge of a loving God. He is as concerned with the small details of our day-to-day lives as he is with big global issues. He is a God who cares.

This couple isn't able to officially rent from us until December 1, due to their current rental agreement. Interestingly, our mortgage payments on our new house in SP don't begin until December 1.

Only God could work out every detail so meticulously to ensure that just the right people are living in our house. Renters who, I believe, will take good care of it as if it were their own home. And a house created for a family of seven, with all of their needs in mind—right down to the extra water heater.

Nope. No coincidences here. Just God-incidences.

And we know that for those who love God all things work together for good, for those who are called according to his purpose. ~Romans 8:28

Family Stuff

Just a little something I jotted out last night after a time of learning, praise, praise, and worship . . .

How to Train our Children:

— to love God with their whole hearts
— to serve God and others as an outpouring of that love
— to worship without inhibition

- worship music playing at all times
- stop to pray, praise, worship at set points throughout the day
- invest time in them for fun
- invest time in them for training in obedience
- invest time in them for discipline
- love God with our whole hearts
- model service to them and to others
- worship without inhibition, inviting them to participate
- family memory verses
- family devotionals
- bring God into every conversation
- share our prayer requests and praises with the children
- teach them to pray out loud, without inhibition
- pray out loud with them, without inhibition
- love one another (as a couple) with passion and purpose
- love one another (as a family) with passion and purpose
- obey God without question or hesitation, and tell the kids about it
- give generously as a couple and as a family
- model the fruits of the spirit
- stop yelling
- stop swearing
- do not be impatient

- do not be angry
- put the needs of others before self (ie., kids before computer)
- do not disobey God
- stop repeat sin

We need to develop a plan as a family. A vision, mission, and values perhaps? A goal to aspire to and the methods to attain it. A common objective.

Train up a child in the way he should go; even when he is old he will not depart from it. ~Proverbs 22:6

Making Friends

I've been reflecting a lot lately on making friends, trying to remember how to do it. As a child it was so easy—see someone about your age at the park or in the school yard, walk up to that person, introduce yourself (although, this step could easily be done much later, or omitted all together), and ask the other kid, "Would you like to be friends?" As an adult, it seems so many more personal insecurities play into the friend-making process. How did I do it several years ago when we joined our church and I felt lost, alone, and depressed? I knew I needed someone, and now I have many someone's—but how did it all happen?

I remember walking into the basement of the church on a Wednesday morning, terrified. So many women, all smiling and chatting over their crafts. Ugh, how I loathe crafts! So I make my way to the coffee pot, feeling tentative but trying my best not to look either afraid or standoffish. I stand back and peruse the tables filled with friends.

Where should I sit? One table seems to be "older" women—ack, one of my high school teachers is sitting there! Another table of very young women (maybe close to my age, but I feel older). There they are . . . a table of women who are laughing loudly, talking back and forth and over each other, shouting out greetings to women walking in the door. They look welcoming. So I take a deep breath, stand up straight, put a smile on, walk myself, my coffee, and my craft supplies (ugh) over and ask, "Is this chair taken?"

I sat, I crafted (ugh), I listened, and every now and then I talked. And though I didn't feel comfortable—no, not for one moment—something in me knew that I could be comfortable in the place . . . eventually.

Wednesday after Wednesday, I went, I looked, I sat. And one week, the dam broke. I had tried a couple different tables over the weeks, but this week I was back with the group of loud outgoing gals. One of them said something that got all my senses firing. I heard her say, "When I had post-partum depression after . . ." That whole morning I waited for a chance to talk to her somewhat privately, because she knew my pain. Eventually, over another craft, that moment came. I can't recall if we made some small talk first and I somehow led the conversation around, or if I just jumped right in. But with a choked voice and tear-filled eyes I shared with her how I was struggling with post-partum depression. And that common-thread drew us together.

The next week she invited my husband and me to join the life group they were part of. Through that group, friendships bloomed. I began to learn who I was, what I was looking for, and who I wanted to spend my time with. Because of the love from that group (which, ironically, included my old high school teacher and her husband), I found healing in my broken places and friendship for my empty spaces.

It's good to remember that time. Though my friendships have changed over the years, and I am no longer connected with the people from that original life group, I will never forget the impact of knowing them and being welcomed by them.

As we step into this next place, I will remember. Be bold. Do not be afraid. Don't allow discomfort to make me shy away. Be real and open and honest. Look for opportunities. Be willing. Friendship will come, if I look for it. But it means stepping outside the bounds of where I feel comfortable, talking to people I don't know, possibly doing crafts (ugh), and looking for that common ground.

We've all had to make new friends at one time or another. What did you do to find those connections?

A friend loves at all times, and a brother is born for adversity. ~Proverbs 17:17

Aching Heart

This week, my heart has been wrenched to and fro.

In addition to the surprise on my date night and the blessing at the church staff meeting, I was blessed and honoured at *Friendship Factor* on Wednesday. You wouldn't believe the trickery of those girls! People who haven't been at FF in over a year were tracked down and invited to take the morning off work so they could attend. (Bless their hearts, several did.)

Nothing is more humbling than feeling really, really loved. Did you know that? I would have thought hearing all these people telling me how great I am (I know they are selectively forgetting the bad stuff right now, but hey) would make me feel prideful and oh-so important. But it just doesn't. It makes me feel a bit shy, a bit confused, and very tender.

I cannot wrap my head and heart around it. It seems only last week I was a just-past-teenage mom with only one friend in the whole world. And these past couple of weeks have shown me that I have more friends than I know what to do with. (You should see my calendar these days as I try to have coffee with everyone I love. I am not getting anything done besides socializing!)

Each blessing I receive just makes the loss more profound. Not that I'm really losing these friends—I know that! I will be back at least once per month, and I will insist that they come my way periodically, and the modern miracle of email will keep us in close touch. But what I am losing is a culture of friendship and fellowship. It's something that took six years to develop, and moving away from this church family is . . . ouch.

Today I had to take one step further yet. You see, today we chose the woman who will take my position. The only job I've held in six years (besides those of wife and mother). A job that exists because it was on my heart and I asked if I could do it. Frankly, I see this ministry more as my baby than as my job. A baby I laboured over, nurtured, prayed for, and loved with my whole heart. And today, I chose an adoptive mother for my baby. I have just over one week to hold this baby close until it is time to extend my arms to the one who will take over the job of its care. And no matter that I know it is God's will, and it is time, and that it is not only for my good and my family's but for the baby's good as well—the ache in my gut just may kill me.

And as I sit here letting the tears flow freely, I hear a gentle whisper in my soul . . .

Jehovah-Shammah, the LORD is there. I AM there. I AM in Red Deer with Women of Worth (WOW), and I will not let it stumble. I AM in Sherwood Park where you will go, and I will not let you stumble. The name of every city you visit, every church you worship in, every ministry you serve with will be: the LORD is there. (from Ezekial 48:35)

Though the ache remains, I know I will live through it, for He is with me.

The Crooked Mat

I often take off my rings (wedding band, engagement/wedding combo ring, family ring) in the evening and set them on my bookshelf. Every now and then, though, I will set them in some other totally convenient location. I once set them on top of the microwave.

The next evening (almost 24 hours later) as I was getting ready to head out somewhere, I began searching for my rings. And searching. I could not find them anywhere, nor could I recall where I had set them the night before. I shrugged it off, thinking it was one of those places that will come to mind later. But as I grabbed my purse from its perch beside the microwave, I discovered my wedding band peeking out from underneath.

One of the kids had likely been grabbing something and bumped them. Or, there's always the possibility that someone thought they would be fun to play with or wear. But I try to think the best of my kids.

I set my purse down and started looking around the kitchen for my other rings. After a minute of two, I stumbled across my family ring on the floor against the baseboard. Unfortunately, no matter where I looked and from what vantage point (crawling, standing, squinting) I just was not finding my precious diamonds! After about five minutes knots began to form in my stomach and throat.

A thought popped into my head . . . *Pray.* That was countered by the thought, *but what a ridiculous thing to pray about! There are children starving and people dying of cancer, families breaking apart and worse.* No matter how I tried to ignore that thought, though, it kept coming back to me. So I stopped and asked the Lord to help me find my ring.

After I prayed I wasn't sure what to do. Wait for an idea to come to me? Continue searching? Stop searching altogether? I took a deep breath, picked up my purse, and prepared to leave the house—trying to trust that God would take care of it. Somehow.

On my way out the door I stopped to straighten out the mat (as I often do—a crooked mat makes me crazy!). A glint of something flickered in my peripheral vision. *Could it be? Nah.* As if God would literally answer my prayer two seconds after I prayed it. I almost ignored that little glint, but my curiosity got the better of me.

A couple inches away from the heat register—was my ring! The tension instantly lifted from my neck and shoulders, I slid the ring on my finger, and headed out the door smiling.

As I hopped in my vehicle and turned the key I felt a little whisper in my heart, *you're welcome*. And I paused again for just a moment to give honour and praise to the One who cares about what's important to me.

Casting all your anxieties on him, because he cares for you. ~1 Peter 5:7

Morning Solitude

I've had a couple friends ask me how to start getting into the Word more regularly. I'm no expert, nor am I am shining example, but I do have some ideas that have worked for me (during those times that I am consistent).

Why do Bible reading, prayer, journaling, etc. in the mornings? I don't know about you, but if there is something I NEED to get done, I have to plan to do it first thing in the morning. If I am in one of those phases where I'm trying to exercise regularly, I MUST do it in the morning. If it's housecleaning day, or laundry day, morning is the time to get it done. It seems that the more time I let pass, the easier it becomes to put off what's important until I eventually decide to take care of it . . . tomorrow.

Time can slip by so quickly in the early morning. If I allow myself to do anything before my time with God, I typically run out of time. It's easy to tell yourself, "I'll just unload the dishwasher. That will only take 2 minutes. Then I'll sit down with my Bible." But we all know how women are about multi-tasking! One small job leads to another, and before we know it half an hour has passed and life is upon us.

So, to prevent the stuff of life from distracting you from your good intentions to spend time with God daily, it needs to be the first thing you do each day.

What if I'm not a morning person? Or I just don't have time in the morning?
It's hard to change your regular routine! I suggest you start small. Set your alarm for just 15 minutes earlier in the morning. Once you sit in your quiet spot: pray for God to speak to you from His Word; read a short passage of Scripture (maybe just a couple verses); reflect on what they mean and how they can apply to you; then get

ready for your day. After a week or two, set the alarm for another 15 minutes earlier.

When I first started getting up earlier in the morning, I found myself very tired throughout the day. Mid-afternoon would often find my nodding off or yawning uncontrollably. Some days I countered the tiredness with an afternoon cup of coffee, some days (rarely, ha) I would do a few minutes of exercise, other days (more often) I'd grab a power nap. By the time evening rolled along, I would have a second wind and end up staying up late, making the next day even more exhausting. But after about two weeks of this cycle, my body fought back! It is not often you will find me awake past 10pm on a weeknight these days. You also won't find me dozing off during my supper prep time anymore.

I'm so tired in the mornings that I'm not remembering anything I read.

Here are a few quick tips to make the most of your learning and retention from your Bible times . . .

- Always pray first, asking God to make His Word clear to you and asking Him to speak to you in your life from what you read.
- Read shorter passages and focus on them, rather than trying to read through several chapters at once. (Personally, I find that most of those 'read the Bible in a year' schedules have me reading far too much at once. Sure, I may have read through my whole Bible, but I haven't taken much of it to heart.)
- Write down a passage that really speaks to you on an index card. Carry it around with you and meditate on it throughout the day. Look at it when you're stopped at a red light, standing in a line, waiting on hold, taking your coffee or lunch break.
- Write in your Bible! Make notes beside passages that hold special meaning for you. These notes will not only help you remember what you've read and how it spoke to you, but they will hold special meaning to the people in your life who love you. I consider my Bible study notes to be a huge

part of the legacy I will leave for my children. My hope is that seeing my faith walk, my joys and struggles, and my spiritual growth will inspire and encourage them as they walk with the Lord.

I want to read my whole Bible, but every time I get started I find myself bogged down in Numbers and I give up.
The best thing I ever did to read through my entire Bible is that I stopped trying to read it in order! The Old Testament (OT) stories are fascinating, but there are books of the Bible that sure do seem to take more effort to dig through. My system (though not necessarily the most theologically sound) is to read from the OT—a book, maybe two if they're shorter—then reward myself for the hard work and focus by reading a book from the New Testament (NT). To keep track of what I've read, I just check off the books in the Table of Contents of my Bible . . . next time through I turn the checks into Xs . . . next time I circle the Xs . . .

Some other ideas I've heard include reading a passage from an OT book and a passage from a NT book each day, progressing forward through each. Many of those 'read the Bible in a year' systems provide you with an order to follow. Or a new thing that I've heard a few people rave about is the Chronological Bible—the books of the Bible are rearranged so that everything flows in order chronologically.

The most important thing is to do what works for you! Personally, I like to have guidelines to follow. If you don't, just pick up your Bible and read, spend time in prayer, write out any thoughts you have, and go with the flow! Either way, God is pleased when we choose to spend time with Him each day. And life just makes more sense when each day is started being filled up. No, it's not perfect or easy, but there is a unique peace that fills our days when we start them out with God.

And rising very early in the morning, while it was still dark, he departed and went out to a desolate place, and there he prayed. ~Mark 1:35

Consider it Pure Joy?

I have a confession to make . . . I struggle between wanting God to answer my prayers and pour out His blessings on me, while also desiring a deeper relationship with Him and experiences that grow my faith to maturity.

I will pray, "Lord, give me a deeper desire to know You and Your Word." Then, when difficult, stressful, frustrating things happen I cry out, "God, what is going on here? Can't You please stop this messy thing that is happening to me?!"

I ask for one thing, then when God begins His work in me—work that will transform my heart and give me that which I've prayed for—I quickly backpedal and begin praying for Him to just put everything back to normal.

It is difficult to remember that life's trials serve a purpose. Our struggles test our faith—we are *supposed* to draw close to God during such times. Experiencing this testing develops perseverance (determination, persistence, doggedness, diligence, resolution) in us. And perseverance grows us into mature Christ-followers. (Taken from James 1:2-4.)

Our trials serve a purpose. So often we ask God to provide what we want—health, peace, financial provision, a husband, children, and so on—without taking into consideration the possibility that God has a much bigger plan. Possibly, not receiving all that we ask for is the path to fulfilling His plan.

Lysa TerKeurst puts it this way, "We want the promises, but we don't want to get any dirt under our fingernails in the process." (Becoming More than a Good Bible Study Girl, pp. 201)

Yup, that's me. I want all of the good God assures me of in His Word, but I sure don't want to have to work for it. I don't want to have to struggle and experience pain and heartache in order to experience blessings.

Yet if I haven't experienced that pain, pushed through the struggles, clung to my faith in God, can I even recognize a blessing?

Having spent years in deep debt and financial struggle, I remember to thank God every time I can go to the grocery store and buy whatever I toss in the cart (even if the cart load includes a box of Lucky Charms). If it had simply always been this way—where we needed an item and could go out to get it—I would likely attribute the state of our finances to ourselves. But having experienced times of huge heartache and trials, I am all the more aware that any financial provision has been provided by our Heavenly Father.

I think this is what James means when he says, "Consider it pure joy, my brothers, whenever you face trials of many kinds." (James 1:2) He's not telling us to be ridiculous and run through the streets exclaiming, "I praise you, Lord, that my child has a disability! I am filled with joy by having a special needs child!" Rather, he's instructing us to have a joy deep in our hearts, because of the knowledge that God is using our trials to mature us and draw us closer to Him.

The name of the Lord is a strong tower; the righteous man runs into it and is safe. ~Proverbs 18:10

Feet First

As a women's ministry leader, I've always had a heart for women who feel like they just don't "fit." I've spent many hours coffee-ing (I know, that's not a word) with lonely, isolated, broken women. One common theme I've noticed among these women is their heartfelt NEED for fellowship with other women. Which is why I've reached out even when it's inconvenient. Even when the invitation includes four children under the age of six (in addition to my own five), a ridiculous mess in my house, and two dozen hot dogs for lunch. *Now don't get me wrong and think I'm some sort of saint—there are a million instances in my memory when I know I should have reached out and I didn't.*

You know what else I've noticed? There are two distinct "types" among women seeking fellowship.

Type 1 is sad and lonely, she complains of being sad and lonely, she may even make pleas for friendship in conversation . . . but she doesn't actually take action. When she meets people she pulls into herself, allows shyness and insecurity take over, and she ends up with no invitations. This woman remains sad and lonely for a long time before someone reaches out and draws her into friendship.

Type 2 is also sad and lonely, feels shy and insecure. But she is different. This woman pushes past her feelings and makes herself do things that are not at all comfortable. She makes conversation when she meets people, even though she has a lump of fear in her throat. Rather than waiting for invitations, she risks rejection and invites near strangers for coffee. She steps out in courage.

Courage is doing what you're afraid to do. There can be no courage unless you're scared.

~ Eddie Rickenbacker

In this new and foreign place, I am choosing to be the second type of woman. In spite of the fear, insecurity, discomfort, and ball in the pit of my stomach, I am going to women's groups and reaching out. I am inviting people to my home for coffee and Christmassy get-togethers.

Some of the women I meet are saying that I'm brave. The truth is . . . I am terrified. But the knowledge in my heart that I NEED other women pushes me to do that which I am most afraid of. Because my fear of having no one is stronger than the insecurity and fear of rejection.

Be strong and courageous. Do not fear or be in dread of them, for it is the Lord your God who goes with you. He will not leave you or forsake you. ~Deuteronomy 31:6

And Again, as I Hop Back on the Wagon

God is speaking to me about my eating again. He's reminding me that He provided me with the perfect "diet" plan—a plan for eating His way. He's showing me that this plan was not intended to be a temporary, short-term suggestion, but a way of life.

I've been plugging my ears and singing, "La, la, la, la!" for a while now. I don't want to sacrifice. I don't want to work hard. I don't want to struggle. There's a little rebel inside of me that doesn't want to do the thing that everyone else is doing (makes sense, doesn't it—refusing to eat healthy and exercise so that no one thinks I'm just trying to be a part of the "in" crowd?).

What I've come to realize, though, is that what I am really choosing is self-abuse. I fill my body with junk that I think tastes good, and I get fatter. I grow more lethargic and lose motivation. I feel queasy on and off all day, I have heartburn at night, my back aches and my feet hurt, I have headaches and feel irritable. All caused by me.

God may not have given me a supermodel's body—thin and willowy, completely flat abs and curves in all the right places. But He did give me this body. He has a vision for how it's supposed to look and feel, and I'm pretty sure He wasn't thinking of this.

Here are some thoughts that I've jotted down the past while as I've pondered this subject:

- Why would God reveal His plan/purpose/calling for me right now, when I'm clearly too fat, tired, unhealthy, and lazy to fulfill it?
- Given the fact that the Holy Spirit dwells within all believers (that includes me), how can I accept giving Him a sub-par,

unhealthy dwelling place? Someone once gave me this evaluation for deciding which shows and movies to watch: if Jesus were sitting right beside you, would you be willing to watch it? The same could be asked about what I put in my body.

— When I eat particularly terribly, I have noticed that I tend to be extra irritable and impatient with my children and husband. (And, my acne breaks out like crazy.) I shouldn't be surprised; it's basic math . . . junk in = junk out.

Quote of the day: Satan comes to steal, kill, and destroy . . . And if we continue to make God's temple our trash can, we are helping the devil accomplish his mission—one meal at a time. ~Sheri Rose Shepherd.

For we do not wrestle against flesh and blood, but against the rulers, against the authorities, against the cosmic powers over this present darkness, against the spiritual forces of evil in the heavenly places. ~Ephesians 6:12

The Tree

Last night, we finally decked out our little tree with lights and ornaments. It is now a gloriously unsymmetrical mess of homemade ornaments.

As we decorated the tree and bee-bopped to some Christmas tunes, my mind wandered . . . *Why do we decorate a tree for Jesus' birthday?* This morning I asked my trusty friend, Google that very question. The answers were many and varied—many completely inaccurate, I'm sure. But I found a couple explanations that resonated . . .

The triangle shape of the tree represents the Trinity: Father, Son, Holy Spirit. The top of the tree points Heavenward.

The colour of the tree, green, represents life. Evergreen means eternal life.

The needles of a tree grow upward, like hands raised praising God.

The lights on the tree glitter and glisten like the streets of Heaven.

And the giving of gifts is an act of love and charity; a reflection of the love Christ has for us.

Looking at the tree, beautiful and shiny, brought to mind another tree. A tree that was roughly carved down, limbs and leaves and bark stripped away, ugly and bare, made into a cross.

It's impossible to reflect on the birth of the Christ child without the mind coming to His reason for being born. As we celebrate the

Saviour birth, we are reminded of His death. A sacrifice of love for our sins. It seems fitting, doesn't it, that we use a tree to celebrate His birth, and tree to celebrate His death?

(Yes, we can celebrate Christ's death, because we know that it was not the end, but the beginning. God raised Him from the dead, just as His Salvation pulls us up from the darkness of death.)

The Christmas tree . . . a symbol of the eternal life we have been promised through Christ.

He himself bore our sins in his body on the tree, that we might die to sin and live to righteousness. By his wounds you have been healed. ~1 Peter 2:24

My Shoulders are no Longer Hunched over by the Weight of the World

When we decided to move, I knew that having Pat home every night would be special, wonderful, and a blessing to all of us. Because God has made it clear that we are to leave our families and cleave to our spouses, I knew that He would bless this decision. In spite of the heartache moving away from our extended family, friends, ministry, church, and overall support network, there was not a doubt in my mind that this was the right thing to do. *(Lest you think that by "moving away" I mean we went far, we are only a 90 minute drive from our old home!)*

You know what I had no idea about, though? Just how much difference it makes in life to have a second pair of hands around on a regular basis! I am not the only one on call in the middle of the night. I don't have to wrangle up friends and grandparents to assist with getting all the kids to activities. I am no longer chef, bus girl, and dishwasher for virtually every dinner. I'm not the only cog in the bath time assembly line. I don't have to do loving and teaching and discipline and homework all tangled together—on my own. Until I experienced the joy of having my husband home nightly, I had no clue how overwhelmed I was without him.

Don't get me wrong, it's not like my husband was never home. But he was away and working late just often enough that I settled into a comfortable (if not slightly harried) groove of doing it all. I didn't realize the weight of that burden until it was lifted from me.

Sure, we've gotten into a few squabbles along the way. I had a good system, but Pat employs different methods. Sometimes I forget that the end result is more important than the methods and

I try to remind him that I know how to do things best. Thankfully, he understands the "planner" part of me and can help me loosen my grip gently.

You know what else has surprised me a bit? The simple fact that I really do **like** my husband! *I can hear you chuckling* . . . It's not that I ever *didn't* like him, but that I was worried that we might get on one another's nerves and grow tired of each other's company after so much "togetherness." But we're not! Well, *I'm* not; I guess you'd have to ask him if I'm getting on his nerves. 🙂

I like talking with him, hanging out with him, fighting over the remote control with him, planning out our week together. It's like we're dating again and don't want to be apart for any lengthy period of time—and I love it! All these gooey feelings kinda make a girl want to do something as an expression of all that love . . . like maybe make a baby. Nothing says "we're madly in love" than creating life together. Whaddya say, honey? Should we explore the possibility of going for #6?

Just kidding . . . Sort of.

Likewise, husbands, live with your wives in an understanding way, showing honor to the woman as the weaker vessel, since they are heirs with you of the grace of life, so that your prayers may not be hindered. ~1 Peter 3:7

From Dishonour to Freedom

Then the Lord God will wipe away the tears from all faces, and the disgrace of his people he will take away from all the earth, for the Lord has spoken. ~Isaiah 25:8-9 (NRSV)

In just two short weeks we will celebrate the birth of the Messiah, the One who removes our disgrace and wipes our tears.

Don't you just love that phrase, "He will take away our disgrace?"

Disgrace (n)—shame, dishonour, discredit, scandal, humiliation.

Disgrace (v)—bring shame on, bring into disrepute, tarnish, stain.

The coming of the Christ child was not just a promise to forgive our sins, but to remove the scandal of those sins, so that our names (and His) could not be brought into disrepute.

Do you find that you sometimes go to God seeking forgiveness, yet you continue to allow the sins you have confessed to stain your own view of yourself? You allow the shame of the sins to linger? I know I do. I'm truly sorry for the wrong I've done, but it never leaves me; it's always in the back of my mind. *I can't share the gospel with this person—I'm too messed up. With my background, I should never be in public ministry. I can't possibly serve God in that capacity! I'm a liar, a failure, a hypocrite. Anyone who knows me will know the truth about who I am and what I've done . . .*

Yet we are promised not only that we will be forgiven, but that our disgrace will be taken away. The redemption of Christ means that the stains on our lives are completely removed.

You know those laundry commercials? The ones where the "testers" grab someone in a grocery store and rub all sorts of goo and gunk onto her white shirt? Then they treat the stain with their special formula stain remover, wash the shirt—in cold, icy water, no less—and it's like the stain was never there.

It's the same when Christ erases our dishonour—like it was never there.

So don't let past sin hold you back. If God is calling you to teach a Bible study, to speak in front of a group, to share the gospel with your neighbour—do it! Your old junk doesn't matter—it was never there. Don't hold onto shame that Christ has already removed. It is the very fact that you are imperfect and you have a past that will bring glory and honour to the Name of Jesus. The fact that our tarnish has been brought to a shine is a demonstration of His greatness and grace.

*Therefore, there is now **no condemnation** for those who are in Christ Jesus, because through Christ Jesus the law of the Spirit of life set me **free** from the law of sin and death.* ~Romans 8:1-2 (emphasis mine)

Pondering

I read some words this morning in my quiet time that brought tears to my eyes and a lump into my throat. They resonated with truth and made me feel so encouraged that I just had to share them. Both of these quotes are from Gary Thomas's "Holy Available" (pp. 124-125).

"Have you ever realized that God purposely sets up our lives to reveal His glory? Speaking of one man's healing, Jesus told His disciples, 'This happened so that the work of God might be displayed in his life. As long as it is day, we must do the work of him who sent me' (John 9:3-4)."

One thing I noticed about this story when I looked it up in my Bible was that this man was blind from birth. He was blind forever, for his whole life. He suffered a long time. Yet God healed him at just the right time that would bring glory to His name. It makes me think of things in my life that seem to be constant battles, going on and on. And I feel encouraged knowing that when God's hand of deliverance comes for those issues, it will be at just the right time to bring His Name glory.

"God has a purpose for you, and He's working to make this purpose come true. And because it's His purpose and because He's doing it, it's never in doubt. It's going to happen. God knows that it is so."

Just before this statement, the author has shared that God put on his heart a passion to write a certain book. He wrote this book and received, consecutively, 150 rejections before it was picked up for publication. And through the whole experience, he continued to feel God pushing him to pursue it. So he did. I know that I often feel God has put a dream in my heart for something, but the longer it takes the more I begin to question it. *Was that dream really from*

God? Maybe I made it up in my own head. Perhaps it's time to give up. For me, these words were a good and timely reminder to "stay the course" and trust that God will do His thing in His time.

I hope that something in these words gives you encouragement as well.

For I know the plans I have for you, declares the Lord, plans for welfare and not for evil, to give you a future and a hope. ~Jeremiah 29:11

The View from Up Here

Not too long ago, we were having a bit of family fun swimming. Abbey was having fun jumping off the diving board, but she suspected that the high board (5m) would be even more fun. Twice, she climbed all the way up that ladder, then climbed right back down.

Seeing a teachable moment about conquering our fears, I gave her a mini lecture/pep talk encouraging her to take the leap. When I finished, Abbey asked me, "Mom, have you ever jumped off that high board?"

As far as I could remember, I had not taken that plunge. You see, I have a small issue with heights. I'm not technically afraid of being up high, nor am I afraid of falling (because I know that they don't let people continue to go up on high things if someone has fallen from it). But there is a physical reaction that occurs in my body when I look down from a high vantage point. And in all my years, the best I've been able to do is breathe deeply, cling tightly, and tell myself I won't fall—every once in a while this actually helps me. Most times, though, I have done what Abbey did—turn around, climb down, and back out.

I asked Abbey, in perfect teenage fashion, "If I do it, will you do it?" She grinned and nodded.

The climb up the ladder wasn't bad. Deep breath in, step-step-step, deep breath out, step-step-step. The walk on the first half of the diving board was manageable. Deep breathe in, hold it, cling to the railing, steeeeepppp, steeeeepppp, steeeeepppp. But there is a point on every diving board where the railing ends and you are left to take those last few steps on your own.

I froze. My pulse hammered at my throat. The walls and pool seemed to shift and move, rocking with the twisting of my stomach. My legs literally trembled. I felt like a blob of jell-o on a plate that someone had just flicked to make it dance.

I took another breath, let go, and stepped. No! I stepped back and grabbed the railing. The board and I danced this way three times. I thought to myself, "I can't do this." I started to turn back. No! I told myself, "You can do this. Your little girl is down there, counting on you to do this. She is watching you, and will take her lead from your choices. Do not let her down!" My legs of gelatin cautiously carried me to the edge of the board, and I stood with hands extended to hold my balance. One, two, three, breathe, plug nose, and ~~jump~~ step right off that board. Victory!

It took a full half hour for my queasy stomach to relax, longer to feel as though my legs could hold me upright. Abbey proceeded to leap off that 5m high board a dozen times.

I could draw a million (or three) parallels and metaphors on how this relates to our relationship with God:

#1 - Sometimes faith is scary.
#2 - There are lots of times that we must simply step out in obedience, knowing the truth that God is with us even when we feel terrified and uncertain.
#3 - Someone is always watching what we do, and making choices about their own faith based on our actions.

But mostly, I just wanted to tell you because it's a darn good story. And hey—I jumped from the high board! Nanananana!

I can do all things through him who strengthens me. ~Philippians 4:13

The Moral of the Story

One of our children has an iron will. This child will dig heels in deep and not budge—ever—on whatever the issue of the day is.

Since school began this year (even before the move), this child has not been participating well in class. I don't know why, but I suspect it has to do with:

#1 - not wanting to look foolish doing silly actions and movements;
#2 - not wanting too much focus to be turned toward the child;
#3 - needing to be perfect and have things mastered before being willing to do them; and
#4 - a little bit of stubbornness deep down in this child's heart.

Said child came home a couple days ago proclaiming that there was no happy face in the agenda from school because the class was doing yoga and my darling wouldn't do it. To be honest, I was so proud of this child that I cannot even tell you—we have had many discussions about yoga and why our family believes it is best not to participate in it at all.

I began drafting an email . . .

Later, with some digging from Daddy, it was discovered that the child did not, in fact, refuse to do yoga, but simply refused to join in on the doing movement (you know, bend down and touch your toes, now reach up to the sky, etc.). Yoga was not for today, but they would be learning it later on, said the child. Perhaps this should have been my first clue that things were not all as they appeared?

I began revising the email . . . I had Pat read the email . . . I re-read and re-revised . . . And then—I hit send.

Yesterday I received a phone message from the teacher. As I did in my email, the teacher first addressed the child's issue and some solutions that had been brainstormed. Then the teacher addressed my concern and request that they not do yoga in school. The teacher informed that there has never been, nor would there ever be, any plans to practice yoga at school. *Ahem.*

The information my child had given us was incorrect, and no one has any clue where that information may have come from.

This morning, I drafted a new email. If email came with a picture, my face would be very red and my eyes averted. How incredibly embarrassing—to have written an email convincing the teacher of my reasons for opposing yoga in school FOR NO REASON. Oh, how foolish of me.

There are three morals to this story:

First, never jump to conclusions.

Second, when you learn information that upsets you the first thing you should do is ask, "is it true?"

And third, never, ever, ever take what a child says at face value!

Do your best to present yourself to God as one approved, a worker who has no need to be ashamed, rightly handling the word of truth. ~2 Timothy 2:15

On the Loose

I am almost off for an evening away with a girlfriend. By the time you read this I will be off (she doesn't know where she's going or who she's meeting, so I scheduled this to pop up after I know she's gone—you know?). As soon as I get home tomorrow, Pat and I are sneaking off for a night. We'll go to his work Christmas party, then enjoy the luxury of sleeping in the next morning. (Yay, Grandma! Have fun at 6am.)

So far this morning I have:

- washed, dried, folded, and put away three loads of laundry
- had my chimney cleaned (unrelated, but it was scheduled for this morning)
- grocery shopped for snacks and quick foods
- packed for one night, stacked packing for the next night
- put tonight's dinner in the crock pot
- fed two children lunch
- taken out the garbage and recycling
- cleaned up 400 mounds of dog doo
- paid bills
- and paced anxiously waiting for the sitter to arrive (who, as I write this, is not yet due for another hour).

If you've never taken a night away with a girlfriend, you totally should. It's almost naughty how free you feel!

If you've never taken a night away with your hubby, you should do that one first. Just 24 hours of escape from the day-to-day can bring months' worth of refreshing to a marriage.

And if you ever have the blessed opportunity to do both in one weekend, be sure to thank the Lord and not take one moment for granted. Because time away—it ***is*** a blessing.

Anyone know how it is that on any normal day it would take every waking moment to complete that list of tasks? Really, getting away is good for the whole family—they've never had such a productive Mommy!

Two are better than one, because they have a good reward for their toil. ~Ecclesiastes 4:9

I came to my garden, my sister, my bride, I gathered my myrrh with my spice, I ate my honeycomb with my honey, I drank my wine with my milk. Eat, friends, drink, and be drunk with love! I slept, but my heart was awake. A sound! My beloved is knocking. "Open to me, my sister, my love, my dove, my perfect one, for my head is wet with dew, my locks with the drops of the night." ~Song of Solomon 5:1-2

Traditionally Speaking

Traditions are the glue that holds a family together, separate and unique from other families. Some traditions become such a part of the daily routine that we may not even recognize them as special, such as praying together at night or talking about the day's high and low points over dinner. Christmas traditions, though, are special.

Do you read the Christmas story together? Open stockings? Have a turkey ~~dinner~~ feast?

Last year, our family began a tradition that I'd like to continue. Together, as a family, we found a way to give to others. The tough part (which was also the most blessed part) of the giving was that it was sacrificial.

I don't think our kids are old enough to understand going with a "giftless" Christmas where we give all of our gift money to a worthwhile project. But there is no age limit on learning to be a blessing, to offer something that may mean you need to have a little less for yourself.

A couple other traditions that have bloomed over the years:

— Each kid gets a new ornament every year, and they hang their ornaments on the tree. (There is a slim chance that I missed a year along the way—baby brain—but I'm going to make sure each kid is all set for next year.)
— On Christmas Eve, the kids get to open a gift (pre-selected by moi). It's always new pyjamas.
— Santa fills the stockings in this house and leaves a gift (typically something that everyone can enjoy together). Of

course, we always leave out milk and cookies for the jolly fella.

— At my parents' house, one of them will read the Christmas story before we devour the turkey and trimmings. Sometimes it's direct from the Bible, sometimes a version from a children's book.

I should share a little trick I came up with a few years back that seems to help with any sibling issues that occur around gifts (you know, no matter how you do Christmas and how much you try to focus on Christ and not the gifts, there is almost always one child who ends up whining to play with something that someone else received—this makes me crazy!). For any and all gift-giving occasions, a gift received by a particular child belongs solely to that child for a full 24 hours. After that day is done, the treasure is now for sharing. The exceptions to the rule are clothing and items that they choose to put in their special box. (The special box is a shoebox-sized Rubbermaid container, which the child keeps in his/her room. No one else is allowed to take items from the box. This little trick helped me deal with the child who was "hoarding" everything in piles on and beside the bed.)

Now, given that time is running short, I need to figure out what we're going to do as a family to be a blessing this Christmas. Pat and I have already come up with one thing, but it didn't involve the kids . . .

What are your family's traditions around Christmas?

And going into the house they saw the child with Mary his mother, and they fell down and worshiped him. Then, opening their treasures, they offered him gifts, gold and frankincense and myrrh. ~Matthew 2:11

Year in Review, 2009

Here's how I learned His ways, His paths, and His truths throughout the year . . .

I asked the Lord to shake me up, keep me from becoming too comfortable, unsettle me.

I asked God to reveal His agenda for my daily schedule and "to do" lists.

The Lord provided peace when I submitted to His will for our special needs son.

Our family settled in to enjoy the snot-nosed, dirty-faced, sweaty-kid days of summer.

I had the amazing experience of attending the *She Speaks* conference, and many thanks to Lysa who inspired me to begin my fast food fast.

An answer to those prayers of mine—the ones to be unsettled . . . God nudged, we listened (albeit reluctantly).

In the midst of preparing to move, God called my husband to take a short walk in the mission field. His heart is forever turned toward the people of Haiti.

I spent some time trying to refocus my prayers and praises.

A month spent glorying in the new lifestyle of our family, but sadly neglecting other important things (such as writing—for my book).

It surely was a Jesus year! I asked and sought and God showed my His ways, taught me His paths, and spoke to me about His truths. My world was rocked more than once. Adventure was had. Much time was spent on my knees. And some people say that following Jesus is boring . . .

But he said to me, "My grace is sufficient for you, for my power is made perfect in weakness." Therefore I will boast all the more gladly of my weaknesses, so that the power of Christ may rest upon me. For the sake of Christ, then, I am content with weaknesses, insults, hardships, persecutions, and calamities. For when I am weak, then I am strong. ~2 Corinthians 12:9-10

Be the Centre . . .

As I ready myself this morning for my first speaking engagement on mother anger, my heart is filled with prayers.

Lord, let my words be Your words . . .

Father, open the hearts of the women who need to hear that they are not alone . . .

Abba, keep me from being bumbling and nervous and doing things that might distract from the message You want the women to hear . . .

Jesus, let me not forget—not even for one moment—that this is all about You and bringing glory to Your Name . . .

When I Wander

I have sometimes heard—even been one of those who has said—when we are not walking in God's will for our lives, our ears become deaf to His voice. Somewhere, in the recesses of my mind, I have believed that God will not heed my prayers if I am knowingly in sin.

In the silent hour of this dark morning, though, I felt His presence.

And far, far away from His will is where I have been.

If our children are rebellious and disobedient, but they come to ask us for food, for a hug, to talk a minute—do we cross our arms and turn away, pretending as though we cannot hear their pleas? Of course not! If our love for our own children is too great to ignore them when they come to us, don't we know that our Father's love for us is that much greater?

For some weeks now—in spite of knowing the call on my life to commit each day to the Lord through prayer and praise, the reading of the Word, and listening for His voice—I have neglected my time of communion with Him. If His will for me is to spend time each morning in His presence, not doing so means that I am walking in sin. And yet, even in my sin, I hear His voice. Without a thought of repentance, continuing in my sin, I cry out to Him in prayer and sense His presence.

Though I have wandered, He comes with me. What a precious gift to find that I was wrong all along!

Humbled by His love and grace, my heart is turned. An extra hour of sleep no longer holds more appeal than communing with the God who loves me, hears me, and answers me—no matter how far I wander.

Call to Me and I will answer you . . . ~Jeremiah 33:3a

Start Dating Again

I can't seem to put together a post this morning because all I can think about is that I get to go out on a date with a very good-looking guy (who I kinda have a crush on) tonight.

We live for date night. Well, I do! I think that there are times Pat would rather just stay home and veg out, but he indulges me. You know why I love it so? Date night refreshes me and strengthens our marriage.

It can be easy to fall into the trap of living our two different worlds, and simply crossing one another's paths at the end of each day. I'm home with the kids, doing the homemaker thing. He's out working, doing the breadwinner thing. And when the "work day" ends, we are both exhausted. I want to run away from homemaking and child-raising stuff and do something grown-up. He wants to turn his brain off and relax.

I am so thankful that Pat resists the urge to shut-down when he walks in the door and instead engages with us. Because I know how difficult it must be to walk in the door and be "on" immediately, I resist my urge to run away. But give us a couple weeks of this hard work, and we can begin to feel pretty disconnected as a couple.

Anyone else feeling this?

About two years ago we began a tradition of having a date night on payday weekends.

For me, date night provides the face-to-face interaction I need to feel emotionally fulfilled. It gives us both time to be together and talk about any family issues without being "on duty" or being continually interrupted.

(Mom, you may want to skip this next paragraph.)

As you know, foreplay for women has a lot to do with feeling emotionally satisfied. So for Pat, date night holds the promise that the *date* will continue once we get home.

Date night refuels us both, so that we have renewed energy and can continue with the hard work we both do.

Are you feeling disconnected with your hubby? Feel like you are not heard? Emotionally drained? Don't *date* in the bedroom as often as you think you should?

Try having a regular date night at least once per month, but ideally twice per month. I suggest getting out of the house if at all possible, to eliminate distractions and your own temptation to "just do this one thing." I would also suggest that you try having a scheduled weekly *date night* (or morning/ afternoon—whatever rocks your boat). Try dating your hubby for just a month and see if you don't feel a little bit more connected and not quite so emotionally drained.

All or Nothing

The song below has been on repeat this morning, while Jesus and I have our coffee together.

I believe that we make a choice each day, each moment, whether we will serve our God or serve this world (and the one who has dominion in it). He is a jealous God, and is not satisfied with any half-hearted effort. He wants our all; He wants to be our Everything. There's no middle ground when it comes to our relationship with our God. We make a choice each day, each moment, whether He is our All . . . or nothing. Today, I pray that I will let Him be my Everything . . . in everything that I do.

God in my living
There in my breathing
God in my waking
God in my sleeping

God in my resting
There in my working
God in my thinking
God in my speaking

Be my everything
Be my everything
Be my everything
Be my everything

God in my hoping
There in my dreaming
God in my watching
God in my waiting

God in my laughing
There in my weeping
God in my hurting
God in my healing

Christ in me
Christ in me
Christ in me the hope of glory
You are everything

Christ in me
Christ in me
Christ in me the hope of glory
Be my everything

Building Your Ministry—1: What Your Team Really Needs from You

Through starting and leading a women's ministry for six years, in a church with a congregation of nearly 2000, I have had a few interesting experiences! Some fantastic, amazing, joyful; others bitterly painful. All of them were used by the Lord to grow me as His daughter and servant and to teach me how to lead *His way*. Lately, He has placed a burden and a passion on my heart to share the lessons I've learned. My prayer is that these lessons will be helpful to other women in ministry—that you might avoid the mistakes I made as well as use anything I did that worked well. I will share the bits and pieces with you as they come to me, in a multi-part blogging series (the number of parts to be determined by how much I find to say) that will appear in random intervals (whenever I feel inspired to say something). How's that for ambiguous?!

In my early years of leading women's ministry, I had a problem keeping leaders on my team. Attending our team meetings was not a priority on most of their "to do" lists. Being available to serve at ministry events was an "optional" activity, it seemed, for everyone but a few hard core volunteers. Women from the team quit altogether at the drop of a hat—no notice, no explanation.

I wondered, "What the heck can I do to make these women care about this ministry as much as I do?" I believed that the core problem had to do with *them*. For reasons beyond my understanding, they were just not sold out on impacting women for Jesus. At least, not sold out enough to actually stick with it for the long haul.

There was one woman who left the team early on who always seemed to have a bone to pick with me. I was heartbroken by this, because prior to being in ministry together she was my friend. One day, I gathered up the courage to ask her what happened.

She said, "Tyler, you are really good at being organized, at planning, and at taking care of the details. But I'm not sure you're the right person to be the leader of women's ministry."

I thought to myself, "Of course you'd say that! You have never liked the fact that I am in this role. You have never respected me as a leader. You have a bone to pick with me!"

She continued, "Even though you're good at those things, you're missing an important ingredient. You don't care. You don't have the heart. You don't love us as people. All you are concerned about is that everyone gives as much as you do. When we have life circumstances that get in the way, you only care about how that affects the ministry. You simply don't care about us and our lives."

The conversation continued for nearly an hour, with many tears on both our parts. It was a devastatingly painful conversation. I had always believed that one of my gifts was empathy, yet she was telling me that I was terrible at it. I believed that God had placed a loud and clear call on my life to minister to women, yet she said I didn't have what it takes to be a leader.

I wept and prayed on and off for five days, begging God to heal my broken heart (read: to show me how wrong *she* was). But the pain in my heart did not ease. On the sixth day I reluctantly changed my prayers and began asking God to weed through her words for me—to show me what words I should ignore, but more importantly to reveal to me the parts of what she said that were true.

Almost immediately, I sensed His answer in my heart. He asked me, "Daughter, *have* you **cared** for these women whom I have placed in your charge and under your leadership?" I knew that the answer was *no*. But I didn't know exactly *how* to care for them better. Thus began my journey in learning to truly love the women on my team—for who they were instead of for what they did for the ministry. Though Satan intended the cruel words of a hurting woman to beat me down and discourage me, God could use them to grow and mold me.

Lesson #1—Women need to feel loved. This is not only true in marriage, but in work and ministry as well. If you want to build a team that sticks together for the long haul, sold out for your (God's) vision, you must learn to love them in a way they understand.

Lesson #2—All advice that is given to you—even that which is laced with vindictive intent—should be sifted by God. He will use every experience (especially the painful ones) to weed out the junk in our lives that prevents us from leading with excellence.

His winnowing fork is in his hand, and he will clear his threshing floor, gathering his wheat into the barn and burning up the chaff with unquenchable fire. ~Matthew 3:12

Building Your Ministry—2: How to Love on Your Team

If it feels like we're starting in the middle of a post, it's because we are! A really, really long time ago, I addressed point #1—invest time. As promised, we'll tackle points #2 and #3 here (if I can remember what they are!).

In developing a new ministry or in building up a ministry that's already running, a team of committed volunteers (and/or staff) are needed to make things happen. Finding people to join your team may not be as difficult as you think (but that's for another post on another day); but keeping people committed to the team, the ministry, you (their leader), and of course to the work God is doing through the ministry—well that task, it takes hard work!

How to make your team feel loved . . .

#2—Pay Attention:

If you are a wife, you already know how important this is. Because the first time your husband does NOT pay attention to the details of life, it hurts! Has your man ever forgotten your wedding anniversary or your birthday? Ouch! Women like to know that they matter. Don't we?

One quick and easy way to show your team that you are paying attention to their needs is to spend five minutes putting their important dates into your calendar—birthdays, anniversaries, vacation days, surgeries, kids' milestones (such as weddings or graduations). Then, let your team know you remember these dates. It only takes a minute to send a greeting card by email. Sometimes, you may want to do something a little "bigger" and get your team in on purchasing a joint gift or throwing a party (big # birthdays and anniversaries, baby showers, etc.).

It's also important to pay attention to what's happening in the lives of your team. At the end of the meeting, when you take prayer requests (isn't that always the way?!), and someone on your team asks for prayer for a sick child or marital struggles, don't just pray for it and forget about it. Check in with her in a few days or a couple weeks (depending on how long-term the need may be) and ask how it's going. Let her know you've been praying. That small act of remembering her needs will make her feel absolutely treasured by you!

As a leader, it's also vital to learn specifics about the women on your team. What is her love language (in other words, what's the best way you can encourage her in her own language)? What are her spiritual gifts (and do you have her serving in a role that's using them)? What are her strengths, skills, and abilities (how can you help her develop these further)? What are her limitations (and how can you help her overcome them or work around them)?

#3—Listen AND Hear

A new friend of mine is involved with the women's ministry of her church. She is passionate about meeting the needs of the women and drawing them to Christ, and she is chalk full of fantastic ideas on how to make that happen in the particular area of ministry that she serves in. God has called her to this ministry, of that I have no doubt!

My friend, though, is dangerously close to calling it quits and stepping away for good.

You see, when she voices her ideas in meetings, she is discouraged by the "old hats" on the team. They always have a reason why her idea just won't work. Half the time they won't even let her get the whole idea out before they shut her down and move on. When she sends an email, IF she actually receives a reply from her team lead (it's about a 50-50 split), the standard reply is, "Thanks for your input."

How to listen:

- — Make eye contact.
- — Let the person complete their thought.
- — Even if your gut reaction is to reject the idea, take time to consider it.
- — Reply to emails promptly.
- — Use more words than necessary (while many of us are "get to the point" kinda gals, more often than not our team feels shut down and/or rejected by brief and abrupt conversations or emails).
- — Always thank people for being willing to share ideas.
- — Remember to whom the credit goes for a great suggestion (record it in your meeting minutes, so everyone knows who is responsible for innovative thinking).

How to HEAR:

- — Always follow-up! If you have said you will consider an idea, make sure you get back to your team member once you've made a decision.
- — Ask, "What do you think?" Then actually pay attention to what she thinks.
- — Wherever possible, allow your team members the freedom to make their own decisions in ministry. (Experiencing our own successes builds confidence. Experiencing our own struggles builds character.)
- — Remember that ministry is not just about the women in the congregation and community. As a ministry leader, your greatest ministry is to your team. Your job is to meet their need for validation, mentoring, and encouragement!
- — Don't forget that God placed each woman on your team with you for your growth, too! Each of them is there to bring wisdom and discernment. Overlooking their thoughts,

feelings, and ideas could just as easily be ignoring where God is leading you!

Want to build a leadership team for your ministry that endures? A team that sticks together? A team that is sold out for your ministry's vision? A team that is loyal and steadfast? **Invest time** in each member of your team**, pay attention** to the small details, and learn to **listen AND hear** what they have to say.

Love each other with genuine affection, and take delight in honoring each other. ~Romans 12:10 (NLT)

Really Random Facts

Because you all really want to know ridiculous, random things about me, right?

* I have an odd affinity for shopping for school and office supplies. (In fact, it's the only kind of shopping I enjoy.)
* I am completely directionally impaired. Sadly, it was only a few years ago that I learned the sun rose in the East.
* Using multi-coloured pens (or in the computer age, colour-coded labels) on my calendar makes me very happy.
* I spent most of my teenage years pumping gas.
* At the young age of 32, I have just discovered what eyeliner can do for me!
* At the slightly younger age of 31, I finally quit biting my nails to the quick. I do, however, continue to gnaw away at the cuticles.
* Do not read over my shoulder. Ever. Especially if I'm writing. Actually, if I'm writing you are safest to back out of the room and go far, far away. You may not ever read anything that is in progress!
* Toilet paper belongs OVER the roll. If I use your washroom, you will discover that I have corrected the roll for you.
* I still periodically have nightmares starring the alien from "Signs."
* I used to bite my toenails. The only thing stopping me now is Pat's disgust and my children's big mouths.
* I love making "To Do" lists. I usually add tasks to my list that I have already completed that day, just so I can cross something off right away.
* It is a bad idea to talk to me in the early morning before I've had coffee. I just can't help myself from glaring at you.

* As a child (an only child until the age of 12), I would entertain myself by pretending I was the narrator/star of a show on Discovery. I especially enjoyed narrating my cooking show while in the bathtub.
* If you touch my feet—even accidentally—I will kick you. I'm sorry; it's as instinctive as the sucking reflex in babies.
* I never make my bed.
* I do NOT like new foods. Until my teenage years, I had never ordered anything but a grilled cheese and fries (with gravy on the side) from a restaurant.
* When I finish reading a good fiction novel, I will begin to panic slightly if there is not another book in my house.
* Though I have a degree in psychology, when asked about post-secondary education I almost always advise against a 4-year program.
* I cannot wear yellow or green or anything with those undertones. They make me look deathly ill.
* I cannot wear purple (or use it to decorate my house) simply because I hate it that much!
* In my first year of driving I hit a dog, a deer, and another vehicle. I also got 2 speeding tickets.
* Since then, I have backed into a concrete barrier and a fence. I have also gotten many more speeding tickets (thanks to the modern-day miracle of photo radar).

There you have it—23 things about me. All true facts. As Amanda Moore has been known to say, "You are dumber now!" You're welcome.

Stirring up the Embers

There has been a crazy dream stirring up in my heart. The first little spark of that dream appeared several years ago—a hint of things to come. Recently, I have sensed God blowing on the embers and fanning the flame.

Like I said, it's a wild and crazy dream . . .

You already know about the writing. It's a passion of mine. Writing what I see, feel, hear, and learn makes it *real*. If it's not written down, chances are it will slip away into the recesses of my mind. I have many stories—a lot of life lived for such a young thang (teehee)—but one particular account has been burning to be told, the anger story (and how God is writing the ending). Once it is permanently etched in the hard drive of my computer, though, I have no doubt that God will blow His wind on other stories. Tales of starting out a young marriage in a faith dichotomy, a young girl looking for love in all the wrong places who eventually finds what she was looking for in the only One who can provide it, walking through post-partum depression and surviving, an ill-equipped and inexperienced "baby" Christian starting a women's ministry that somehow (in spite of her and all because of Him) thrives . . . There are volumes just waiting to be poured out!

Chronicling God's work on paper (or hard drive), however, is not the only way to get a message out there. Though I resisted, I have long sensed God pulling me to share the message not only through my fingertips, but with my mouth. It is a terrifying prospect, accompanied by many conflicting emotions. Fear of failure. Fear of letting God down. Fear of fumbling so much that the listener can only focus on my ineptitude and doesn't see God's greatness. Fear of being good at it. Fear of growing prideful. Fear of public scrutiny and harsh judgment. Fear of letting all my baggage lay on the ground in front of others. F-E-A-R.

I can let fear win, or—with Christ's strength—I can conquer it. Here are some things that have inspired me to go with the latter:

* When Moses refused God's call and asked Him to send someone else, "The LORD's anger burned against Moses." (Exodus 4:14) I would rather not be the one to incite God's wrath.
* I was told that, when God calls us to "minister to the masses," we have a responsibility to pursue our calling and fine-tune our gifts/talents/abilities so that we can effectively reach a great number of people. (Thanks, Shannon Ethridge.)
* A friend, with similar passions and fears, is walking alongside me. (Having a friend on the journey always makes it easier, doesn't it?)
* A verse was given to me at the time of my greatest doubt. Proverbs 1:21, "At the head of the noisy streets she cries out, in the gateways of the city **she makes her speech** . . ."
* A couple other friends are cheering me on: this one, this one, this one, and most importantly—this one.

One tentative step at a time, I will move forward, laying down the kindling, striking the match, then stepping back to let the wind of God to fan the flame.

The Writing on the Wall Headstone

A good name is more desirable than great riches; to be esteemed is better than silver or gold.
~Proverbs 22:1

Have you ever been in a course where everyone is asked to participate in one of those "life application" activities that involves capturing the essence of your character—who you are and how you lived your life—in short captions? Basically, it's a slightly morbid exercise in selecting the phrase that you would like to see embossed on your own gravestone. Then, of course, the instructor usually makes everyone read it for the rest of the class . . .

I recently told my husband that if we were to develop a family mission statement I would like it to include the phrase "radically obedient." Because obeying the Lord as soon as He speaks, without question, even when it seems insane (like Noah or Abraham), is a trait that I want to characterize our family's faith journey. *That* is how I would like to be remembered.

After much contemplation, I've decided that I would like my gravestone to say:

God led, she followed.

Except that I probably won't be the one who actually gets to decide what is written at the head of my burial site. No one says we can't offer suggestions in advance, though!

What would you like your stone to read?

Unexpected Blessings are the Best Kind

This is a story about a big surprise. Now, some people don't like to be caught unaware—but that's not me! I LOVE to be astonished! Surprises are unexpected blessings, things of joy, miracles, full of excitement, extra special, and they make my heart happy. (Yes, feel free to throw me a surprise party. Just make sure lots of people show up.)

Not quite seven years ago (October of 2003, to be exact), we thought our family was complete. It wasn't a difficult decision for Pat to get the surgery because I was struggling with post-partum depression and we both believed that we were maxed out. But then my medication kicked in, family pitched in, and life felt closer to normal. And that decision that had seemed so easy became a burning regret deep in my heart. I was too ashamed to tell Pat of my regret (I mean, he had a sharp knife cut things down there!), but I did take it to God in prayer. Fervent prayer!

To my great joy (and Pat's), I came to him in August of 2004 with the news that our family was not complete after all! On April 13, 2005 we greeted the baby I had spent 10 months praying for—our beautiful fourth child and third daughter.

I consider Shea to be our miracle baby, a gift from God, an answer to prayer. The Hebrew version of her name, Shai, means gift. I chose her name before knowing the meaning, then searched and searched for a middle name that meant gift or blessing—until I stumbled across the meaning of her first name. God knew her name before I did!

I cannot imagine our family without Shea's big, blue eyes and infectious giggle. I praise the Lord that His plans prevail over ours

(Proverbs 19:21). Whenever I fear that I may have messed things up, I need only to look at my precious Shea to be reminded that God can redeem any mistake.

As Shea grows up, I am so thankful that she isn't "growing into" her eyes. They continue to be breath-taking blue and so wide. When I look into the depths of those gigantic blue pools, I always think of the Precious Moments figurines, and I know that Shea *is* our precious one! Five years ago, God answered our prayers with the gift of a real, live precious moment that would last a lifetime . . .

Parenting is Tough

Have you ever heard the saying, "You can deal with it now, or you can deal with it when she's 16?"

We had one of those "its" to deal with this weekend.

Megan (almost 7) is a leader. You know how I know this? Because she will not allow anyone to boss her! Nope, not a soul. Not even her parents. When she's older, and if she's received proper training and encouragement, she will be an amazing leader. Her charismatic personality draws friends like flies. Once she develops the skills to tamp down her short fuse and her tendency to be oppositional, there is no telling what the girl will do for the Kingdom!

As parents, we (meaning Pat and I—hopefully you are better at this than us!) tend to operate in a cyclical manner. For a while we are strict and firm, offering clear guidelines and distinct consequences. As we see troublesome behaviours easing up, our strictness eases up in kind. We float along effortlessly for a time. Then the behaviour of concern creeps up again. We then take a deep breath and tighten up our parenting belts once again.

You think we'd learn to just **always** be consistent! But consistency is hard work and requires superhuman effort (on rough days), so the allure of taking a break is difficult to resist. I think it's fair to say that we have been on a little consistency break these days. Sigh.

Back to the "it . . ." While I don't think it's fair for me to give out specifics of Megan's struggles, I will tell you this much—they were plentiful, and they involved more people than just the parents. There have been issues—while small in and of themselves—that, once stacked up, amount to a very big pile of disrespect. Very Big.

To us, disrespect is a heart issue. One that must be dealt with swiftly and with unflinching firmness. And while it broke our hearts to make this decision, we informed our almost-birthday-girl that the big sleepover/movie-going party she had planned to celebrate her upcoming special day would not take place.*

Seeing Megan's tears nearly undid me. After all, who wants to break their own child's heart? But through all our discussion and prayer on how to deal with a situation that appeared to be getting out of control, Pat and I had two verses resonating in our minds . . .

Proverbs 22:6 *Train a child in the way he should go, and when he is old he will not depart from it.*

Proverbs 13:24 *He who spares the rod hates his child, but he who loves him is careful to discipline him.*

I do acknowledge our own responsibility in this big "it." If we consistently adhered to the first passage, it is unlikely that we'd have run into a pile up of disrespect. If we consistently trained our children, without taking little breaks, I am certain that heart issues would be dealt with before they ballooned this way. I pray that God gives us the strength, wisdom, and patience required to truly train our children.

But, I also recognize that, regardless of where the trail of responsibility tracks back to, failing to discipline at this point is as much as telling our child that we hate her. Harsh words, I know. Our love for her is so great, though, that we cannot risk allowing this character issue to take root. Which is exactly what would happen if we were to allow our compassion to overrule our discipline.

Man alive, this parenting thing is tough with a capital "T!"

* Before I get all sorts of flak for being a "mean mom" (ahem, Grandma) I would like to clarify that the birthday party will still take place, but has been revamped to no longer include going to a movie or friends sleeping over. The revised party will be the

basic hot dogs, cake, presents, home kinda party. We felt that this compromise of sorts would send a clear message about our expectations, while still showing love and compassion.

Of course, I welcome your thoughts on the matter and/or stories of how you've dealt with parenting issues. Just don't beat me up and call me mean!

Our Greatest Weakness is NOT Knowing Our Own Strengths

I have been reading Now, Discover Your Strengths (Buckingham & Clifton). The premise of the book is based around two core assumptions:

1. Each person's talents are enduring and unique.
2. Each person's greatest room for growth is in the areas of the person's greatest strength.

Is it going too far for me to say that I think EVERYONE should read this book?!

So often we focus on all the things we need to "fix" in ourselves that we lose sight of the fact that God has placed unique talents, abilities, and passions in each one of us. There is nothing more affirming or empowering than to spend a few minutes reading true words about what you're good at.

An added bonus (especially for a girl who loves doing surveys, inventories, and assessments) is that the book comes with a code for an online Strengths Finder evaluation, which helps to identify your top 5 strengths.

Since you already know way too much about me, you are probably dying to hear what they are. Right? Here they are, all changed to first person since I'm talking about myself. Okee-dokey?

1. Relator—I am pulled toward people I already know. I don't necessarily shy away from meeting new people, but I do derive a great deal of pleasure and strength from being around my close friends. I am comfortable with intimacy. For me, a relationship has value only if it is genuine. And

the only way to know that is to entrust myself to that person and share openly (even if it means I risk being taken advantage of).

2. Strategic—This perspective allows me to see patterns where others may simply see complexity. Mindful of these patterns, I play out alternative scenarios, always asking, "What if this happened?" This helps me to see around the next corner, discarding paths that lead nowhere, that lead to resistance, and that lead to confusion until I arrive at the chosen path—my strategy. Armed with my strategy, I strike forward.
3. Arranger—I am a conductor. When faced with a complex situation involving many factors, I enjoy managing all of the variables, aligning and realigning them until I am sure I have arranged them in the most productive configuration possible. I spend time mulling over just the right combination of people and resources to accomplish a new project.
4. Empathy—I can sense the emotions of those around me and feel what they are feeling. Intuitively, I am able to see the world through their eyes. I do not necessarily agree with each person's perspective, nor do I necessarily feel pity for their predicament. I do not necessarily condone the choices each person makes, but I do understand. People tend to be drawn to confide in me.
5. Communication—I like to explain, to describe, to host, to speak in public, and to write. I want my information to survive, to divert other's attention toward my idea and then capture it and lock it in. This is what drives my hunt for the perfect phrase.

Now, didn't that make you want to run out and discover your own strengths?!

P.S. This review was completely unpaid and unsolicited, done of my own free will on a book I paid for. Just so ya know.

My Will or His?

What is God's will?

In decision-making time your greatest difficulty may not be choosing between good and bad but choosing between good and best. You may have several options that appear to be equally attractive. At a time like this, begin by saying with all your heart, "Lord, whatever I know to be Your will, I will do it. Regardless of the cost and regardless of the adjustment, I commit myself ahead of time to follow Your will. Lord, no matter what that will looks like, I will do it!"

What if God's will isn't convenient?

If you cannot say that [above] when you begin to seek God's will, you do not mean "Thy will be done" (Matt. 6:10 KJV). Instead, you mean "Thy will be done as long as it does not conflict with my will." Two words in a Christian's language cannot go together: "No, Lord." If you say no to God, He is not your Lord. If He really is your Lord, your answer must always be yes, Lord. In decision making, always begin at this point. Do not proceed until you can honestly say, "Whatever You want of me, Lord, I will do it . . ."

What if I cannot seem to discern His will?

. . . When God gets ready for you to take a new step or direction in His activity, it will always be in sequence with what He has already been doing in your life . . .

What if I just can't do what he's asking of me?

. . . Truth stands . . . to say, "Believe Me. I will never give you an order without releasing My power to enable it to happen. Trust Me and obey me, and it will happen."

~ all quotes from: Experiencing God: Knowing and Doing the Will of God, study guide (pp. 123, Blackaby & King) ~

Get Serious

In church yesterday I was amazed to learn that Muslim children memorize the entire Koran at the age of 6! I imagine that their parents spend countless hours reciting passages to the children, diligently training them in the tenets of their faith.

It got me reflecting on how diligent (or not) I am at instilling faith in Jesus Christ in my kids. We say a prayer of thanks before meals (most of the time). We say prayers at bedtime (usually). I help them practice their school memory verses (sometimes).

But do they really know the Word of God? Do they think of what the Word tells them to do when they encounter difficulty? Is it imprinted, permanently etched in their hearts and minds?

Heck, do I set aside time 5 times per day to focus solely on prayer or worship? I'm lucky if I get in one good session in the early morning hours (generally).

I wonder how many of us give our religious practices the same consideration as Muslims give theirs . . .

No wonder the rest of the world doesn't take Christians and Christianity seriously—tossing prayer out of schools, using the Lord's Name in vain as common language, perverting Scripture to suit immoral agendas.

Isn't it time we get serious?

Maturity, does it equal boredom?

Do you ever wonder what happens to us when we become "mature" Christians? What changes? How do we get there? How did others get there?

A few things come to my mind when I think "mature" Christian:

- — long walk with God
- — enduring in faith through life's ups and downs
- — in the Word every day
- — praying for hours at a time
- — faith that is calm (in contrast to the "fiery" and exuberant faith of a new believer)
- — serene
- — bored and boring (yes, I said it!).

There is a part of me that admires and aspires to be like the women I know who have walked with God for what seems like forever. But there is this tiny part of me that whispers, "Please Lord, don't let it be boring!"

Maybe you remember my prayers for the year of 2009? I prayed for God to unsettle me. I asked Him not to let me get too comfortable. He answered, and answered, and answered, and answered again!

This year, I began praying that the Lord would consecrate me (make me holy and set apart for His purposes). I didn't want to settle for a faith that was simply "good enough." But in the back of my mind I was also reminding Him that I didn't want to be bored (or boring).

For a short time, I let my heart drift away from His. I was bored AND boring. I had created my own little self-fulfilling prophecy (think that it will be lackluster and you will surely end up disinterested).

But I was not, as I feared, uninspired *because* of maturity. I grew apathetic because I was slowly emptying of that which fills me—His Spirit. What little of Him I had inside of me was seeping out through my many cracks. As those cracks are pieced back together, and I feel the filling up happening again, *things** are happening.

Guess what—deciding to be a "grown up" in the faith is far from humdrum! No, I sense that I am about to embark on an escapade of God-sized proportions!

I suspect that maturity is not tedious at all, but that it comes from maintaining a sense of peace, faith, and trust while riding life's ups and downs, over and over again. I am beginning to realize that the quest to become established and settled is probably one of the most adventurous journeys we can embark on!

No one is ever bored on a roller coaster! Some people—those familiar with its nausea-inducing motion—may appear a bit blasé as they take their hundredth loop-de-loop, but we must be careful not to mistake their composure for apathy. If we were to hook them up to a biometrics machine, the heart rates of the experienced rider would be no slower than the shrieking 13-year-old boy's in the front row. Their composure is gained by holding fast, practicing lots, and the total faith (that comes with much experience) of knowing that they will not fall.

* *things* defined: life's ups and downs; stretching; growing; finding oneself in need of God's amazing provision; praying; seeking; obeying in spite of obstacles and doubt

In other words, not a single prayer said on our behalf would be wasted right now!

Family Funnies

Our family had a fantastic long weekend in the mountains! We drove, we hiked, we toured a town of days gone by, we hot tubbed, we rode a train, we visited the world's largest cuckoo clock, we toured a mine, we swam, we ate too much and slept too little.

Shea: Dad! Look at that mountain! It's so big! The trees are higher than the sky!

Abbey: Sometimes, when the trees are waving in the wind, it kinda looks like they are worshipping God.

Mom: I bet they are! It says in the Bible that even the rocks cry out to worship the Lord.

Megan: Mom, what about the rocks that aren't Christians?

Malakai, at age 2 1/2, is really becoming a talker! Here are our two favourite sayings of his:

Shake a booty! (said in a sing-songy way while bopping his head up and down)

I nu no. (I don't know. His standard reply to any question beginning in "Where is . . . .")

The Tragedy of the Unopened Gift

In his book If You Want To Walk on Water, You've Got to Get Out of the Boat, John Ortberg speaks of those people who stop growing and allow themselves to become stagnant "boat potatoes." He quotes Gregg Levoy's description of the "common cold of the soul."

To sinful patterns of behavior that never get confronted and changed,
Abilities and gifts that never get cultivated and deployed—
Until weeks become months
And months turn into years,
And one day you're looking back on a life of
Deep intimate gut-wrenchingly honest conversations you never had;
Great bold prayers you never prayed,
Exhilarating risks you never took,
Sacrificial gifts you never offered,
Lives you never touched,
And you're sitting in a recliner with a shriveled soul,
And forgotten dreams,
And you realize there was a world of desperate need,
And a great God calling you to be part of something bigger than yourself—
You see the person you could have become but did not;
You never followed your calling.
You never got out of the boat

Ortberg goes on to say, "there is no tragedy like the tragedy of the unopened gift."

Are You Burying Your Talents? Or Do You Even Know What They Are?

I am surprised by the number of Christians who have no idea what their spiritual gifts are! (This is coming from a girl who LOVES to fill out quizzes, personality tests, and so on. I mean, don't we all love to do those? Or is it just me?) We all seem to be aware that God gives us certain gifts when we accept Christ, but many believers (even many long-time believers) don't seem to be too interested in finding out what they are. Or perhaps we are interested, but no one has given us the tools to figure it out!

I believe that it is vital for us to try to understand our gifts (to the best that we can in our limited human knowledge), so that we can ensure we are using them to serve in Kingdom purposes.

To that end, I would encourage you to search for an online tool—there are many that are similar to the paper one that is typically used in evangelical churches.

Before you complete an inventory, here are a few things to think about:

—In school, how did you BEST complete multiple choice exams? Did you do best going quickly and with your gut instinct, or slowly and thoughtfully? It's best to view this in the same way. (I told one friend to go with her gut—like I tend to—and her results were fairly skewed, but when she went back and did it her way—methodically—the results made much more sense for her!)

—Are you an "all or nothing" girl? Or do you tend to be more "middle of the road?" (Some of us will have a few gifts that we score VERY high on and a few that are VERY low, while others will see less of a range between the top and bottom numbers. For example, if I recall correctly my top score was 29 or something ridiculous! My best friend's top score was 15. The score does not measure the strength or intensity of the gift! The actual number does not matter as it compares to others; only use the numbers to gauge which of your gifts appears to be strongest and which are weakest. What matters is—which gifts come in the top half of your scoring?)

—Over time, our spiritual gifts may appear to change. The truth is that God imparts every spiritual gift He intends for us the moment we accept Christ. Our gifts remain for our lifetime. BUT, we may not discover some of our gifts at first. It is through relationship with God and serving Him that we grow spiritually and develop the gifts He has given to us. (An example from my life: Six years ago I completed a spiritual gifts inventory and found exhortation and pastoring to be smack dab in the middle. This led me to think I wasn't really gifted in those areas. Now, they are among my top few. I believe that God gave those gifts to me, but until I spent some time in ministry using those gifts and developing them, they didn't show up as strongly. You might find that evangelism sits in the middle for you, and if you're like me you'll breathe a sigh of relief! LOL! But then God may put a few people in your path who need to know God . . . Do the questionnaire again in a few years and you may find that evangelism is higher.)

Well, go ahead! What are you waiting for? I assure you, reading the list of spiritual gifts beside your name will be encouraging, inspiring, and FUN!

Every good and perfect gift is from above, coming down from the Father of the heavenly lights, who does not change like shifting shadows. ~James 1:17

On Daddy's Shoulders

One of my kids' favorite places to be is up on Pat's shoulders. When chubby, little legs tire of walking, up they go! When big, round, peering eyes cannot see what's up ahead, Daddy hoists them up.

There comes a point, though, in each of our children's lives, when they can no longer ride on Daddy's shoulders. It usually happens somewhere in the fifth year of life, when that 50 lb mark is attained on the scale. At that time, it becomes awkward and cumbersome to get the child up there and keep him or her safely perched.

I thought of this as I listened to the lyrics of a song by Francesca Battistelli, "Free To Be Me." She sings:

'Cause I got a couple dents in my fender
Got a couple rips in my jeans
Try to fit the pieces together
But perfection is my enemy
On my own I'm so clumsy
But on Your shoulders I can see
I'm free to be me.

I have heard this song, sang along with it hundreds of times. Yet never caught on to that phrase, "on Your shoulders I can see." But the other day, it just struck me and stuck with me, and I've been mulling it over ever since.

All too often I find myself navigating through life as a blind woman. I hold my hands out in front of me and ask, *This way, Lord?* Bump. *This way?* Crash. *Which way do I go? Where do I turn? What can I do for You? Where am I?* ***Who*** *am I???* I want to do it right, but on my own and in my own strength, I am nothing more than a bumbling mess still trying to "find myself."

If I would just stop flailing around in the dark for a moment and ask Him, *Daddy, will you put me up on Your shoulders?* I would see. I would see that He has good plans for me (Jeremiah 29:11); I would see that He has purpose for me (Psalm 138:8); I would see the person that He created me to be (Jeremiah 1:5); I would be free to be that person.

What about you? Have you found yourself bumping into things, trying to figure out who you are and why you are here?

If so, try taking one of the three Scriptures listed above and meditating on it. Ask God what He wants to say to you through that verse.

Framed and Stoned

Early in our marriage, I established an annual family tradition—the Rowan family photo session. Over the years, "annual" became a flexible term, depending on finances, motivation, and scheduling. Family photo day, though, has often been a day of dread and obligation for our crew. Why is it that people who spend hours of their day hamming it up for the camera at home are unable to do the same when their mother needs them to?!

It has been two years since our last family photo session, and I could not let it pass by any longer! Children change so much in these young years, and I want to have that growth documented. On Sunday, we headed out to a construction site in hopes of capturing all the little faces in a smile—at the same time—just once.

Thanks to my beautiful and talented friend, Loni (of Loni Bourne Photography), our photo session was absolutely painless! Loni was FAST—in just over half an hour she got at least 300 shots. She was able to capture each of the kids in moments when they were posing themselves, so we didn't need to beg and cajole anyone to "stand here" and "look there." For their awesome cooperation and participation in mommy's annual tradition, the kids earned themselves a yummy ice cream.

I find that our daily lives are full of frame-able moments. I would love to capture the moment when an older sibling imparts words of wisdom to one of the younger ones. Or the silly, giggling faces around the dinner table as we each try our hand at being the joke-master. Those moments in our lives when we know we have just witnessed the hand of God over our family. But those instances will have to live on as still shots in my mind, because by the time I get the camera the perfect picture has vaporized.

Instead I will take our latest 11x14 family shot and put it in the frame on the mantle, tucking it in front of the photos from years before. As I do this, I will gather the family around me to wander through the years. And we will remember as many moments as we can, captured in one still frame.

Lord, your faithfulness goes on through the generations! Thank-you for these children and for every moment with them. We praise You and You alone for where our family is today, and how You brought us here.

While I may not be able to take a snapshot of every instance of God's faithfulness in our lives, each family photo will be as a pile of stones—an altar of worship and praise—representing our family's journey with the Lord for the past year. The Rowan family Gilgal.

I Don't Have the Energy for That

I've noticed that us women who have struggles with anger, frustration, and impatience in our parenting seem to have one common refrain, "I know they need consistent discipline, but I just don't have the energy for that right now."

I have said it. I have heard others say it and nodded and "mmm-hmmm" ed my understanding. Today, I am compelled to call it what it is: bullcrap! (Yes, I said that on here!) The fact is, believing that I am too tired (or too ill, old, alone, worn out, beaten down, abused, hurt, whatever) to actively parent is—for most of us—buying into a lie straight from the pit of hell. (Here is where I will insert the caveat that I am referring to the general population of mothers, not to those who are in the throes of critical illness or family tragedy. In those instances, I have no doubt that "I can't handle it," is the absolute truth. These are the circumstances where family, friends, and especially the church must step in and help.)

If I am nitty-gritty honest, when I say "I just can't do it anymore! I'm so tired," what I really mean is: *I am too selfish*, *I am too lazy*, *I am too busy*. Too selfish to set my own agenda aside, to stop what I am doing, to focus on child-training. Too lazy to get up from the couch/ office chair or walk into the next room in order to exact discipline. Too busy with my stuff (housework, ministry, writing—ahem) to take a break from the task at hand in favour of raising good people.

Funny thing is, my selfishness, laziness, and business ultimately create more work, cause me to expend more energy, and take up more time than active parenting. By being selfish, lazy, and busy, I am leading my children to be needy and demanding. "Mooooom, will you/ can you/ I need/ I want!" When I am doing my own thing too often, the kids will do what they can to garner my attention.

Attention-seeking children can quickly turn into patience-sucking monsters, and next thing I know I am bellering at the top of my lungs in hopes of regaining control.

Out-of-control children = out-of-control mommy. But as James Dobson says, "Trying to control children by screaming is as utterly futile as trying to steer a car by honking the horn."*

So, how does one find the energy to dive wholeheartedly into the murky waters of active parenting, immediate discipline, and an in-control household? Well, I'm working on that! I'd love to hear the strategies you use, both for training your children AND for motivating yourself. What works in your home?

* Dr James Dobson, *The New Dare to Discipline*, pp. 36

A Couple Life Lessons I'm Learning

To be a good leader: Lead in such a way that those you are leading become empowered and equipped; do your job in such a way that it can be taken over with ease. In other words, work yourself out of a job.

To be a good friend: Love in such a way that shows you are willing to sacrifice personal selfishness for your friends; make yourself indispensable. In other words, work yourself into a lifelong job.

Ministry: When God calls you to a ministry, it becomes etched in your heart. Even without a formal "ministry," you will find yourself ministering. Even if you try, you cannot turn away from the group of people whom God has given you a passion for. Also, ministry should fill you up. If you feel drained, perhaps you and God should have a chat about where you're supposed to be serving. For example, serving in the church nursery is not where I'm supposed to be (the babies and I have all learned that one together!).

Marriage: No matter how long you've been at it, it is always work. It is a constant battle between selfishness and self-sacrifice. Having a good marriage is not easy, you have to invest lots of time and energy to make it good and even more to keep it that way.

Parenting: The only rule that matters is consistency. Love and cuddle consistently, regardless of behaviour. Discipline firmly and consistently for any and all wrong behaviours. Have a consistent schedule, no matter how busy life is. Our kids are programmed to watch for weakness, and they will attack if they see any break in consistency. Also, yelling never really works (each time you yell, you have get louder in order for the little darlings to respond; this equals way too much wasted energy). FYI, parenting makes you tired. I think it's supposed to be that way.

Homemaking: Housework is no fun, but a messy house causes stress and makes it hard to show hospitality. Figure out one or two tasks that make the house look clean and make you feel calm, without having to do the whole cleaning routine. For me, clean floors and an empty sink help me relax and keep me chill if unexpected guests show up.

I'm no expert. In fact, most of the time I find myself failing in several of these areas at once. That's where the lessons get learned—in the failures. Hopefully, I will eventually remember these lessons and be able to stop learning them over and over again.

I am an Orphan

I was conceived, and the boy-child God chose to be my father made his own choice. He left. **Discarded**. Leaving my mother, barely more than a girl, to be both mother and father, nurturer and provider. Once in my growing years and twice in my grown years, I implored him to accept me, acknowledge me. I was told that he did not need a reminder of his sinful past. **Despised**.

There was a "Dad" in my world for a short hiccup in time. At least that was the name I called him. But a name does not a father make. My childhood memories of him are laced with the lingering sting of disappointment. **Unloved**. As a woman-child with baby growing inside, I pleaded with him to love me more than he loved his whiskey. That baby, now 12, knows nothing of this man I once called "Dad." **Unwanted**.

I was a teenager, and he tried to be "Dad." But in my heart I knew the truth about men. He would leave me, too. He didn't have a chance. Rather than risk more heartbreak and rejection, I turned away first. He gained the disdainful title of "step-dad" and his efforts were met with sneers and defiance. I already bore the names Discarded, Despised, Unloved, and Unwanted; I would not take the name **Rejected**. Instead, I gave it to him.

Time passed, life's pages turned. In the irony of this world, I chose a man who was destined to leave me. We started out a mess, did everything backwards and upside-down, we believed differently and lived as polar opposites. He didn't leave, and today he is Dad with a capital "D" and husband with a capital "L-O-V-E." But that is a story in its own right.

Time passed, life's pages turned, and he (the "step-dad") remained. I was a broken and bitter orphan, and his mistakes were repeated assurance to me that he would leave. But he did not leave. Though I named him Rejected and even Hated at times, he remained, he endured, he waited, he loved.

In my children, as all good grandparents do, he grasped onto the opportunity to rewrite his mistakes. He has laid on the floor smiling and chatting with each of my babes. He has driven remote control cars, put on pretend make-up, danced in the living room, built bird houses and sandboxes, cuddled, and wrestled. In those twelve years of seeing him be Grandpa to my brood, I watched and realized two things:

1. He will not leave me.
2. He *is* **Dad**.

I wasted many years keeping my distance, not trusting, being afraid. But the Lord is true to His Word, and He says, "*I will repay you for the years the locusts have eaten.*" (Joel 2:25) A swarm of locusts came in and devoured my trust in men, yet God gave me ~~Step-~~Dad to restore that devastation.

For those of us left orphaned, God is *Father to the Fatherless.* (Psalm 68:5) We can (and along the way I did) find our strength, love, and hope in His paternity. He renames us: **Indispensable, Esteemed, Loved, Wanted, Accepted**. But every now and then, He sees us in our hopeless state and determines to go to great lengths to show His love. In my case, He did that by giving me the desire of my broken heart—an earthly Dad.

While I may still call him **Lee,** his very name writes the word "Father" on my heart. He chose to be the Dad he didn't have to be.

Kids Say the Darndest Things

Not long ago, while Malakai and Shea were spending the week at Grandma and Grandpa's house, I had the pleasure of overhearing the following conversation while on the phone with my mom.

Grandma was getting the kids into the bath, and just moments after she helped Kai get in we both heard him tell her, "Gama, I peed! Gama, pee!"

Before Grandma could say a word, Shea chimed in to reassure Kai, "It's okay, Kai. I do that *all the time*."

Needless to say, our telephone conversation was effectively over. It would have been impossible to talk over our hysterical gales of laughter.

Note to self: Make sure little people go pee *before* climbing in the bathtub.

Secrets to Make a Marriage Last

We are coming up on 11 years of marriage next month and the past 5 have been great! So what secrets did we unearth along the way to make things go from unbearable to enjoyable?

1. **Grow up.** Arguments went unresolved for days, issues were brought up over and again, and the goal was not to find unity, but to win. Eventually, we both realized that it could not always be about who was right.

2. **Communicate.** A little-known fact about communication: it is a two-way conversation. And the hearing part is much more important than the speaking part. I always thought communicating well was about presenting my argument better, convincing him of the superiority of my perspective. We learned that it is okay to let disagreements *rest* unresolved, as long as we both felt that we had been "heard."

3. **Learn to speak Klingon.** We all know men are from another planet, so why do we expect them to speak the same language as us? I may say "I love you" by doing his laundry or making his favorite dinner and thus expect him to say he loves me in the same way. But he prefers to say "I love you" by asking me to sit by his side and watch hockey with him. Learn what makes him understand your love, and try showing it that way. It is also okay to ask him to do the same for you.

4. **Assume the best.** My emotions tend to get the best of me, especially during a particular week of the month. My emotional response to careless words is, "He hurt me. He doesn't love me. He doesn't know me. He never did." My entire world shifted on its axis when I began to tell myself, "He didn't mean to hurt me. He loves me. It was not intentional. I should just forgive this and move on."

5. Laugh. We struggled with keeping our emotional cool during arguments. Things would move from heated to inferno with two misplaced words delivered on a raised voice. It was a cycle we couldn't break. So if things began to feel out-of-control, one of us would shout "Pickle!" in the midst of it. We would laugh, realize we needed to take a break, and schedule a time to revisit the issue. Annoyed by his bad habit of dropping dirty laundry on the floor, but knowing (through trial and error) that nagging would not change his habits, I offered him an apology. "Honey, I am sorry that I constantly put the laundry basket just three feet away from the spot where you'd like your dirty laundry to go." He laughed. Interestingly, the laundry is in the hamper at least 90% of the time.

6. Date. I've said it before—never underestimate the power of having time alone together doing something fun! Our dates nights help us remember that we actually *like* each other.

7. Absence *does* make the heart grow fonder! Spend time with friends. Encourage him to do the same. Same-sex friends provide an outlet that is completely different from the marriage relationship. We have found that we enjoy our time together more after having some time with friends. (As long as the time of absence is not greater than the time of being present, which is generally not very helpful for the marriage.)

8. Bless him. Recently, Pat was beyond busy at work and he was stressed. I knew that I couldn't do anything about his work, but I could reduce his stress here at home. So for those couple months, I took over the "blue" job of doing the garbages. Pat knows that I hate cooking, so on days when I'm particularly tired he frequently takes over for me.

9. Pray. For him to be the husband God wants him to be. For you to be the wife the God wants you to be. For a strong marriage. Together, if possible. We are still growing in the whole praying together thing, but I am certain that I can feel God's pleasure when we step out of our comfort zone and do it.

10. Don't neglect your "ministry."(nudge, nudge, wink, wink) If that was a bit too vague, perhaps it will help to know that this is the only ministry you will ever do fully un-clothed. (No personal examples here.)

I can't guarantee that using our secrets will work a miracle for you, but I wouldn't be surprised. After all, the fact that we are still married *and* happy is an absolute miracle for us!

Don't be a Moses

I am reading Exodus right now, and it's definitely one of my favourite parts of the Bible. As I read I can envision scenes from "The Prince of Egypt" playing in my mind. Of course, those images are overlapping with visions of Charleton Heston standing on the mountain, beard waving in the breeze, holding two tablets of stone in his arms.

Rather than allowing myself to be carried away by the story (as I usually am reading the great history laid out in the Old Testament), I am trying to take things more slowly—a couple chapters per day—in an effort to glean more wisdom from the pages. Today, I am reflecting on Moses' calling from God and his response. (Below is my paraphrase of the whole situation.)

— Moses sees a bush on fire that is not burning up. The bush (the Lord) speaks to Moses, telling him that he has been chosen by God to lead the Israelites out of Egypt and into freedom.
— Moses says, "Who am I, that I should do this?"
— God reassures Moses that He will be with Moses the whole time.
— Moses asks, "Well, what if the Israelites don't believe You sent me?"
— God tells Moses to say "I AM sent me."
— Moses then asks, "Well, what if the Egyptians don't believe You sent me?"
— God gives Moses miraculous powers AND assures Moses that He will reach out His hand over Egypt and they will recognize the Lord.
— Then Moses tells God, "But God, I'm no good at public speaking!"

- — God reassures Moses that He will put the words right in Moses' mouth.
- — Next, Moses whines and asks God to pleeeeease send someone else.

***Then the LORD's anger burned** against Moses.* (Exodus 4:14a)

By the time I arrived to that verse, *my* anger was burning against Moses! I was so annoyed with him, thinking, "Moses, you dufus. He is GOD! Stop questioning Him. Just do what He says and trust that He will lead you every step. Sheesh, dude!"

And then I felt a quiet question whisper in my heart. How much time do I waste questioning God and His call? How far do I push with my lack of faith and trust? Do I bring the Lord to a place of anger or frustration before I finally listen and obey?

I can think of two areas where I'm pretty sure I've provoked God's ire . . .

God called me to write this book at least a couple years before I wrote the post about it. Part of the writing, I'm sure, is for me and me alone. While there have been huge improvements in my struggle with anger, there continue to be days where I feel as though I've fallen right back to the beginning. I believe that God's full deliverance will come once I have finished what He asked me to do. I'm still (slowly, and at times barely) working on it.

When we moved, I had a strong sense of awareness that God was calling me to a new ministry. A shift of focus in my ministry to women. I think that God knew I would not be able to let go of WOW to do something new (but would instead try to do it all). We arrived here and I knew that I was supposed to make my ministry focus threefold: writing, speaking, and ministry consulting. That was eight months ago.

Man, I am burning in anger *at myself*! What happened to my desire to serve? When did I become such a wuss? Why in the world have I been holding off on doing what I believe God has called me to do? Fear. Insecurity. Loneliness. Laziness.

Taking the BLAST course has been instrumental in building my confidence in my calling and teaching me the practical steps to take in order to move forward. And signing up for She Speaks this year has given me the kick-start I desperately needed to actually take those steps. I am ready to stop annoying myself and God by acting like Moses. Instead, I want to be an Isaiah.

Here am I, Lord. Send me! (Isaiah 6:8b)

How about you? Is there an area in your life where you've been a Moses lately?

The Perfect Mom—1

Do you have a picture in your mind of who the perfect mom is? Perhaps she's a real person that you know. Maybe she's a proto-type that fits a list of characteristics and qualities. Have you found, over the years, that your image of what makes a perfect mom is changing?

Us women, we are all about perfection, aren't we? It's not okay to just be a good mom (or even a great mom). Nope, the goal is Super Mom! Unfortunately, when we fall short of our perfect goals, we carry around a big backpack of guilt. After all, if so-and-so can handle this and do it that way, why can't I?

I am here today to throw that monkey off my (and your) back! Get lost, guilt!

Here is my image of the Super Mom:

- She stays home with her children (probably a dozen of them).
- Her house is usually immaculate.
- She bakes yummy goodies for her family all the time.
- She provides colourful and well-balanced meals three times per day.
- She has a set snack time, where her children eat at the table.
- Her laundry is virtually always caught-up.
- She probably home-schools her children.
- Her kids are incredibly well-mannered.
- She leads the children in Bible study and prayer time every single morning (and/or evening).
- She dresses nicely and wears make-up every day.

— Her children are the recipients of utterly consistent discipline (though they rarely need it).
— She wears nice shoes.
— Her kids don't really fight with one another (not even at home).
— Her cupboards don't contain sugary cereals or potato chips.
— She is always patient with her children.
— She never raises her voice.
— Her husband is greeted with a hug, a kiss, and a hot meal the moment he walks in the door each day.
— She always has a smile on her face.
— Her children seldom watch television or play video games, unless there is educational or spiritual merit to it.
— She never swears, even if she stubs her toe really, really hard.

If you know me, and you're keeping score, I get 1 point for staying home with my children (but maybe it's only half a point, because there are only 5 of them . . . and I was in university and then worked until the birth of the third). I'm curious, what would be on your list and how many points would you get?

Here is something I think we all need to remember—there is an enemy, and his goal is bring death and destruction to our families. And he will start his nasty work right at the family's heart—the mother. He's got two dirty little strategies that manage to catch all of us at one time or another: the "I'm not good enough" and the "I've got it right."

I think that the enemy likes to lure us into the trap of "all-or-nothing" thinking. He wants us to believe that we must be everything on our list to be good enough. And if he can't wear us down with guilt, he'll fill our heads with a sense of superiority. If we are doing all (or many) of the things we think are right, we are certain that our way is the only way and those who don't do what we do are falling short.

Before we go one step further, I just want to name the devil's tricks for what they are—PRIDE. The latter is obvious, but keep in mind that thinking badly of yourself is still simply "thinking all about yourself." Whether we think we're awesome or pathetic, we are caught in the trap of being solely focused on ourselves (aka: prideful).

Here are some questions that wander through my mind (and maybe yours) a lot. Do I have to be a full-time stay at home mother to be a good mom? If I work outside of the home, am I a bad or neglectful mom? Must I homeschool my children in order to truly fulfill God's parenting requirements? Is sending my children to school a cop-out (or even detrimental)? Does every mom really bake and cook like Betty Crocker?!

This post is getting long. My four younger children are being cared for by the "electronic babysitter" and Hannah Montana. My eldest has been sent away for the week. My house is dirty. The laundry pile is enormous. And I haven't brushed my teeth yet. So given my multiple failings (according to my list of perfection), I better get to work! But tomorrow, I'd like to tackle the answers to some of those questions. (Said tongue in cheek.)

*Disclaimer: Lots of what I have to say on this here blog spot is solely my personal opinion. But I don't say much on here without hitting God's Word to see what He has to say on the matters I think about, and I seldom click the "publish" button without praying. I pray that my words will not offend, but will encourage (and I pray the same for your thoughts posted in the comments—so if you disagree, don't be mean, okay?! *grin).*

The Perfect Mom—2

Okay, I did promise to help throw the monkey of guilt off our backs, didn't I? So let's get started.

Am I a bad/neglectful mom if I work outside of the home?

Me—No, that's ridiculous! First, some moms don't have a choice. Family finances dictate that mom needs to bring in some income (especially in single-parent homes). Second, while quantity of time certainly does matter, I do believe the old adage that quality is more important. If your time with your child(ren) is limited, you may need to be more intentional about how your time together is spent to feel that you are engaging with and training up your kids, but the fact is you are MOM. Especially in the younger years, your influence has the most impact (regardless of how much or little time you have).

In fact, dare I say that many working moms are better at engaging with their kids than us SAHMs?! Being a SAHM gets you into a particular routine with the household and the kids, and I (maybe you, too?) frequently find myself saying things like, "Not now/ later/ soon/ I just have to get this done first." I tend to think that working moms are less inclined to "put off" their kids in this way.

God's Word—I wonder if, like me, you've read about the Proverbs 31 woman and secretly hated her? She's got it all together! Here are a few things I've noticed about her lately:

—In verse 15, it says she gets up really, ridiculously early to provide food for her family and servants. We often assume that means she's doing the day's cooking in the wee hours. But could it mean that she is out working? Or out in the fields? Or at the market? She may be working outside of the home, while her servant girls are there to tend the children. Maybe not, I'm just sayin'.

—Verse 16 refers to earnings. How does a woman earn money? By working, I presume.

—In verse 17 it says "she sets about her work vigorously." It doesn't say that she sets about her housework, or cooking, or child-rearing.

—While many people use P31 to make their case for being a SAHM, I believe that may be a case of using the Scripture to suit your own agenda. In fact, throughout God's Word, when I search for the word "mother" I cannot find any absolute direction that states, "a good mother must stay home all day long with her children and should never find work outside the home."

Must I homeschool my children in order to fulfill God's parenting requirements?

Me—First, let me say that I have nothing but admiration for parents who homeschool their kids! You gals (and some guys) rock my socks! And I am aware that many of you may disagree with MHO, which is totally cool with me. I welcome your thoughts on the matter!

Of course, you know I am going to say, "no, I don't think God requires us to homeschool our children." If I did, I would be. I know that many homeschooling parents do so because they feel that HS is how God intended children to learn. But there are also many HS parents who do so because they believe it's a matter of personal preference, gifting, and calling. I tend to be from the same camp. *Some* parents are definitely called to educate their children at home! Some are not. While I admire HS parents (and somewhat envy their ability to do what they do), I want to state clearly that I do NOT believe that either way is the only right way. Neither method is superior, preferable, or without its issues. Both options come with big, fat lists of pros and cons. Good mothers homeschool. Good mothers send their children to public school. Good mothers send their children to private school.

God's Word—One of my favourite passages, Deuteronomy 6:7, is often quoted to encourage parents that they are solely responsible for the education of their children . . . and for ensuring that all aspects of that education include God. What the Lord is referring to in Deut 6 are the 10 Commandments He laid out for His people in Deut 5.

Can you impress the importance of following God's Commandments on the hearts of your children while they attend a public school? Surely you can! The fact is, our children learn much more about our faith and morals by observing how we live than they do by what we tell them. So we can spend 3-6 hours per day incorporating God's truths into our children's school curriculum, or we can spend every moment we have with our children living out our faith (even if they are spending 6-8 hours of their day, 5 days per week, out of our care).

Research has shown that, regardless of where children spend the majority of their time, their parents remain the #1 influence on their attitudes and actions. There is also substantial evidence to support the assertion found in Proverbs 22:6, *Train a child in the way he should go, and when he is old he will not turn from it.* (*Faith Begins at Home*, Mark Holmen)

Does every good mom bake and cook like Betty Crocker?

Well, I think you get the point . . .

Here is the thing: God's Word does not tell us the specifics of how to live out our lives. He has given us The Ten Commandments, The Greatest Commandment, and The Way of Salvation. For all the rest (such as how to be the best mom you can be, or rather—how to be the best mom God wants you to be), He has given us the Holy Spirit to guide and direct our paths. You cannot look in the Bible to find answers to questions like: Which job should I take?

Should I go on a mission trip to Kalamzoo? Am I supposed to be a stay-at-home mother?

Want to be the perfect mom? Here's my suggestion . . . . Love God. Let your kids see how much you love God. Love your kids. (If loving your kids is easier for you (as it is for me) when you have something fulfilling to do—such as work or ministry—do it.) Do your best in all the things to do with being a wife, mother, homemaker, friend, servant of God. Sometimes that means getting help—having a housekeeper or a babysitter is NOT unscriptural! And if you've got tough decisions to make, pray and seek the guidance of the Holy Spirit.

The most important thing we can all do to be the mothers that God wants us to be is to ABIDE in Christ, wage battle against the enemy, and not let guilt or pride influence our decisions or our relationships. Oh, and for goodness sake, get some other mom friends! Nothing brings more freedom than knowing that we are not alone.

In case you are still looking at your list and tallying your points, know this: God chose YOU to be the mother to YOUR children for a REASON. Trust His judgment.

Just my Imagination?

Did you ever entertain the question, "What if this is all just a big dream?" As a teen, I recall wondering about that a lot. Perhaps the life I was leading wasn't my life at all, but merely a vivid dream that I would soon awake from.

Sometimes, I hear that same concept applied to faith. "What if God is just a figment of your imagination?"

These are good questions. What if? How do we know that we're not all really asleep? Or living in a computer grid world of some sort? Or that God really exists?

Basically, it all comes down to faith, doesn't it?! At some point in our lives, we must all decide what we believe to be true and what we sense to be true in our hearts. Believing that I am awake and alive and living in a real world requires faith. Believing the opposite—that we are all living in a dream, or perhaps we are all living in a fabricated world where others watch our lives on TV, or perhaps we are being controlled by alien forces—requires faith. Believing that a grand explosion turned a minuscule fragment of an atom into living, breathing matter takes faith. Believing in a God that created us, the world, and everything in it—you guessed it, takes faith. *(Frankly, I think it takes less faith to believe in a Creator than in some of those other concepts. But anyhoo . . .)*

There are no "right" answers to explain the hows and whys of God. All we can offer is our faith and our testimony. The story of how God has worked in us and changed us is the best evidence we can offer to back up our faith. Our testimony is better than any scientific argument, better than any intellectual debate. Our testimony is OURS, and whether someone believes it or not, they cannot argue against it. They can only choose to accept or reject is as true, on faith.

This leads us to a tough question. Does our testimony offer evidence of that which we believe? Does Jesus really work? Are we actually different because of God in our lives?

(The concepts listed above—such as living in a dream world, computer world, and movie world—are fantastic imaginative ideas borrowed from the silver screen. Movies referenced are: "Inception," "The Matrix," and "The Truman Show." I'm sure there's a movie about how we live in a world controlled by aliens as well, but it's not coming to me. Also referenced is a theory on how the earth came to be, called the "Big Bang Theory," which is also a relatively hilarious TV sitcom that actually has nothing to do with said theory. The theory referenced which I put my faith in is aptly named "Creationism.")

My Kids Robbed the Bank

Being a mom, or anyone who spends a lot of time taking care of children, is what many would call a "thankless job." There is no pay cheque to speak of, much of the work done doesn't show tangible results, and days off are few and far between. Raising kids is huge investment of our time, energy, mental capacity, patience, prayers, and finances. But it's more like an investment in today's economy than a few years ago—unbelievably slow-growing, taking years before showing a return.

In order to keep it all in perspective (and help keep our cool), it is so important to watch for, recognize, give yourself credit for, and thank God for those "paydays."

A great report card or meeting with the teacher—cha-ching!
Your pre-teen sits close and lets you snuggle with him for a few minutes—cha-ching!
Your toddler poops in the potty—cha-ching!
Someone shares with a sibling (without a lecture from you)—cha-cha-cha-ching!
Your child asks Jesus to be her "forever friend"—cha-CHING!

We need to take these paydays and store them up in our hearts. Because in the 20-or-so years we spend raising our children to be good and Godly grown-ups, their withdrawals from the bank of mom will far outnumber their deposits. When that one particular child says, "No!" to you for the thousandth time and makes you want to scream and shake your fist—stop for a moment, think back (sometimes waaaay back) to that one time that child said, "Okay Mom," without arguing (cha-ching), then discipline the disobedience with the knowledge that the child truly is capable of willing obedience and all hope is not lost.

This advice was especially helpful for me this week, as long summer holidays with little structure provide enough withdrawals from the bank of mom to put me into overdraft.

What about you? Has it been a long time since you've experienced a payday as a mom (or childcare provider)? What are some great paydays you can remember?

If I Only had a Brain

Sometimes our job is to plow the fields, getting them ready for planting . . .
We may be the very first Christians some people meet that they don't hate.

Sometimes our job is to sow the seeds . . .
We live our lives for Christ, allowing those around us to witness the difference He makes in and for us.

Sometimes we are the rain, the sunshine, or the fertilizer . . .

We have opportunities to pour out love, shine the light of God's Word, and bring the Truth alive by sharing how God is working in our lives.

Sometimes we get to bring in the harvest . . .
We may even get to lead someone to accepting Christ as Lord and Savior.

Sometimes we are the scarecrow, keeping pests away.
We do our best to drive away the enemy when he tries to distract them and help them stay focused on their growth.

I spend most of my time being a scarecrow. (Feel free to envision my face on the body of Scarecrow in Wizard of Oz, singing the famous—and fitting—song, "If I Only had a Brain.") For some reason, when people are afraid, stressed, confused, and losing their faith, they come to me. My job is to wave my arms around and holler until the crows fly away. Wait, I mean my job is to love them, encourage them, bring them back to Christ and His Truths through prayer and Scripture.

Being a scarecrow isn't the most glorious job. The harvesters really have the job that offers the highest dividends. The scarecrow job description is kinda like the spiritual janitor—helping sweep away all the junk and clutter so that the Truth shines through. The thing is, clean-up is a never ending job. Just as soon as you think you've got it all gleaming, someone walks through your hard work with their muddy boots. Or, back to the scarecrow analogy—as the crow flies away it poops on your head. It can sometimes be a rather inglorious occupation.

Every now and then, though, the scarecrow gets a blessed reminder about the importance of his job.

Last week, a 12-year-old boy from my old home church was killed in a freak accident. These are the things that can make or break the faith of everyone involved.

So far, two women have contacted me to help them process this situation. One was on her way to be with the family, another a friend with an "overprotective" nature when it comes to her children. They didn't come to me for wisdom or advice; I'm pretty sure they don't think I'm all that sage. They came to me because they needed someone to help them cry out to Jesus and scare away all the fears and worries that were threatening to overtake their minds.

So I grabbed my Bible, took to my knees, flapped my straw-filled arms in the air to keep those nasty pests away, and together we found our Source of peace.

I may not get to bring in the harvest, leading people to a new faith in Christ. I may not get to spend a lot of time with people who don't know Him, preparing the ground, sowing seeds, fertilizing. My job is to tend the fields where the "hard work" has already been done. But I am reminded that each step—each person—in the cultivation process makes a difference in the final crop. Even brainless, straw-stuffed, human-like figurines with sticks up their butts . . .

No amount of discipline will make up for a lack of training!

What does that mean? It means that you can give consequence after consequence but you will see a significant difference if you take the time to teach your child not only what to "put off" as Eph. 4 tells us but what to put on. Don't athletes practice, practice, and practice some more before actually going out to compete? So why not give our children time to practice obeying during a fun, non-confrontational training time?

During training time, you can teach your kids what you mean by first-time obedience. Tell them what you've seen them doing: talking back, grumbling, ignoring, etc. You can even act out what you've seen them doing. This usually makes a huge impact and the kids think it's hilarious seeing Mom and Dad acting like them. Next, explain using Scripture such as Ephesians 6:1-2 and Phil 2:14 why what they've been doing is wrong. Carefully explain and/or act out what you would like to see. Then let them know what the consequence will be if they don't obey cheerfully, right away, all the way and no matter what.

Now it's practice time! Give them a task to perform.

Example) "Becky, please take these two toys and put them where they belong." Becky says cheerfully, "Yes, Mom." When she finishes, she comes back and reports, "Mom, I put the toys away. Is there anything else I can do to help?" You encourage her with, "Thank you, Becky, for obeying cheerfully and right away!"

You can also use this time to practice all kinds of things like how to resolve an argument with a sibling, the best way to ask for a toy, how to sit quietly in church, what to do when a friend says something unkind, how to look an adult in the eye and carry on a conversation. Whatever you want to work on, use this time to practice it. The more you want to work on, the more often you schedule training time. If you have littler ones, you may want to set aside two nights a week. For older kids, once a week or every other week might do.

I will say try to make it a set night if possible. It will help you to remember and actually do it if you know it's "Tuesday Training Time."

I love how Mrs. Duggar puts it, "Practice makes progress!" That's what we're looking for, progress . . . not perfection.

Lastly, **don't forget to praise, encourage and thank your children when you see respectful, loving behavior.** When someone praises you for something, doesn't it make you want to do it again? And if we're only correcting what we don't like, they will become discouraged. They need to be assured that they are on the right track. "Thank you, Lucy, for showing love to your sister by sharing that toy!" "Wow, Cameron, what a kind boy you are!" "Good job, Molly, obeying so quickly! Thank you."

While teaching first-time obedience calmly, consistently and in love will bring peace and order to your home, it is equally important to remember when Jesus said there was no greater commandment than to "'love the Lord your God with all your heart and with all your soul and with all your mind and with all your strength [and to] love your neighbor as yourself.'"

If our children are outwardly obedient but inwardly defiant, or outwardly respectful to you and others but don't love others, it is worthless. We lead first by example, then through teaching what the Word says and allowing the Holy Spirit to do His work in their lives. Parenting is not a part-time job. It takes a lot of time, patience, love, and proactive, intentional teaching and training. What an awesome responsibility is ours. I want to be found faithful.

It's been almost seven years since my husband and I were first introduced to the godly parenting information that changed our lives and the vision we have for our family. I don't know where we'd be without it. I am so very grateful that God led a woman at our church (who is now my mentor) to facilitate a parenting class which was a series of videos by Reb Bradley of Family Ministries called *Biblical Insights into Child Training*. Since then I have worked with Mr. Bradley and even had the opportunity to have him stay with us recently. I love this man's heart and am so grateful he has used his God-given gifts of wisdom and teaching to share with parents a biblical, practical, and counter-cultural way to raise up warriors for Christ. Thanks to him, I understand what the Bible means when it says that children are a blessing and reward.

What are you going to try doing differently?

How to See

I want to see. Really see. I don't want to merely look, but to see with eyes that take in the truth and a heart that understands.

As a little girl, I would watch the hour-long TV specials put on by World Vision and weep. My insides torn apart and spilled out at the very thought of children starving to death. Now, I change the channel. I hide from the truth of this broken world.

Where can I go from Your Spirit? Where can I flee from Your presence? . . . I say, "Surely the darkness will hide me."

It is not poverty or sorrow or pain or truth that I hide from. It is the very Spirit of God. I hide not because I do not want to see, but because I don't want to be seen. For I am destitute and starving, greedy for more. More money, more food, more clothes, more entertainment, more things. But if I am seen, those icky inner parts that I want to hide in the dark will be exposed.

O LORD, You have searched me and You know me. You know when I sit and when I rise; You perceive my thoughts from afar. You discern my going out and my lying down; You are familiar with all my ways. Before a word is on my tongue You know it completely O LORD.

I am seen. I am known. I am exposed. I was all along, but am just now realizing it. The inner darkness cannot be hidden. There is nowhere to hide that He is not there.

If I go up to the heavens, You are there; if I make my bed in the depths, You are there.

In this moment, as my impoverished state is exposed raw, I remember. Like scenes from a movie reel, one by one, the memories scroll. Beautiful, broken people, truly starving. Literally hungry every moment of every day. A scraggly man sporting foul body odour on the boulevard with a cardboard sign. A dark-skinned girl with a round belly—not full, but bloated with starvation and parasites. Three-thousand images brought home from Haiti almost one year ago.

And I feel it again. The true, raw pain that sears the heart with the seeing. And I know this is why I've been hiding. I can hardly bear it, this eyes and heart wide-open feeling. Yet now that it's back, I can't understand how I ever lived without it.

I need to be seen. Really seen. *We* need to be seen. Because until we are torn and exposed ourselves, our eyes are blinded to the pain around us. We change the channel to avoid it, because we cannot understand. It is in being seen that we learn to see. To really see, with eyes, mind, heart, and spirit.

When we finally see—really see—only then can we be used as agents of healing . . . giving Life, Bread, and Living Water.

All the days ordained for [every impoverished soul] were written in Your book before one of them came to be . . . You hem [us] in—behind and before; You have laid Your hand upon [us].

** Scripture from Psalm 139*

Obsessed by Unbelief

In my life, I have noticed a direct link between worry and prayer. I believe it's referred to as an inverse relationship. That is, when I am filled with worry over something, chances are good that I haven't been praying about it very much.

I have spent many mornings this month confessing my worry to the Lord and asking Him to replace my fretting thoughts with the peace and truth of His Word. But not until this very moment did it occur to me what is really going on . . .

First, all the while I've been calling it "worry" or "fear" or "fretting." The plain truth is that what I am allowing to go on in my mind is nothing short of **unbelief**. I am not believing that:

— God is who He says He is, and
— God can do what He says He can do. *

I have allowed my heart and mind to slip away from, what I believe, are the **foundational truths** of my faith.

Second, I have become **obsessed**. "What we allow our minds to dwell on, there our hearts will be also." (I feel as though that should be in quotes, because I'm certain they're not my words. But for the life of me I cannot recall who said them or where they might be in the Bible. Feel free to fill in the blank.) My thoughts have been so focused on this one "problem" that it has become this thing that I am constantly thinking about. I wish that I were as **obsessed with God** as I have become over this small issue. Imagine if all I could think about all the time were God and His Word!

Third, (and I don't know why it has taken several weeks for this to occur to me) this is a **spiritual battle**. Given all the God-sized plans we see in our family's future (missions trip, speaking to women, new church connections, and more); I guess it's not surprising that the enemy would try to come at us. But if I know anything about spiritual warfare, it's this—**victory is ours**! All that we need to do is claim the authority we have been given in Christ and the enemy will be utterly defeated!

** From Beth Moore's "Believing God." (If you've never done this study, you should! Foundational, faith-growing, life changing.)*

Seven Steps to Stop Anger in its Tracks

I pray that my story, at the very least, has shown you that you are not alone! This mothering thing can be so hard, and it's okay to admit that we aren't perfect.

Today, you will find that I've added some tips for moms dealing with anger. If you stop by again tomorrow, I'll have some tips for others (that is, for those whose spouse or friend or relative struggles with anger). I do hope that you'll come back!

If you'd like to share your thoughts, you can leave a comment at the end of this post. (Please do! You have no idea how much I love your comments! They are my encouragement and source of inspiration.) To leave a comment, simply click on the word "comments" at the end of the post. Then follow the instructions in the pop-up window. If you don't have a Google account, or would rather not leave your name, just click "anonymous."

The other morning I was supervising Braeden (12) as he went through his morning routine. Because of his cerebral palsy, Braeden's motor control isn't always the greatest, and I suspected that he wasn't doing the best job brushing his teeth. I was watching and coaching, "Okay, now the bottom. Do the back part. No, not there, the inside. Okay, now the outside. No, no, no, here!" He brushed the same areas over and over again, missing the same two spots with every back-and-forth of the brush. It was clear to me that this was not really a motor control issue, but more of a pre-teen laziness thing. My jaw clenched just a little bit as my frustration mounted.

I stepped in to place my hand over his and guide him in moving the brush over to the neglected teeth. He made one of those rude adolescent noises (a cross between a whine, a grunt, and a growl) and swung around to pull away from me. His scowl lit a spark in me that has been dormant for some time. I felt heat climb up my neck, a knot develop in my stomach, and my teeth ground together so tightly I could hear them crunch. In two seconds flat, I went from frustrated to mad.

I grabbed back on to his hand clasping the toothbrush, and we brushed! A muffled, "Ow!" tried to make its way around the frothy brush jammed into his mouth. I continued. "Ow!" A bit louder this time. With everything in me I wanted to grab on to the back of his neck, make him be still, and brush all my fury away. I wanted to scream at him to, "Shut up and stop whining! If you did a good job in the first place I wouldn't have to help you!" I could feel it bubbling to the surface . . .

And then I felt this little pinprick in my spirit and words from James echoed in my mind, Human anger does not produce the righteousness God desires . . . The balloon of anger didn't burst, but developed a slow leak. I could tell that it would deflate soon, if I just gave it time and quit puffing more air into it. I shot up a dart of a prayer, "Lord, I need you to interrupt me right now, so I don't completely lose it." Without a word, I let go and stepped out of the bathroom. I breathed deeply once, twice, three times. While smaller, that balloon still rested at the back of my throat. I took the three steps into my bedroom, closed the door, stuffed my pillow into my face, and hollered with everything in me, "Aggggghhhhhhh!!!" Then I breathed again—in through the nose, out through the mouth, again, again.

I realized that the rushed morning hours may not be the best time for teaching. I returned to find Braeden rinsing his mouth. I said sorry that I was rough and asked if he was okay. He nodded. I asked him if we could practice brushing his teeth properly on Saturdays, to make sure he's getting all the areas. He nodded. I asked if I could have a hug. He smiled and nodded and wrapped his one good arm around me, "I love you, Mom. You're the best."

As I sent my big boy out the door to his bus, I reflected on how differently that could have gone. How differently it would have gone in the past. And I thanked God for working in me and for interrupting me when I need Him to.

How to stop anger in its tracks:

1. Learn to recognize the physical feelings of anger that precede the emotional outburst. Respond to those physical feelings by stepping away.
2. Find Scriptures that remind you why you don't want to be angry. Write them out on index cards, carry them around, read them out loud. Eventually, they will get lodged in your heart and mind.
3. Ask God to interrupt your typical reactions.*
4. Breathe.
5. Pay attention to the times of day (or month) that you are easily triggered. Make those times of day as routine as possible and avoid things that add more stress (such as trying to teach a new skill or send an important email).
6. Always ask for forgiveness.
7. Don't forget to thank God for each and every success.

Have you experienced that pinprick in the spirit recently, where God interrupts your natural reaction to turn you around? Maybe when you were about to speak those snarky words to your husband? Or share that juicy morsel of gossip with a girlfriend? Perhaps it's your own anger story? I'd love to hear how God has been working in your life!

** This phrase is adapted from a live talk given by Lysa TerKeurst.*

How we made it through alive

I believe that, as soon as we step out and try to teach spiritual truths to others, the enemy has a game plan. He thinks, "Sure, she says that she is free in Christ . . . But does she live like it? Let's test her out. Mwahahahaha." Okay, I'm not sure if he does that evil laugh, but I wouldn't put it past him.

In these situations, I tend to see God as the third base coach. He's standing right there, telling us what we need to do, encouraging and coaching, hoping and praying, cheering us on. I'm pretty sure His reply to the devil's questions goes something like this, "You better believe she's free! Go ahead, just try and tempt her. You'll see. She may stumble, but she will not fall!"

I stumbled a bit first thing in the morning. The boots issue—that brought out my "outside voice." The shelf, well that one had me hollering at everyone for a minute or two. Honestly, those are the kind of situations that would typically get my anger flaring. I hate, hate, hate running late and everything about yesterday morning screamed of "We're all gonna be late!!!" I was tempted to skip out on my women's group altogether, rather than show up late. But something inside me told me that keeping me starved for fellowship was another trick of the enemy, and I knew I needed me some girl time!

When I closed myself in the bathroom to tackle my hair and make-up in twenty minutes flat, and I began my frantic work, I felt a pause. I knew that I needed God to work quick in my heart if I wanted to turn the day around. I began praying, but my prayers felt like whining and complaining and I couldn't bear to listen to myself. Instead, as I pulled my hair into a ponytail and covered up pimples, I began reciting Scripture. (Last year I memorized 24 verses, this year about 6, and I gave those 30 verses my best shot.

I could only recall about half of them, and I was definitely not at 100% accuracy. But I spoke those slightly out-of-order Bible verses with my whole heart.)

No more than fifteen minutes later, my hair and make-up were done, my teeth were clean, I had a fresh layer of deodorant on, and I was dressed. The best part, though, is that I felt victorious. I didn't feel stressed, frazzled, late, or angry anymore. In fact, the peace of God was so strong over me that when Kai refused to go into childcare and insisted sitting with me ALL morning, it didn't even annoy me! (Seriously, if you know me, you know that this is a miracle! I am never one to turn down an hour of childcare!)

So if you were with me on Saturday, and you were wondering whether the stuff I was talking about really works, it does. Does speaking Scripture really hold the power to halt our anger? Absolutely! Remember "Thing 2?" Words are powerful. Especially the Word of God. It's sharper than any double-edged sword. (Hebrews 4:12)

Yesterday is living proof.

Thing Six: What to do when you mess up

This morning I am packing up to take my kiddos and dog home from a weekend of worship and fellowship. For many years I volunteered at the Freshwind conference, hauling chairs around and cleaning bathrooms (okay, honestly, I usually tried to delegate the bathrooms), but this year was special. At this year's conference, I had the huge privilege of being one of the workshop speakers. Can I just say—my body and mind are just as exhausted as they have been every other year! (Honestly, though, I do know those volunteers had to deal with a lot more crap than I did! If you were there, you know what I mean)

Not only did I enjoy the hours of catching up with some old friends (you know who you are), but I had the opportunity to meet some new ones. I just want to send a quick shout out to them: Rhiannon, Kathy from New Sarepta, Heidi, Monika, Pam, Charlotte and friends from Calgary, and Pam and Wendy from "the Park," and about 90 others whose names I didn't learn. Hi girls! Thanks for spending your time with me Saturday afternoon.

If this is your first visit to my blog, here are a few things that will help you get involved. **Got something to say?** Excellent! I love comments! Just click on the phrase "__ shared their thoughts" at the bottom of this post and follow the prompts. **Don't know how to sign in?** If you have a Google account, sign in to it to leave your comment. If not, you can choose "Open ID" and just type your name in the box; you can click "Name/URL" and if you type in your own blog or website address I can come visit you; or you can choose "Anonymous" and either type your name at the end of your comment or remain anonymous. **Want to come back and read all the time?** It would make my day if you clicked to "follow it" and "find me on Facebook" or decided to "receive posts by email!" (All of these options can be found in the sidebars to the right of this post.)

Okay, let's get on with the good stuff!

In my session, *Mommy, why are you Angry?* I shared five things God has taught me in our journey to break free from my "addiction" to venting my anger and frustration on my kids. (I sure hope that, if you were in my session on Saturday, you've had a chance to review the handout and are thinking about your first steps. Are you going to start exploring your children's' love languages? Do a spiritual gifts inventory for yourself? Have you started writing out those verses and sticking them all over your world?) But there is an important sixth point that I still need to talk about—what should I do when I mess up?

Heaven knows that I have messed up more times than I can count on this journey! I don't know about you, but I tend to be an "all or nothing" girl. When I am trying to lose weight (when am not?!), for example, I jump in with both feet—I count points, I exercise, and I am diligent. But then someone has a birthday and messes with my system. You see, I am powerless to resist a good, fat slice of cake. And once I let that one piece pass my lips, I begin to feel defeated. *I lost the battle, so I may as well quit trying.* And I fall face-first, mouth wide open off the wagon. This all or nothing mindset carries to most areas of my life, including yelling. I resolve to never yell again, and when I slip up and let a frustrated holler go I feel weak and discouraged, so I just give up. Then I'm just "a yeller" as opposed to being a mom who is trying to change but is a failure.

Is anyone relating to this?!

Here are three quick tips on dealing with the inevitable mess ups:

1. **Celebrate every little success.**

We can't experience success if we look at life through the all or nothing lens. If our goal is perfection, we will constantly fall short. So stop resolving to be perfect! Start resolving to do better next time. Take it one frustrating experience at a time. And if next time you want to lose your cool but instead give yourself a time out—you have succeeded! Write it down! Celebrate! Pat yourself on the back! And don't forget to praise the Lord!

2. **Always ask forgiveness.**

There will be next times when the yelling still sneaks out. The one thing we can never afford to do is ignore those mistakes. When we ignore sin and pretend it isn't there, it grows. We need to allow God to bring our sin into His light, so He can remove it. When we confess our sins, He is faithful to forgive us—every single time (yes, even if it's the 10,000th time). Remember, too, that God isn't the only One we need to seek forgiveness from—so many angry words can be instantly healed by the simple act of telling our children that we're sorry.

(See 1 John 1:9. Use a concordance to look up some verses containing the words "repent," "forgive," and "confess.")

3. **Pray about your anger every day.**

Event today, when I am (finally) less "angry mommy" and more "mommy who sometimes messes up and gets angry," I still ask God to help me with my anger every single day. I plan to continue to do so until the day I die. You see, when something begins to gain victory over us, we will (in most cases) always be particularly susceptible to that struggle. For example, I quit smoking nearly eight years ago. Obviously, I am no longer addicted. Yet put me in a certain situation, especially with other smokers, and my foolish mind begins to entertain thoughts of having "just one drag." The enemy knows our areas of weakness, and he is relentless in his pursuit of our failure! The best guard we have against his tricks and temptations is daily prayer for protection and strength.

Basically, it all comes down to changing our thinking. (Sound familiar?) To continue the whole diet analogy, we have to stop thinking like we're on a diet, and begin living like we're making a lifestyle change. It's not all or nothing, but one step at a time toward the goal. And while our daily weigh-ins may not all show the results we're looking for, if we begin to track progress over time (remember #1—write down those successes) we will see positive change!

One last thing I want to say to you. When you mess up, you are not a bad mom. Wait, I'm not sure you're really hearing that. You are not a bad mom! When you mess up, you are a good mom who messed up. So say, "Oops," and keep moving forward. Because you are a good mom! You are exactly the mom God chose for your children. Say it with me, I am a good mom!

How to Repair a Cracked Vase

It is fall again. While the leaves fall to the ground and all of nature begins to lie dormant, I sense a revival coming. A time of renewal. A time of glorying in the presence of God. As I feel the spark in my spirit fanning to flame, I felt it important to look back a bit and reflect on where He has brought me from.

Last fall was a time of some major highs and lows in our family.

Pat gets offered a promotion—high.
We need to move—low.
Asking God to provide and seeing it happen—high.
Settling into new everything—low.
There were, of course, many others, but you get the picture.

Through the entire roller-coaster ride, we leaned hard on God. It was a new thing in our marriage—to pray together—but we pushed through our discomfort and did it, daily. Regardless of my emotions, I felt the presence of the Holy Spirit over every moment of every day.

We are settled into our new life and its routines. The kids seem to be comfortable at their new schools. We have decided to make our new church our "home" church. Along the way we've even had a few free moments to make some friends.

But there's an underlying sense of . . . something. Sadness? Emptiness? Unfulfilled-ness? (Yes, I do realize that's not a word!) There's this thing that's nagging at me. God feels far away. I know that He didn't take a step back from me, which means I'm the one that moved.

Last year (2009) I memorized 24 Scripture verses; this year, zilch. Last fall our family was a family of prayer—Pat and I prayed together, we prayed with the kids, we prayed with friends, we prayed over every single decision; this year, at least we still pray at mealtimes and bedtimes with the kids. Last year I committed to getting up at 5:30am for my quiet time with the Lord and I rarely missed a morning; this year I rise a little bit early on random days and try to squeeze in a few minutes. I used to be responsible for mentoring many other women in their walk with the Lord, and I took that calling seriously; without that level of accountability I have allowed myself to slack off.

Just as it is no surprise that I gained back all my lost weight when I decided to "take a break" from exercising and eating well, I shouldn't be surprised that taking a break from vital spiritual habits has placed distance between me and God.

So here I am, working to piece together the fragments of my faith. I am like a vase that developed a hairline crack, and as time wore on little shards of clay fell out here and there. Not broken, not destroyed, but fractured and in need of repair.

How to Repair a Cracked Vase:

Step one: Pick up the section of the vase that seems easiest to fit back into place. For me, this means returning to the basics of Scripture memory.

Step two: Be generous with the crazy glue and hold it there until it dries. I need to allow the Holy Spirit to do His work settling the Word of God in my heart and mind.

Repeat steps one and two until each segment and sliver of clay is picked up off the floor. A few of the larger chunks I can see are morning time, praise, and prayer. It's the smaller fragments, though, that will take great concentration to fit back into place.

Things like a hunger for God's Word, peace in my soul, and sensing those little nudges from the Holy Spirit.

While the vase may never be restored to its original beauty, it will be whole again. The shadow of those cracked places will forever be a reminder of what caused the vase to crack and the hard work invested in its repair. And those cracks, they will serve to let the Light shine through a little bit more than it did before the fracture happened.

Hypocrisy

One of the biggest criticisms that other folks have of church folks is that we are hypocrites. I have two things to say in response to that assertion:

1. They're right.

Unfortunately, there are many Christians who don't act very . . . Christian. Have you ever accidentally upset another driver, had them wave their hands (or flip the bird) angrily at you and whiz past, only to see a Jesus fish on their rear bumper? Or maybe that fish-toting vehicle is yours (or mine, *cough*)? This is just one small example, but I'm sure we can all name hundreds more.

Sadly, when *some* Christians demonstrate actions that oppose what they claim to believe, they give the whole lot of us a bad name. Worse, they give God a bad name. Worst, I'm pretty sure I'm one of those *some*one's all too often.

As followers of Christ, we have a responsibility to do our best to live like Him in all aspects of our lives. If we preach the gospel of love and forgiveness, we should actually love and forgive others. Our walk should match our talk.

2. They're wrong.

Often, people who aren't familiar with faith in Christ get the (incorrect) impression that all Christians think they (we) are perfect. Thus, when we fail to behave as perfect people, we prove their case. We're no better than them, our faith is no better than theirs, but because we think we are and it is—we are hypocrites. But this reasoning is false.

I don't know about you, but I don't claim to be perfect. I don't require the people around me to be perfect either. What I do claim is that Jesus Christ is perfect, and with my whole heart I *want* to be as like Him as I possibly can. Messing up doesn't necessarily mean I'm a hypocrite; it just means I'm human.

I love how James M. Reeves, author of *Refuge: how "hospital church" ministry can change your church forever* and founder/ pastor of Celebration Fellowship puts it, "The church has to be a safe place for people to tell their secrets and have a safe process for people to experience spiritual and emotional healing." Reeves asserts that, rather than holding to the popular view of church as a place for "good, Christian people," we need to begin to view church as a hospital, where people of varying levels of illness and disease come to receive care.

Huh?

So what are we to do? How can we, as followers of Christ, show the world that the church isn't full of judgmental hypocrites?

I think we can:

1. **Be real.** We don't need pretend to be perfect, flawless, or sinless to the church crowd. We don't need to pretend to be important and successful to the world crowd. We need to be who we are—the same person—with everyone we encounter, both in front of others and behind closed doors.

Better to be a nobody and yet have a servant than to pretend to be somebody and have no food. ~ Proverbs 12:9

2. **Be holy.** Jesus is perfect. He is holy and righteous, and His ways are true and right. We are not and cannot be as perfect as Jesus, but we can *try* to be like Him in as many ways as possible (and not just at church!).

Anybody can observe the Sabbath, but making it holy surely takes the rest of the week. ~ Alive Walker

3. **Be honest.** When we mess up and don't act like Jesus at all, the most Christ-like thing we can do is to confess and seek forgiveness.

Therefore confess your sins to each other and pray for each other so that you may be healed. ~ James5:16a

4. **Be love.** We need to love people. Loving others means being kind to them, welcoming them, accepting them without trying to change them. Our job is not to point out for others their sinful ways. Our job is to point them to Christ. He'll take care of their hearts.

"Everyone thinks of changing the world, but no one thinks of changing himself." ~ Tolstoy

Basically, we need to be people of integrity. What we do should live up to what we say. And ~~if~~ when it doesn't, we need to be truthful about how who we are doesn't always match up with Who we want to be like.

What do you think?

I'm Just a Yeller . . .

An anonymous friend posed a really great question last week that I've decided to tackle this morning. I don't really want to talk about anger today because, well, I've been feeling pretty pi#%ed off with my kids all week. Which means, as much as I don't feel like talking about it, I probably should.

Our friend asked, When and how did you discover that you were angry, and not just doing what Moms have to do—yell at our kids to get them to do anything?

Can I be to-the-gut point-blank honest here? For me as much as for you? Thanks . . .

The fact of the matter is, we moms do NOT have to yell at our kids to get them to listen to us. While certain circumstances will require a raised voice (safety concerns, a massive brawl of 14 children that needs to be stopped, a generally loud situation), if it seems as though every circumstance is one of those, we need to take that as our first clue that something is amiss. A raised voice should be the exception, not the rule. **If we are yelling regularly, we have a problem.**

If you were a fly on my wall, you would likely listen in on the odd conversation between Pat and I where one of us is asking, "Why do we have to yell at the kids to get them to listen and obey?" It's one that we revisit more regularly than I'd like. Really, though, we both know the answer . . . **If we need to yell at our kids to make them listen and obey, it is because we have taught them that they don't have to listen or obey until/unless we are yelling.**

I assure you, I am the last person who will ever pass judgment on another mother! I know how hopeless it feels, how impossible it looks. I am the queen of yelling and swearing, and I often catch myself thinking, "I am never going to be able to NOT yell!" So as you read my gut-honest words, do not feel condemned. Everyone has their issues . . . anger happens to be ours.

If you think you may have anger issues but are not totally sure, here are seven questions you can ask yourself:

1. Have I ever told myself or someone else, "I'm a yeller. That's just who I am."?
2. Have I ever had the urge to hurl an object across the room in frustration?
3. Whether or not I speak them, do I think curse words in my head when I'm frustrated?
4. If my child(ren) does thinks like slamming doors and shouting, "I hate you!" am I tempted to respond with those same words and reactions?
5. Do I frequently find myself feeling annoyed with my children's constant interruptions and requests?
6. Do I sometimes react in ways that are disproportionate to the situation? (For example, feeling *truly angry* about a spilled cup of juice.)
7. Am I a different mother behind closed doors than I am out in public?

There's no magic formula, no points system, but if you found yourself answering "yes" to a few of those questions, it's probably time to get alone with God and ask Him if you have a problem with mommy anger.

And you know that hopeless, impossible thing? For the record, that's a lie. It's a big, fat, ugly lie that Satan wants us to believe so that we *don't even try* to overcome this struggle. **Victory is possible.**

I believe it with everything in me. If I didn't, I wouldn't be out here on the World Wide Web (and hopefully, eventually in book format) publishing all my shortcomings for the world to see. The only way it's hopeless and impossible is if we try to do it on our own.

For nothing is impossible with God.

~Luke 1:37 (NLT)

Giving starts right here

What comes to your mind when you hear the word "giving?" Do you tend to think of feeding the homeless, sponsoring a child, and the like? While I believe this type of generosity is absolutely vital, I believe there is another form of giving that many of us neglect.

Giving to the local church. I'm not referring to tithing here (though we should all do that), but to the offering up of our time and talents. Do you serve within your church? In a capacity that makes use of your spiritual gifts?

We worshippers tend toward one of these two mindsets: "I have done my time, it's someone else's turn," or

"If I don't do it, nobody will." I propose to you that both of these thought patterns are flawed.

Everyone should serve in a volunteer capacity.

Yes, everyone. Those who are paid staff of the church should find a way to serve elsewhere that is unpaid. Full time mothers with fifteen small children need to find a place to volunteer. Hard working men ought to seek out a ministry to get involved with. Every single person in the church body has a vital role to fill, and without me, without you, the church is merely functioning—not thriving.

Just as a body, though one, has many parts, but all its many parts form one body, so it is with Christ. Even so the body is not made up of one part but of many . . .

Now if the foot should say, "Because I am not a hand, I do not belong to the body," it would not for that reason stop being part of the body. And if the ear should say, "Because I am not an eye, I do not belong to the body," it would not for that reason stop being part of the body. If the whole body were an eye, where would the sense of hearing be? If the whole body were an ear, where would the sense of smell be? But in fact God has placed the parts in the body, every one of them, just as he wanted them to be. As it is, there are many parts, but one body . . .

But God has put the body together, giving greater honor to the parts that lacked it, so that there should be no division in the body, but that its parts should have equal concern for each other. If one part suffers, every part suffers with it; if one part is honored, every part rejoices with it.

Now you are the body of Christ, and each one of you is a part of it.

~1 Corinthians 12:12, 14-20, 24b-27

Each person should use their God-given gifts in service.

When I had small children, I volunteered in the nursery. Because I "should." Those nursery Sundays were the most mentally, physically, emotionally, and spiritually draining 90 minutes of my life. I would get up in the morning dreading it, and would leave exhausted and short-tempered with my family. Until I discovered my spiritual gifts, one of which is administration.

Have you ever thought about how much work goes into the oversight of the church nursery? Creating spreadsheets and name tags, writing newsletters, keeping track of sign-ins and clearances. (If you're from a smaller church, perhaps this list of "need tos" has you shaking your head. All I can tell you is that large church culture is different and requires more extensive security precautions.) Needless to say, I discovered that there were ways to give my time to the nursery ministry that used my spiritual gifts.

God doesn't call us all to fill the vacancies in church ministry (although, I won't dare say never . . . sometimes He will ask us to do something completely stretching), He calls each of us to serve Him in a specific way. In a way that He has equipped us to serve, to give.

In his grace, God has given us different gifts for doing certain things well. So if God has given you the ability to prophesy, speak out with as much faith as God has given you. If your gift is serving others, serve them well. If you are a teacher, teach well. If your gift is to encourage others, be encouraging. If it is giving, give generously. If God has given you leadership ability, take the responsibility seriously. And if you have a gift for showing kindness to others, do it gladly.

~Romans 12:4-8 (NLT)

Just give!

Giving love, money, and time to the needs at home and abroad is necessary. As is giving time, talent, and effort in our local church. Doing one without the other is like . . . well, I don't know, exactly . . . incomplete. Like baking bread without yeast.

How to be Superwoman (or not)—1

I have been asked questions like: How do you get everything done for your family, not neglect your relationship with God, and find time to write too?

So I figured it would be helpful share my four-step tutorial on *How to be Superwoman (or not)*. Because I prefer to use more words than necessary, I'll split this into two posts. You'll thank me later.

Step One: Never neglect time with God.

I delight in Your decrees; I will not neglect Your Word. ~Psalm 119:16
Okay, that's not to say that I *never* neglect time with God. But I shouldn't. And neither should you. Know what I mean?

In my world, experiencing quiet time cannot occur if children are awake. And given my bent toward complete and utter couch vegetation after they're tucked in for the evening, the twilight hours are ruled out. By process of elimination, I've found that my relationship with God is best fostered in the wee hours of the morning.

A number of years ago I started rising an hour before the kids so that I would have enough time for coffee, prayer, listening, Bible study, Bible reading, Scripture memory, and worship. No, I don't do all of those things every morning! But I do probably tackle each of them once or twice over a two-week period.

I also don't view my quiet time as my only time of day to be in relationship with the Lord. He and I converse throughout the day. If I'm unsure about making a certain purchase while out grocery shopping, I ask God. If I am running late for an appointment but make it on time anyway thanks to low traffic and lots of green lights, I thank Him. If I have six million things on my "to do" list that day, I ask God where to start, and what to do next all day. Whatever doesn't get done, I trust is something that He didn't need me to take care of that day.

If you ever hear me being frazzled, flustered, or stressed, you can pretty much be assured that I've forgotten step one. The tough thing for me is that all of my secrets are revealed in my writing. Although, the knowledge that you will be able to tell when I'm not in close fellowship with my Abba is a pretty good accountability tool!

Step Two: Schedule, schedule, schedule.

She watches over the affairs of her household and does not eat the bread of idleness. ~Proverbs 31:27
I like to feel organized. I didn't say that I *am* organized, but I like to *feel* as though I am. One thing that helps me is to schedule everything that I can.

Social life—While building friendships is very important to me (and also one thing God has called me to do), I tend to be very particular about *how* I make and take time to do so. If we're going to have coffee and a visit together, we will often email back and forth a few times to schedule a date and time—frequently up to two weeks away. But when I make these dates, I commit to myself to keep them (I really, really try not to cancel). Things like girls' night out, home parties, and so on only happen for me a couple times a year. It's worth saying that I have great friends who understand my priorities and my calling. I pray that they can say the same of me.

Marriage—I book a date night roughly every second weekend (on paydays). This has been an integral part of our marriage for several years. I also try to schedule my "work" during the day, so that my evenings are free to hang out with my man. I like to sit on the couch reading a good book next to him as he watches the hockey game. (Really, there is only so much hockey a girl can take! Even a Canadian one.)

Household duties—I used to try to get all my housework done on one day of the week. A grueling five-hour day of utter exhaustion. This house is too big for that, and the laundry far too demanding! We've recently begun doing the house cleaning as a family on the weekends, and I am really enjoying it! We tend to be homebodies on the weekends anyway, so it's not cutting into anything, and everyone seems to enjoy working together. I haven't fine-tuned the laundry thing yet, but so far it seems to be working well to simply toss in a load whenever I pass by the machines. The kids all put away their own laundry (well, put away is used very loosely).

When it comes to meals, I do best with a meal plan. Having a monthly meal plan helps me know what are the essential purchases, what meat to pull out of the freezer in the morning (or the night before), and how much prep time I'll need. Planning meals means I can decide which days require crock pot cooking in advance (activity nights) and which days I can do something bigger. I must confess that I have been lacking a meal plan for months now. The unfortunate solution has been too much eating out and too many dinners of kid fare (mini pizzas, grilled cheese sandwiches, etc.).

Family time—Busy or not, it's hard to get quality time together with a family of seven. So we try to get our time where we can . . . Family movie night, swimming, skating, walking the dog, going to the playground (neither of those last two really happens for 8 months of the year).

Pat and I also try to take individual dates with each child once or twice over the course of the school year. What works for me is to "blitz" them—I email Pat with four occasions (we don't really need to take Kai out yet) that all occur within two weeks. I try to combine our date nights with things that need to get done anyway. For example, I'll take someone for dinner and then we'll grocery shop together.

How to be Superwoman (or not)—2

Step Three: Make time.

There is a time for everything, and a season for every activity under the heavens. ~Ecclesiastes 3:1

We've all heard it said that people make time for what's important to them. It's true. Writing is important to me, so I tackle it early in the morning before doing much of anything else (besides getting the kids off to school). I won't even start a load of laundry before writing on my blog, because I know that I am far too easily distracted.

I used to give myself "Facebook time" while I ate my lunch, until I realized that I was allowing myself to waste an hour (or more) every day doing nothing! Instead, I now watch BLAST* teaching videos while I eat my lunch. (Just a note, on weekdays I don't eat lunch with the kids. I feed them, and once they're done and into quiet time/nap I sit down for mine.)

Not only do we need to make time for the important stuff and get rid of the time killers, we really need to allow ourselves to become okay with leaving some things undone (whether for today or forever). There are times when my house looks like a sty and I make the kids pull out the "cleanest" jeans from the dirty laundry pile. There are times when my desk looks like a hurricane victim and I will actually choose to throw away some things that could/should be done. I have only been parent helper at school once so far this year and probably only two or three times last year (whereas some moms—the really good ones who I want to be like when I grow up—are there twice a month). And I have not placed a photo in an album since Megan's birth more than seven years ago. So yeah, I don't do it all! Not at all.

Step Four: Find your own super power.

Each of you has your own gift from God; one has this gift, another has that. ~1 Corinthians 7:7b

Do not neglect your gift . . . ~1 Timothy 4:14a

I just need to say one more thing about how I get done all that I need to . . . It's all about personality and giftings! I like to be busy, I thrive on a full schedule, and I function best with my hands full. It's a fine balance between really busy and too busy, but I'd like to think I'm self-aware enough that I usually pick up on the signals that I'm doing too much fairly quickly.

The fact is, I'm a deadline girl and I always have been. Homework assignments, exams, pumping gas, waitressing—all were done best when I was under pressure. Recently, as my schedule began to fill up with Heart to Heart stuff and Logos society things, Pat told me he was excited—excited for me to finally be busy because he knew he'd be fed yummier meals in a tidier house, all while I was actually (finally) getting to work on my book.

Maybe it's not even that I thrive on being busy so much as I am too lazy to be allowed to be idle.

If you're not built like me, then you'll never be the kind of non-Superwoman I am. Each of us needs to find our own super powers. If you do best with the slow and steady method, that is your super power. Work with it. Embrace it. And for goodness sake, tell me how you always seem to be so calm, cool, and collected!

How to Change the World

The needs of this world are great. Sometimes, the idea that my little bit of help can't possibly make a difference discourages. We can't all go on missions trips, and even those of us who can may wonder if what we've done can truly change lives in the long run. We can't all volunteer at our local shelter, and for those who can, they must sometimes wonder what it will take to stop seeing the same faces in the lunch line, day after day, week after week, year after year.

But our God did not call us to fix all the world's ails, He simply calls each one of us to obedience. Imagine every single person listening and doing the one thing He asks of them. What might the impact be?

It was a bitingly cold February morning, and the four of us walked the downtown sidewalks between our warm, comfortable hotel and the luxuriously equipped conference centre.

At the halfway point, about two-and-a-half frigid blocks into our trek, we ducked into the coffee shop to soak up some warmth and drink down some fortitude. Armed with steaming paper cups, we ventured out for the final couple blocks. I opened my lid and sipped burning liquid into icy cold lips while we tromped the snowy concrete.

There he was, up ahead, hunched forward against the piercing wind, clothed in heavy coveralls designed for snowmobiling. All his life's possessions carried over his shoulder in a black plastic trash bag.

He must be so cold. I really should give him my nice, warm coffee. But I already drank from the cup. Too bad. Lord, bless this poor man who is without his own four walls of shelter, without a bed, without hope.

The morning worship was moving, the speaker inspirational. I think. I can't be sure because the whole time my heart was distracted. I heard His voice whispering to me, "You could have been his hope, his blessing. Oh how I wish you had listened to Me. Don't worry, someone else will hear my prompting and obey, and he will experience the soul-deep joy that only comes from obedience. He will know that he is making a difference."

Over lunch (convenience food served in under five minutes, purchased with pocket change, consumed in the heated food court of a shopping centre rife with opportunities to spend more) I shared how I felt compelled to give away a cup of love and how I ignored the voice of God. My story was met with the echo of three voices sadly confessing, "Me too."

No, our obedience would not have given world peace or brought an end to world hunger. Armies from many nations try to bring peace and fail. Organizations pour out missionaries to feed the hungry from here to the ends of the earth, yet people starve. All that our meager gift could offer was hope for a cold and lonely man who had none. Perhaps changing the world is about giving what you have, when you have it, when God tells you to do it. The cure to all that ails this earth might be as simple as a little cup of hope.

A few days later, when I heard His voice again, I listened.

What do you do to change the world?

Good Fruit: Patience

"Hurry up!"

"Come on!"

"Let's go!"

Phrases I exclaim to my children daily. More than daily.

I often think of patience as having less of that. Less rush. Less hurry. Less "go, go go." When I pray for patience it is usually because I have been dealing with discipline issues impatiently. I want to *feel* more patient, *be* more patient. Somewhere along the way, we have come to understand patience to mean serenity and calmness.

What if we've got it all wrong, though? What if the word we use to define patience isn't really what God meant in Galatians? Perhaps that type of patience (calmness) is really more of a self-control issue, and God had something else in mind when He used Paul to exhort us to have love, joy, peace, patience . . .

I looked up patience as it is in the context of the letter to the Galatians, and it is defined as: endurance, constancy, steadfastness, perseverance, and slowness in avenging wrongs. Am I the only one a little bit surprised to find that patience actually means staying power, persistence, and lack of vengefulness?

Can you think of a time when you exhibited this type of patience? Go ahead and share it in the comments.

Frankly, I'm a little relieved. No more striving to feel calm about everything! Well, until I get to tackling that self-control thing . . .

Year in Review

I began with a goal in my heart. Here's how I worked toward a more consecrated life for those twelve months . . .

January—Right from the first day of my year of consecration, God called me out on my anger issues. Sure, I had been "working" on it, but He was asking me to step it up. It was time to come to God in true submission, sincere obedience, and let Him bring real transformation.

February—I recognized that there were things I allowed to take up valuable time in my life that could better be used for Kingdom purposes. One of those things was Facebook. So Facebook and I took a 40 day break from each other for Lent.

March—This month began with a reminder (written largely for myself) on the importance of consecrating our finances to the Lord by committing to tithing.

April—I was convicted of the lack of emphasis we (as a western society, as a family, as a church body) place on knowing the Word of God.

May—May had me realizing how far I was (and will ever be) from holiness. But I knew that I could come closer to the Lord than I was. I was in need of some repair . . .

June—A tribute to my Dad, inspired by my Abba.

July—The summer months were filled with moments of family togetherness and fun. I chose to be fully there, and felt God's pleasure in each moment.

August—God worked out some hard issues in my heart while I was at She Speaks.

September—As I prepared to answer God's call to begin speaking about my anger, I began to recognize moments of true success in the journey. That transformation He began in January was beginning to bear fruit in my life.

October—It's always difficult to get back into the routine of spiritual disciplines after the flexibility of summer. I found myself starved of the Word and in need of some serious feasting.

November—Usually, getting deep in the Word gives me good fodder for writing. But I found myself at a loss in November, in spite of my feasting. So I turned to floor over for some questions.

December—This year is wrapping up with a big case of distractedness and lists, big dreams and goals, wondering what the focus for 2011 should be.

Tomorrow, Lord willing, I will have an answer.

Good Fruit: Joy

Sometimes we have joy because of our circumstances.

When an acquaintance asks the standard question, "How are you?" our reply is "Great!" or "Excellent!" or "Wonderful!" rather than the usual "Fine." We have work that we enjoy. Our family is healthy and/or wealthy. We feel on top of the world. Our joy comes from the fact that *life is good*.

Sometimes we have joy in spite of our circumstances.

Life is not good. Economic downturn, financial struggles, illness, troubled (or ended) marriage, rebellious children, and so on . . . Even though these circumstances completely stink, we do our best to find joy *somewhere*. This kind of joy sounds like, "We may be out of work, but at least everyone is healthy."

True joy, though, is not found *in* our circumstances or *in spite of* our circumstances. **True joy is found in Christ alone.**

"I am the vine; you are the branches. If you remain in me and I in you, you will bear much fruit; apart from me you can do nothing. If you do not remain in me, you are like a branch that is thrown away and withers; such branches are picked up, thrown into the fire and burned. If you remain in me and my words remain in you, ask whatever you wish, and it will be done for you. This is to my Father's glory, that you bear much fruit, showing yourselves to be my disciples.

"As the Father has loved me, so have I loved you. Now remain in my love. If you keep my commands, you will remain in my love, just as I have kept my Father's commands and remain in his love. I have told you this so that my joy may be in you and **that your joy may be complete**.

~ John 15:5-11 (emphasis mine)

It seems that Christ has given us a formula for joy:

1. Remain in Him (and His love). (vs. 5, 7, 9)
2. Let Him (and His Words) remain in us. (vs. 5, 7, 9, 10)
3. Bear fruit. (vs. 5, 8)
4. Give God glory. (vs. 8)
5. Keep His commands. (vs. 10)
6. Let His joy be in us. (vs. 11)
7. Our joy is complete. (vs. 11)

Call me crazy, but I don't see anything in here about our circumstances. Good or bad, they are beside the point. Our joy comes when we abide in Him.

When You've Lost Your Faith

There have been a couple times in my life where God has felt far, far away. It wasn't just that He seemed hard to reach, but more like He had abandoned me. Certain difficult circumstances in my life had happened—circumstances that He could have prevented—and I felt as though I had been thrown to the wolves to fend for myself.

One such time was during the pregnancy and after the birth of my third child. Early in the pregnancy we moved for the promise of a job that would have my hubby at home more often. Turns out he was away more than ever, and I was on my own with two children in diapers, pregnant, working full time, in a city where I had no friends and family. This move had also given us hope for some restoration in our struggling marriage. Instead, the battles became louder, angrier, more frequent. Not long after the baby arrived, I found my hope slipping away as I sunk into post-partum depression.

As we moved into summer at the end of a long, lonely year, I was convinced that God had forgotten me. Or perhaps I had done something to make Him turn away. Maybe it was me who created the distance. The only thing I was sure of was that I had once known God and felt His presence and His protection, but for a long time I had not sensed Him nearby.

Over time, though, I found Him again. I heard His whispers to my heart once more. And *eventually* I even began to see how He was using that dark year to bring about good in my life. I have some friends who are living in one of those seasons of empty heartache, wondering where God is and how to find Him again. This post is dedicated to you, because I love you and I understand. My prayer for you is that you, too, will not only experience the presence of God in your lives once again, but that you will eventually see the good that He is making from all the no good, terrible, horrible, really bad stuff.

How to Find a Faith that's Been Lost . . .

I can't pin down the rediscovery of my faith to three easy steps done in a special order (even though the writer/speaker in me did somehow find a way to compile my thoughts into three points, ha). Because we're all different, I know that some things that helped me won't work for you. Yet I can see now, in retrospect, that there were some things I did that drew me back to God. My hope is that some of these things will work for you, too.

1. God never leaves.

The first thing I must share, though I'm sure you know it in your head just as I did, is that God never washes His hands of us. He has promised that He will not abandon us. If we feel like orphaned children, we need to remember that this is *our feeling*, **but our feelings do not always reflect the realities of God**.

The LORD himself goes before you and will be with you; He will never leave you nor forsake you. Do not be afraid; do not be discouraged. ~Deuteronomy 31:8

2. Go to church.

One of our instincts when we feel abandoned is to stop doing the things we've done. We convince ourselves that the reasons we did these things (such as going to church, reading our Bibles, etc.) was out of routine and obligation, thus making it easy to quit. We tell ourselves that if God has left us, we may as well leave Him. We also do it as an act of self-preservation—we know that the people there will ask us how we are, and we either become very good a lying or we are more emotionally raw than we ever really want to be.

But we need to remind ourselves of the truth—at some point in our faith walks, we went to church because it filled us up, fed us, gave us pleasure. The people there, they also meant something to us; they became family.

If you've stopped going to church, going back may be one of the most difficult steps in the journey to reclaiming your faith. Nothing is more terrifying than the thought of facing the people and the pastors who are likely to ask questions and bring up all sorts of emotions. I am tempted here to suggest trying a new church (and for some people that may be necessary), but I believe that most of us need to return to home, not just to any church. As they say, "home is where the heart is."

There will be moments of pain, moments of great discomfort, and some people who will be judgmental rather than welcoming. But your home church is filled to the brim with people who love you, who want to pray for you and bless you, who have missed you but simply didn't know how to reach out. And chances are, if you felt abandoned by God you also felt abandoned by your church—the only path to healing those hurts is to go back.

3. Go after Him.

While we know that God has not truly left, the lack of sensing His presence is one that we often don't know how to rectify. So we do nothing. But in reality, knowing that somehow we are the ones who put distance between ourselves and God, we need to do *something* to close the gap. We need to seek Him.

There are many ways to seek Him, but one thing that works for me is worship music. I choose a song or two that have been meaningful to me and I listen, sing along, whisper the lyrics as a prayer, and believe that God will hear me and respond.

I've tried reading the Bible, or looking up Scripture verses that are familiar or meaningful. I've googled "promises of God" and read them aloud to myself. Sadly, these things didn't bring the Word of God alive for me again. They may work for you, though, so still give it a try.

You will seek me and find me when you seek me with all your heart. ~Jeremiah 29:13

My friends, these suggestions for finding your faith again are not coming from some goody-goody, happy, perfect Christian girl who's never strayed a day in her life. No, they are the words from a battle-scarred woman who has walked the lonely road of lost faith more than once, and who has fought tooth and nail to find it again. My words come from a heart of deep love for you, my dear friends, and the understanding that your hearts are broken and cannot be fixed until you once again feel the peace and comfort of your Abba. Please, don't give up. Keep on fighting for your faith. I love you.

Stuck in a Rut

We've all heard someone say it. Many of us have said it ourselves. And everyone wants to know how to get out of it. How to get moving again.

Before we can determine the best path to free us from our rut, we need to figure out what kind of rut we are in. Is it a pit of yuck? Dark, lonely, depressed, anxious, insecure? Or is it a crevice of comfort? Nice things, worldly success, security?

The path out of any rut is virtually the same, except for the starting point. I dare say dragging oneself out of a vat of despair is somewhat less difficult and painful than launching oneself free of the quicksand of coziness.

In the pit of yuck, we need to recognize that we are stuck, desperate, and unable to free ourselves. Then we must turn to the only One who can free us, reach a hand up out of the pit, place it in the hand of the Master, and lift our faces toward the light.

To get unstuck from this rut has us moving from an undesirable place to something better. Stepping forward brings hope. And so our feet are no longer trapped, but move out onto the path. The path, though, is a lengthy journey with feet dragging weighty mud clumps along the way.

The crevice of comfort is a rut we are reluctant to recognize. The first step in acknowledging that we are stuck is the nagging sense that there is something more than this, something missing. There needs to be a humbling of the belief that we are the makers of our success. The first step out of this rut is more like jumping off a cliff. It means being willing to give it all up. Rather than seeing our first step as one of hope, it brings trepidation, fear, doubt, worry, and resistance.

Getting unstuck means stepping down from our self-made pedestal and bowing prostrate before the only One who can free us. This first step is agonizingly slow—crawling hand and knee in His footsteps until the weight of our success tumbles from our shoulders and we can stand on the path—but getting through it places us on a road of joy and exhilaration.

No matter the rut, the path is the same. It is a journey of revival. We turn our hearts away from our circumstances and toward our God, who is above and beyond our experiences. We are sojourners on the path to change. The only thing constant is continual transformation, brought on by an abandoned love for the Guide.

And so the only question really worth asking ourselves is this . . .

Am I on the path of transformation or am I stuck in a rut?

Bumped off Self-Centre

I started reading a new book this morning. I am in the midst of a couple, but they were boring me, so I decided to crack a fresh binding. I've had this piece of literary handiwork gathering dust on my desktop for a couple months, certain that, while it might be a good read, I was not really in need of the message it purported.

I am on page five, and am now thoroughly convinced that this book will be one that marks a turning point in my life.

The book begins with a science lesson of sorts . . . The world was flat and the earth was the centre of it, until Copernicus and then Galileo began challenging the status quo.

[Copernicus] tapped our collective shoulders and cleared his throat. "Forgive my proclamation, but," and pointing a lone finger toward the sun, he announced, "behold the center of the solar system."

What Copernicus did for the earth, God does for our souls. Tapping the collective shoulder of humanity, he points to the Son—his Son—and says, "Behold the center of it all."

"God raise him [Christ] from death and set him on a throne in deep heaven, in charge of running the universe, everything from galaxies to governments, no name and no power exempt from his rule. And not just for the time being but *forever*. He is in charge of it all, has the final word on everything. At the center of all this, Christ rules the church" (Ephesians 1:20-22 MSG).

When God looks at the center of the universe, he doesn't look at you. When heaven's stagehands direct the spotlight toward the star of the show, I need no sunglasses. No light falls on me.

Lesser orbs, that's us. Appreciated. Valued. Loved dearly. But central? Essential? Pivotal? Nope. Sorry. Contrary to the Ptolemy within us, the world does not revolve around us. Our comfort is not God's priority. If it is, something's gone awry. If we are the marquee event, how do we explain flat-earth challenges like death, disease, slumping economies, or rumbling earthquakes? If God exists to please us, then shouldn't we always be pleased?

*Max Lucado, *It's Not About Me: rescue from the life we thought would make us happy* (pp. 4-5)

Maybe it's just me, but I suspect we could all use a good, healthy bump off self-centre these days.

Does the message of this work seem "not applicable" to you (as it did to me)?

Living Life with Purpose

I received this in my inbox today, and knew I had to share it . . . First, because his words impacted me so. Second, because I read his book several years ago and it did, in fact, change my life.

You will enjoy the new insights that Rick Warren has, with his wife now having cancer and him having 'wealth' from the book sales. This is an absolutely incredible short interview with Rick Warren, Purpose Driven Life author and pastor of Saddleback Church in California.

In the interview by Paul Bradshaw with Rick Warren, Rick said:

People ask me, What is the purpose of life?

And I respond: In a nutshell, life is preparation for eternity. We were not made to last forever, and God wants us to be with Him in Heaven.

One day my heart is going to stop, and that will be the end of my body—but not the end of me.

I may live 60 to 100 years on earth, but I am going to spend trillions of years in eternity. This is the warm-up act—the dress rehearsal. God wants us to practice on earth what we will do forever in eternity.

We were made by God and for God, and until you figure that out, life isn't going to make sense.

Life is a series of problems: Either you are in one now, you're just coming out of one, or you're getting ready to go into another one.

The reason for this is that God is more interested in your character than your comfort; God is more interested in making your life holy than He is in making your life happy.

We can be reasonably happy here on earth, but that's not the goal of life. The goal is to grow in character, in Christ likeness.

This past year has been the greatest year of my life but also the toughest, with my wife, Kay, getting cancer.

I used to think that life was hills and valleys—you go through a dark time, then you go to the mountaintop, back and forth. I don't believe that anymore.

Rather than life being hills and valleys, I believe that it's kind of like two rails on a railroad track, and at all times you have something good and something bad in your life.

No matter how good things are in your life, there is always something bad that needs to be worked on.

And no matter how bad things are in your life, there is always something good you can thank God for.

You can focus on your purposes, or you can focus on your problems:

If you focus on your problems, you're going into self-centeredness, which is my problem, my issues, my pain.' But one of the easiest ways to get rid of pain is to get your focus off yourself and onto God and others.

We discovered quickly that in spite of the prayers of hundreds of thousands of people, God was not going to heal Kay or make it easy for her—It has been very difficult for her, and yet God has strengthened her character, given her a ministry of helping other people, given her a testimony, drawn her closer to Him and to people.

You have to learn to deal with both the good and the bad of life.

Actually, sometimes learning to deal with the good is harder. For instance, this past year, all of a sudden, when the book sold 15 million copies, it made me instantly very wealthy.

It also brought a lot of notoriety that I had never had to deal with before. **I don't think God gives you money or notoriety for your own ego or for you to live a life of ease.**

So I began to ask God what He wanted me to do with this money, notoriety and influence. He gave me two different passages that helped me decide what to do, II Corinthians 9 and Psalm 72.

First, in spite of all the money coming in, we would not change our lifestyle one bit. We made no major purchases.

Second, about midway through last year, I stopped taking a salary from the church.

Third, we set up foundations to fund an initiative we call The Peace Plan to plant churches, equip leaders, assist the poor, care for the sick, and educate the next generation.

Fourth, I added up all that the church had paid me in the 24 years since I started the church, and I gave it all back. It was liberating to be able to serve God for free.

We need to ask ourselves: Am I going to live for possessions? Popularity?

Am I going to be driven by pressures? Guilt? Bitterness? Materialism? Or am I going to be driven by God's purposes (for my life)?

When I get up in the morning, I sit on the side of my bed and say, **God, if I don't get anything else done today, I want to know You more and love You better.** God didn't put me on earth just to fulfill a to-do list. **He's more interested in what I am than what I do.**

That's why we're called human beings, not human doings.

To have eyes of Wonder

I had the pleasure of being parent helper at Kindergarten yesterday. It was a good day to be signed up to help—the kids had chapel, then library, snack, all wrapped up with a carol sing in the gym. I wasn't so much a helper as I was an observer.

During chapel, the grade five class acted out the Christmas story. They had quite a few scene changes, which resulted in some loud chatter from the audience. I caught myself wishing they'd "get on with it, already." But the Kindergarteners' attention did not waver. Their eyes were transfixed on the stage, even during scene changes, soaking it all in.

Oh, that I would come to the greatest story ever told with the eyes and heart of a five-year-old! With a heart of amazement and excitement . . .

It is a sad thing to realize that you have lost your marvel at the miracles: virgin birth, angels appearing, a guiding star hung in the sky, God in a baby's body, salvation come to earth. Somehow, after years of retelling and hearing, the marvel was lost.

But to hear young Joseph share the words that the angel spoke to him, "All this took place to fulfill what the Lord had said through the prophet: 'The virgin will be with child and will give birth to a son, and they will call him Immanuel'—which means 'God with us.'" To see that ten-year-old Mary holding her pretend baby, looking upon him with adoring eyes, treasuring these things up in her heart. To watch the wonder in the faces of children to whom the story is not yet familiar . . .

I felt again the joy of His salvation. I was struck by the plan He fulfilled, detail by detail, to save the world through a God-baby. I, too, treasured these things in my heart.

Father, never let Your story grow old to me. Help me each year (each day) to look at the elaborate plan of Your salvation with amazement and great thankfulness. Remind me to use the eyes of a Kindergartner, so that I will not miss the significance of a familiar story, but will continue to experience it as miraculous.

Has the Christmas story grown old and familiar to you? It had for me, until my eyes were made young again . . .

Things my Grandma Taught me

What does a family give to a Grandma who isn't fond of the frivolous, who doesn't like attention, and who has more dish towels than any one person should ever need? This year, our family (I mean our large, extended family of 6 aunts/uncles, 4 spouses, 9 grand-kids, 4 spouses, and 6 great-grand-kids) decided to give Grandma the gift of memories. I thought you might get a kick out of my contribution. (Language warning!)

1. Me: "Grandma, I'm bored. There's nothing to do."
   Grandma: "Go shit in a shoe."
2. If you fall down and hurt your knee, your wrist, your dentures, or smash up your whole face . . . Get up and keep on walking.
3. Liquid dish soap is not to be used in a dishwasher. (Actually, that lesson may have been taught by my older cousin, at Grandma's expense.)
4. Even in your eighties, you can still play chase with your great-grandchildren.
5. Never waste anything! Old cereal boxes can be cut down and used for holding spice jars. (Evidence of her frugality can be found throughout my kitchen today.)
6. Socks don't come clean unless you scrub them by hand, in the sink, with bleach.
7. There is a special way of humming that soothes fussy babies. This method works for all babies throughout the generations.
8. You're never too old to work hard!
9. Low German lullabies are often morbid.
10. You can be thrifty and generous at the same time.
11. Mennonite food. Mmmmmmm good!
12. Measuring ingredients is for the birds.

13. Aging causes you to confuse someone offering you a cup of tea with them asking if you need to go pee.
14. It's always appropriate to stick your tongue out at the camera. No matter how grown-up you are.
15. Phone people on Sundays when it's cheap.
16. Removing a full set of dentures and "smiling" frightens small children.
17. It is possible to conceive six children without ever allowing a man to touch you. ☺
18. Butter goes on everything.

Unconditional Love

Last night, as I tucked my "baby" boy into bed, he wrapped his arms tightly around my neck and said, "I'm not yetting doe, Mommy! I'm never yetting doe!" (Translation: I'm not letting go. I'm never letting go.)

I smiled, closed my eyes, and let his love fill me up.

He didn't care that I yelled at him earlier. He forgot that he's spent countless hours in time-outs by my hands. It didn't matter to him whether I cooked dinner, did dishes, or cleaned the house. He wasn't worried about whether I had been kind to people I encountered that day, or whether I'd spent time in prayer.

He just loved me because I'm his Mommy and He's my son. He loved me—he loves me—because of who I am, not because of what I do (or don't do).

As we clung to each other for those few minutes, I thanked God for my children and for the way that they love me . . . no matter what. The love of a child is, I think, as close as we'll get on this earth to understanding unconditional love. I marveled that God's love could possibly be better than this freshly-bathed, wiggly, four-year-old's tight grip.

As He does sometimes when I'm talking to Him, God whispered a reply into my heart.

This is the way I love you. You are my daughter, and I am your Father. It will never matter what you do or don't do—your actions and choices cannot possibly change My love for you. You could turn your back from Me, immerse yourself in a life of sin, and I would not love you less. Or you could pour all your energies into doing good, and I could not love you more.

My love for you is because of who you are, and has nothing to do with what you do. I'm not letting go; I'm never letting go. My arms will stay tightly wrapped around you, for always.

My sweet friends, some of you are walking through dark and lonely valleys right now. Your celebration of the Christmas season has been tinged with the color of heartache, and it feels like life will never be okay again.

I cannot assure you that your life will get better, that your days will feel brighter and less empty. (My hopes and prayers believe that they will, though!) But I can assure you that you are not stumbling in the darkness alone.

You have a Friend, a Counselor, a Father, and a Guide. He is holding tight to you, with a love that cannot be tainted by anything. His love is wholly unconditional and complete. His arms are locked around you, and His promise to you is this . . .

I'm not letting go. I'm never letting go.

(Im)Perfect Family Devotions

For years, I've had a vision of how family devotions ought to be . . .

The cheery and calm children all gather 'round with their Bibles, waiting eagerly for Mama and Papa to read from the Word. The family takes turns reading, each taking a verse or two until the whole chapter has been read. Then they engage in a thought-provoking, intelligent discussion about the Scriptures, with the children sharing profound insight and understanding of God's Word. The family prays, each family member speaking poignant words of praise and intercession. Devotions are concluded with the voices of angelic children singing a closing worship song. The end.

Beautiful, isn't it?

Here's what family devotions really look like.

The family gathers in the living room, children arguing over who gets to sit where. Mom and Dad call for attention and lead in a decidedly brief word of prayer (if eyes stay closed for too long, someone's bound to poke, pinch, or push a sibling).

Dad opens the Bible to Genesis chapter 6. It's been a few weeks of family devotions, but taking it one chapter at a time, two days per week doesn't move things along very quickly. As Dad begins reading, Mom realizes that the children have ants in their pants.

Mom calls a halt to the proceedings in order to direct the antsy children to the craft cupboard. Perhaps having paper and markers, creating a picture of what Daddy is reading about, will help them to focus. It's an ingenious idea that works amazingly well . . . the first time or two, anyway.

Dad reads. Kids listen. Mom shushes the four-year-old who's never really had to sit still in his life. Mom wonders how long the chapter is.

Time for discussion! Mom asks, "What did you think of that story? Can you imagine how hard it must have been for Noah? Everyone was making fun of him, there had been no rain for years, and yet he obeyed God and built the ark. Do you think it would be scary to be obedient to God even when what He asked you to do didn't make sense?"

One child nods an answer to Mom's questions. Another flashes her artwork, "Look! I drew two of every animal. Even fire-breathing dragons!" (At least she heard something.) Another child raises a question of her own, "What did they do with all the animal poop? Wouldn't that be gross? Oh, and did you ever find out if Adam and Eve had belly buttons?"

The four-year-old begins making shooting noises, aiming the gun he drew at his siblings. Mom shushes him. One kid yells at him to stop. One kid asks for another chapter. Another kid asks, "Are we done yet?"

Dad and Mom give one another a half-smile and a shrug, attempt to quiet the masses, and offer up another decidedly brief prayer. The unspoken prayer in their hearts is that, in spite of the crazy chaos that makes up their family, the children will learn something from this time.

They may not learn a whole lot about the Word of God, at least not yet. But if they learn that their parents put priority on reading God's Word, if they learn that their parents put priority on spending time with them, if they learn that their parents will not give up on establishing this family devotional time (no matter what distractions the kids attempt), then the time spent has been of value.

And one of the promises God gives is that *His Word will never return void*. So even if it seems that little learning or understanding is taking place, those parents can rest in God's promise that His Word is taking root in their crazy, busy, distractible children's hearts.

Sunday and Tuesday evenings are when we have Bible time in our home. It's not perfect. But it is real. And it is a beautiful thing, in all its imperfection.

Changing the Way our Family Works

Last week I shared a sermon illustration that really impacted us. After church that Sunday, Pat and I spent a long time talking about what the "big rocks" are in our lives, and how to put them first.

One of our big rocks that tends to get sidelined too often is parenting. Not just plain, old parenting. Obviously we raise our kids, clothe them, feed them, help them with their homework, mediate disagreements, etc. But our goal as parents was never just to "get by" and survive.

We want to thrive. We want to raise our kids to love God and love others. We want to be invested.

But in the reality of daily life, survival can easily take over. Because investing can take a fair bit of energy, and the selfish us prefer to be lazy.

So we asked ourselves, *How do things get done around here?* The answer—if it's on the calendar, it's booked, scheduled, and written in stone.

Since we turned off the TV on school days, and taken a break from extracurricular activities, our kids have had a lot more flex time in the evenings. Instead of replacing that TV time with something productive for our family, up until now it's just been free play time. For us, too. (Free play on Facebook, reading a novel, taking a catnap.)

We thought about all this free time that has been wasted. Which is probably no different than if we'd left the TV on. Together, we decided to leverage this pocket of time to take care of one of our big rocks. *Intentional parenting.*

The calendar had four days that were, as a general rule, free and clear of major commitments. Four evenings that we could spend investing in our children.

So we booked it, scheduled it on the calendar, and wrote it in stone (well, Outlook). Small pockets of time . . . just 30 minutes 4 days of the week. And by the kids' reactions to this scheduled time, they are feeling invested in. They are feeling loved. And they are not only learning to love God and others, but they're learning some tools that they can use when their time comes to be parents.

Who Are You?

When I introduce myself to a group, I usually say something along these lines, "I'm Tyler. I'm married. Mom to five kids. (Then I pause for a moment to allow anyone gasping to catch their breath.) I spent the past eight years as a stay-at-home mom, while also serving as leader of our church's women's ministry. I'm a (developing) writer and speaker for women's groups. And recently I went back to work, where I found the job of a lifetime working for Break Forth Ministries as their Speaker/Artist Coordinator."

It's a nice, easy introduction. But it says a lot more about what I do than who I am.

Sure, I want to know the basic facts about you. But what I really want to know is who you are . . . what makes you tick . . . your story. (These are the details that build relationship.)

It's been a while since I've actually shared who I am. I'm rusty. So I figure I'll start here. You don't mind, do you? But promise me something—promise me you'll share a bit about who you are in the comments today.

I'm Tyler. That's not my first name, but I've gone by my middle name since junior high. When I think of myself, I think "Tyler." When I hear God speak to my heart, He usually calls me Tyler (or daughter).

I'm an emotional girl. Some people might call me too emotional. I cry easily. I hurt easily. I'm sensitive. But I've learned that my emotional side is a gift. I also love easily and deeply. I forgive quickly (some might say too quickly). Within minutes of meeting someone, I can probably tell you if he or she is hurting.

I'm bossy. It comes from being an only child for most of my growing-up years. I was the boss of all that I did. I like to be in charge, take control. This probably rubs a few people the wrong way. But my take-charge attitude really comes in handy in leadership situations. I can lead a group toward consensus with relative ease, and if consensus isn't reached, I feel comfortable and confident making a decision anyway. Things get done.

I love structure. Spontaneity scares me. No, it stresses me. I like to have a schedule, a list, and a plan. I've been referred to as anal and OCD numerous times. But all my planning means that I'm fully invested. If I've scheduled an appointment three months in advance, you can trust me to keep it. If I've laid out every kilometer of a vacation, you can count on me to have thought of everyone's needs in planning. The last thing in the world I want to do is let someone down, so I lay out a plan.

It's funny how each personality trait has both positive and negative qualities. I used to focus on the negative, and see these traits as character flaws. I'm too emotional, too bossy, too structured. But is there a such thing as being too loving, too decisive, too organized? And I learned that I can't have one without the other. You can't have a coin with only one picture on both side. All I can do is work to emphasize the positive and minimize the negative.

So, there's a little picture of who I am (not just what I do).

How to Have a Good Day

I find that some seasons of life tend to be filled with more bad days than good. During those seasons, it can be easy to feel overwhelmed and discouraged. However, I've learned that we don't have to have bad days—there are things we can do to make every day a good one.

1. We can't control our circumstances, but we can control our reactions.

I hate to be the bearer of such news, but it truly does come down to attitude. Do we let things get to us? Or do we deal with them in stride?

Every situation presents us with a choice. We choose our reactions.

For example, my kids can be at each other's throats—arguing, crying, tattling, even hitting. I feel frustrated. Correction, I feel very frustrated. I mean, it just isn't that hard to be nice to each other! There are a few things I can do to stop the fighting. Choice one (my too-frequent go-to)—yell at them and lecture them. Choice two—calmly inform the culprits that they'll be spending the next while separated in their rooms. Choice three—call a halt to the fighting by introducing an activity that engages everyone, such as a board game tournament or a walk to the playground.

Regardless of how I feel, I still have a choice in how I react.

2. We need to set ourselves up for success.

A good day begins the night before. Often, the less we prepare the night before, the more frazzled, frustrated, and frantic we feel throughout the day.

It should be a no-brainer, but we're all guilty of ignoring the importance of a good night's sleep. I once heard that the number of hours we sleep before midnight are the ones that really count. Who can have a good day after a mere six hours of rest?

In my life, I find that half an hour of work in the evening saves me about two hours the next day. I ready the coffee pot and set the timer so that it's freshly brewed when we get up—2 minutes in the evening or 5 groggy, bumbling minutes in the morning plus time spent waiting for the brew. Choosing what to wear, especially on a tired brain, can take an hour some mornings; but the evening before it's a 5-10 minute procedure. And supper. Oh, the dreaded dinner plan! I can either fret on and off all day about what I'll cook for dinner that night, or I can decide after dinner the night before and have it pulled out and ready to go.

The same is true for our kids. They can choose clothes, pack school lunches, get backpacks ready, bathe, and more the evening before, cutting a lot of stress and pressure from their (and our) mornings.

3. Press the pause button.

Do you feel like some days rush past on fast-forward? Rush here, hurry there, don't stop, can't wait, go, go, go! I think those days are often the worst. Here are some great moments to push pause throughout the day.

Wake up time—Before jumping out of bed, pause. Invite God to take control of the way your day plays out. Ask for the Holy Spirit to fill you up, so that each moment is filtered by His guidance.

Rush hour traffic—You can either hurry up and wait, or you can take advantage of all that waiting. Waiting times (including line ups, doctor's offices, etc.) are excellent moments for prayer. And not just prayer that we won't lose our minds waiting! Pray for someone who's sick or unsaved. Pray for co-workers. Or worship. The car is a great place to pour out your heart in worship! Nobody can hear if you sing off-key.

Interruptions—Every day has its share of interruptions . . . stuff that gets in the way of what we really wanted to accomplish. When an interruption crops up, try asking God to use that moment for His glory. An angry person interrupts your schedule with his/her venting—pause . . . try to be the person that turns his/her day around by being kind, understanding, and smiling. A financial hiccup interrupts your day (or week)—pause . . . try taking that $20 in your wallet and using it to bless someone in need (chances are that hiccup won't seem so major). A health concern interrupts your plans—pause . . . try the optimistic view and make a list of all that you have to be thankful for.

The funny thing about pressing pause is that it doesn't actually slow your day down. In fact, a short pause can often help the rest of your day run more smoothly and efficiently.

Today, I plan to have a good day. What about you? What are a few things that might try to make your day a bad day? And what are you gonna do about them?

Categories of Crazy People

Sports fans are kinda crazy. No offence if you're a sports fan, or if you're my husband or father. Actually, I don't know if the men in my life are huge *fans* so much as sports *watchers*.

True fans tend to be a bit fanatical. They are fiercely loyal to their favorite team. Even if said team hasn't won the Stanley Cup in, oh, 22 years. (Okay, maybe my dad is a true fan.)

True fans know their team's schedule. They seldom miss a game. They know stats and history.

True fans with money buy season tickets. Some of them paint their faces in team colors, buy jerseys and other team paraphernalia.

True fans believe in their team, back their team, talk about their team, and ***delight*** in their team.

Parents are kinda crazy. No offence if you're a parent.

Parents tend to be obsessed with their children. Given the opportunity, they will talk about their kids until your brains fall out.

Parents go to their kids' sporting events, music festivals, and school performances. They sometimes stand and cheer and do embarrassing things.

Parents display their children's artwork on the fridge. They brag it up and show it to other parents. And they really, truly believe it's good.

Parents love their kids, support their kids, fiercely believe in their kids, and ***delight*** in them.

Christians are kinda crazy. No offence if you're a Christian.

Christians tend to . . . Oh wait.

Do we follow God like we follow a favorite sports team?

Do we brag on God like we brag on our kids?

Are we so in love with God that we cannot get enough of His Book?

Do we ***delight*** in the Lord?

Delight yourself in the Lord and He will give you the desires of your heart. ~ Psalm 37:4

Do *you* delight in the Lord?

If You Can't Get it All Done . . .

In a society where the "me first" attitude reigns supreme, many Christian women have flung themselves to the opposite corner, living in a world where pleasing everyone else becomes top priority. It's no surprise then, that many of us live life in a flurry of busy. *Rush here, hurry there, don't be late, do this, do that, juggle those balls, don't drop anything, don't let anyone down . . .*

Do you ever feel like you're juggling too many things and something's about to drop to the ground?!

Here are three keys to getting it all done for today's busy Christian woman.

#1. Ask God.

I have a bad habit of evaluating my own life. I decide whether I have time to take something on. Or I look at an opportunity that's offered to me and convince myself that, even though I don't really have enough time in my day to add it, I can "push through" short-term. Saying no is not an easy thing.

Make it a habit to never give an answer (either a yes or a no) immediately. Reshape your standard reply into something along the lines of, "Let me get back to you on that tomorrow, after I take some time to pray about it." And then—this is the hard part for me—actually do take the time to pray about it.

You won't regret the peace that comes from giving your yes or no based on God's guidance.

#2—Make the most important thing the first thing.

When tasks are harder, require more time or attention, or feel more important, I have this tendency to put them off. I convince myself that I should work through my list of quick and easy chores first, building up to that more important thing. The end of the story is usually that I run out of time and energy, I don't feel like I can do that job justice, and it gets put off. I think the correct term for my condition is procrastination.

But if I face my list in the morning and ask myself, *If I can only get one job done today, what is most important?* and tackle it before anything else, I end up motivated to keep going and get the smaller tasks done, too.

#3—Turn off the TV and computer.

It's true. I'm so sorry. But we spend countless hours of our lives being mindlessly entertained. On those days when I didn't have enough time to get the house cleaned or make dinner, I'd guess that greater than 50% of them could have been avoided by making the choice to turn off the screen and walk away. Even for just an hour.

One thing I learned to do was to set up my blog/Facebook surfing time as a reward. *Once I finish cleaning the bathrooms, I'll give myself half an hour on the computer.*

Following these three keys has changed my life. When people ask how I am, my standard reply is no longer, "Busy!" (said with a breathless smile) but "Great, thanks! And how are *you*?" Of course, I still have my moments . . .

If you can't get it all done, it means you're trying to do more than God intended for you to do (or, possibly, that you're watching too much television). ~ Rick Warren, *The Purpose Driven Life*

Impress or Influence?

Several years ago, I felt God's call on my heart. He was drawing me to ministry to women. To be honest, no one was more surprised than I at His calling.

I've never really worked well with women. Women—myself included—are prone to taking things personally, to monthly fits of moody irrationality, to backbiting and gossip. (Sure, there are exceptions to the rule. But coming from someone who has worked solely with women for pretty much her entire adult life, I still stand behind the truth that women can be *very difficult* to work with!)

But God, He tends to do things like that. He calls us to step into the uncomfortable. Not to make us suffer, but to increase our ability to serve Him with joy. More often than not, when we obey, we discover a surprising joy in doing what we once thought "not our thing." Which is why I now love doing ministry for and with women.

When I began leading that ministry team, I was afraid. I had this continual sinking feeling that everyone would find out the truth about me and tell me I wasn't fit to be doing God's work. I dreaded the moment that they all discovered my fraudulent ways.

So in order to protect myself from that shame and pain, I stood aloof. I didn't let anyone in too close. I couldn't have anyone finding out that my marriage struggled on and off, depending on the day. I could not risk everyone discovering the anger I struggled with behind closed doors when dealing with my children. They would surely fire me from my volunteer position!

A funny thing happens when you don't let anyone get close—no one lets you into their lives, either.

I was a leader, with no heart connection to my team. I had no friendships, no one I could turn to and unload. I remained distant, and one by one, team members began to distance themselves.

It was during our team-building summer Bible study that God turned my life around. You see, we were sharing prayer requests, and I felt that Holy Spirit shiver. You know the feeling—your heart pounds so loud that you can barely hear, your hands tremble, you're covered in goose-bumps, your throat is dry, and you just know that you must speak up.

And so I asked for prayer. Through tears and snot, I hiccupped the confession that I was an angry mom. I yelled. I swore. I felt resentment in my heart. I felt out of control.

The burning feeling that I needed to share ebbed, and stone, cold fear took its place. What had I just done? Surely I sealed my fate. My gig was up. But it wasn't . . .

That day is when I truly began to minister to women. You see, real ministry begins in a heart that is willing to be transformed. Those things we keep hidden in the dark will only be turned around when we allow them to come into the Light. When you let the Light of the world shine on your weaknesses, you move from a place of merely trying to impress others into a place where you can influence them.

As Rick Warren says in The Purpose Driven Life . . .

Our strengths create competition, but our weaknesses create community. At some point in your life you must decide whether you want to *impress* people or *influence* people . . . You must get close to influence them, and when you do that, they will be able to see your flaws.

Are you ready to open yourself up, reveal your struggles and weaknesses, in order that you can begin to influence the hearts of others for the Kingdom of Christ?

A Life of Purpose

I just finished reading The Purpose Driven Life: What on Earth are you Here for? by Rick Warren. Correction . . . I just finished *re-reading* it. Between the markings from 2003 and those from 2011, there is little text left in the book that is not circled, starred, underlined, or highlighted.

If I could, I would send you all a copy of this book today. Since I can't afford to do that, I thought I'd share a few of my favorite gems, and let you choose which ones I write a post about. Sounds like fun, eh?!

- #1. If you can't get it all done, it means you're trying to do more than God intended for you to do (or, possibly, that you're watching too much television).
- #2. God doesn't owe you an explanation or reason for everything He asks you to do. Understanding can wait, but obedience can't.
- #3. You cannot fulfill God's purpose for your life while focusing on your own plans.
- #4. God's ultimate goal for your life on earth is not comfort, but character development. Every time you forget that character is one of God's purposes for your life, you will become frustrated by your circumstances.
- #5. Everything that happens to a child of God is *Father-filtered,* and He intends to use it for good even when Satan and others mean it for bad . . . Accidents are just incidents in God's good plan for you.
- #6. Being a servant means giving up the right to control your schedule and allowing God to interrupt it whenever He needs to.
- #7. Our strengths create competition, but our weaknesses create community. At some point in your life you must

decide whether you want to *impress* people or *influence* people . . . You must get close to influence them, and when you do that, they will be able to see your flaws.

#8. When God's at the center, you worship. When He's not, you worry. Worry is the warning light that God has been shoved to the sideline.

Preparing our Kids for the Reality of Marriage

I was reminded of how much hard work is involved in keeping a marriage healthy . . .

When I was a teenager, I remember getting in an argument with a boy I was dating. At the time, it seemed quite devastating that we were arguing. I was crushed over our first fight. A friend advised me, "If you have to work so hard to be happy with him, it isn't meant to be. True love is natural and easy."

During those teen years, my favorite reading materials were romance novels. Stories where hatred turned to love and love was so overpowering and passionate that it was impossible to resist. Love wasn't as easy in these novels as what my friend said, but it always swept you away. Love always won.

The thinking of my parent's and grandparent's generation was that children should be shielded from marital disagreements. Secret arguments took place late at night and behind closed doors. The same was true for any form of physical affection.

With all those conflicting and equally inaccurate views of love and marriage, it's no wonder I was an unhappy young wife! And it's no surprise that marriages are dissolving at a break-neck rate.

We are part of a generation of marriages that are falling apart at the seams.

So what can we do to stop the divorce epidemic for our children and their spouses?

I think, perhaps, it's time we eliminate the mystery and allow our children to observe and experience the realities of marriage just a little bit more. Here are some things we do to help prepare our kids to build marriages that last . . .

1. We let them see us argue.

While we don't necessarily involve our kids in the content of the argument, we do let them see that we're frustrated or disagreeing about something. We don't try to hide it and pretend life is all roses all the time.

2. We let them see us work things out.

Again, while we are careful not to burden the children with details that are too much for them to handle, we don't pretend in front of them. Our kids are familiar with the request, "Please give us some space so that Mommy and Daddy can finish our discussion and work this out."

3. We let them see us make up.

If we have disagreed in front of them, or even if we haven't, we make apologies and offer forgiveness to one another while they're watching. We don't gather everyone in a circle or anything, but we also don't generally leave the room and make up in secret. We also let them see us smooching, and giggle at their exclamations of, "Ewwwww! Gross!"

It's no secret to our kids that marriage is hard work. They have no illusions that it's always beautiful and perfect. They see struggles and sacrifices, and sometimes disappointments. But they also see offerings of love, fun, a bit of sarcastic banter and teasing, kissing and hugging . . .

And I pray that, when it comes time for my kids to walk the aisle and they proclaim "for better or for worse," they fully understand that there will be moments of worse. But they will be equipped to handle those moments with grace and strength, doing the hard work to build marriages that last "until death do them part."

What do you think? Do you let your kids see you argue (and make up)?

Counter-Culture Decisions

In the spring, Pat and I spent some time re-evaluating what our family does and why we do it. We had gotten so very busy—overwhelmingly busy—and needed to figure out how much extra-curricular involvement was really necessary.

When we first moved here, we enrolled the kids in sports. Gymnastics, soccer, skating, karate . . . We felt that having an activity to engage in would help the kids "feel at home" in our new community. Our hearts were in the right place.

The results, however, were not at all what I'd hoped for. Rather than finding that one thing, each of our kids wanted to try a smorgasbord of activities. When one activity's eight-week cycle ended, the next would begin. We were all over the place, practically every day of the week.

So we began to ask ourselves what really mattered to us . . .

Building a close connection with a small group from our church.

Investing in others in our church and community, through acts of service and good old friendship.

Learning to love the people in our family deeply.

Having time to read the Bible and pray together as a family.

Being a family who is active and healthy.

Having lives of peace.

Interestingly, none of our goals included driving around every night of the week, being frenzied and impatient because we always have somewhere to go, training up Olympian gymnasts and black belt karate experts.

We made a tough decision in May—we decided that we would take a break from extra-curricular activities, with a couple exceptions. (I insisted that Pat continue to play hockey, as most games are later and don't interfere with family time and I believe in the importance of him having an outlet and some "guy time." We also chose to keep Braeden (13) enrolled in Air Cadets. We've seen a marked change in his level of independence, confidence, and attitude, and as such saw value for our whole family if he continued.)

But the other stuff that had us going like crazy people all week—it's gone. For now.

Last night, we spent some dedicated time as a family reading God's Word and praying together. This is the second time we've done so since school started.

Before that, the kids were out riding bikes, getting exercise *and* having fun together. They've been able to do that almost every day.

Once everyone was tucked into bed for the night, I commented to Pat on how much time we have this fall. Then I smiled, because I felt peace in my heart.

Later, Pat and I talked about our plans for small group this year, and sent an email off to the other couples about our start date. Rather than dreading the weekly commitment, we're excited!

I won't say that we're done with activities forever. But I can't say that I'm eager to sign anyone up for anything anytime soon.

Going counter-culture isn't easy, but sometimes it's the only way to set things right again. Kinda reminds me of our TV and video game decision . . .

What side of the fence are you on? Pro activities? Anti-activities? Somewhere in the middle?

Protection? Or Presence?

I mentioned a couple difficult situations that my children (and I) are walking through . . .

I've been thinking and praying about those things on behalf of my kids. A lot.

God's been answering me, speaking to my heart about life's struggles. What He's been saying surprised me. For example . . .

I asked Him for help for Malakai. I prayed that drop off time at daycare wouldn't be so difficult for him, that he would be less sad and afraid. I asked God to be with him, protect him, and comfort him. I asked God to turn Kai's experience around, so that he would be excited about the fun days he would have.

At first, I heard what I expected to hear from the Lord . . .

Tyler, I love your little boy even more than you do. I have his best interests at heart. I am always with him, protecting and comforting him. You can trust Me with him.

But then, God started saying (not out loud, but into my heart) things that took me by surprise.

Just as I use every situation—especially the difficult ones—to shape you to serve Me, I will use this trial in Malakai's life for My Kingdom purposes.

Do not think that your children will be exempt from hardship simply because you love and serve Me. If their faith and strength and character are "by default," they will be weak. But a faith in Me that comes from truly needing Me will be their own. Yes, daughter, even in their preschool years I am already shaping them for My service.

Imagine the great things that a child named "Messenger of God" can do for My Kingdom. Then multiply that by 1,000. Those are the kind of plans I have for Malakai . . . and for each of your children.

But just as you needed to walk through hardships, grow in faith, allow yourself to lean into My strength, and become mature in character in order to serve Me—so will they. If I protect them from these trials that come their way, they will miss out on something greater I have for them.

Trust Me.

As God and I had this conversation, and I wanted to argue with Him about what was best for my children, I was reminded of how Beth Moore prays for her daughters . . . She has often mentioned praying along the lines of, "Lord, please do not protect these children from that which will bring them into Your Presence." (Not a direct quote. But if someone has her exact words handy, please share!)

I've often thought how wildly brave that prayer is, and how cowardly my own prayers for my children seem in comparison. I ask for His protection for them, but fail to ask for them to experience the reality of His presence in their lives.

And that begs the question . . . What would I rather have for my children—His protection or His presence?

Have you ever prayed that wildly brave prayer for your children?

Just a Mom—1:
It's Okay to Want More

A question I often hear, especially from young moms with one or two little (busy) ones, is some variation of "How do you do it all?" What they mean is, "How can you possibly be involved in other things, like ministry or writing or a small group or (fill in the blank) when you've got five kids? I can't imagine being able to do anything else. It's so busy with these little people!"

When I'm asked that, my heart fills with a mixture of compassion and excitement. Compassion . . . because the long, lonely, overwhelming days of being a new mom are never far from my memory. Excitement . . . because I love watching the thrill overtaking the face of a new mom who discovers she is not (and was not meant to be) *just a mom*.

I realize that what I just said may ruffle some feathers, but before anyone gets too worked up let me add this . . . I do believe that motherhood is one of the most important, profound, blessed callings. I also believe that many of us have a tendency to fill our lives with other stuff and neglect the importance of interactive, intentional parenting. What I'm saying is not to oppose the importance of mothering, but to enhance it.

For many of us, those first years of motherhood are a time of isolation and loss. We begin to question . . . *Who am I? What is my purpose in life? Will the rest of my days be marked by an endless cycle of changing diapers and sweeping floors?* In my experience, even a woman who's always dreamed of becoming a mother experiences some level of identity crisis when her child(ren) are young.

So when a mom of young children asks me how I do it, I try to encourage her with these five thoughts:

1. It is less a matter of *how* I do these other things than how I could survive *without* them.

There's is nothing more refreshing to an overwhelmed mom than hearing someone honestly say to them, "It's okay to want more. Don't feel guilty. I want more, too."

2. Grandma always said, "Don't put all your eggs in one basket!"

In twenty or so years, these children of mine won't need me (at least not the way they do right now), and if they are my everything, I will eventually be left with nothing.

3. Doing things other than being a mom helps me be a better mother.

Spending a couple hours in a committee meeting with six other women as we plan our church's women's retreat, for example, fills me up. I feel energized and rejuvenated, both by the fellowship and the sense of purpose. So when I come home to my family, my joy spills over into how I interact with them.

4. Being a mom doesn't mean I can't or shouldn't serve in my church and my community.

In His Word, God calls us to show a special love to fellow believers and to take care of widows and orphans. Nowhere does it add, "unless you're busy being a mother." Having small children changes *how* we do ministry, but it does not make it impossible.

5. Being involved in other things is a beautiful example to my children.

It is good for my children to see me serving God and others. Seeing that the world doesn't revolve around them helps to tame their selfish nature. Sacrificing a small amount of time with mom teaches them that it's better to give than to receive. Observing my passion in ministry inspires them to ask God how He's calling them to serve.

Ultimately, we all make time for things that matter to us. We find time to go on Facebook, read blogs, and watch our favorite TV shows. We shuffle our schedules in order to get to the gym, create scrapbooks, or even attend appointments. It's not impossible or insurmountable to get out of the house and get involved in something. But it does require making a choice, making a plan, and being a little creative.

Just a Mom—2: 5 Key Principles to Getting Started

Some principles that will help turn our desire into a reality.

1. Make a list.

Are you surprised that my first suggestion involves list making? Really, though, the list is the most important step.

List all the things you wish you could do but don't have the time for. List all the things you used to do but felt you *had* to give up. List your personal hobbies, interests, dreams, and goals. Write it all down!

Once your list is written, begin sorting the items on the list according to a few categories: no longer important to me, something for later (whether a different phase in your life or your kids' lives), and important for today. If your 'important for today' list is fairly long, you'll need to rank the items by priority.

On my list of things I'd like to start doing today: writing, building friendships, regular dates with my husband, being involved in my church. For lots of women fitness makes its way onto the list, or a crafty hobby like scrapbooking, or volunteering at the kids' school.

2. Start small.

For most of us, going on a diet doesn't work if we attempt to revamp our entire lives in one day. It's the gradual, consistent implementation of changes that convert our lifestyles and our waistlines. The same is true of finding time for ourselves apart from our children. Slow and gradual just works better.

Choose one item from your list that you'd like to fit into your life and only focus on that item.

When we first moved (nearly two years ago now), building friendships ranked number one. Little by little, I saw that beginning to happen. So then I bumped writing to the top. I'm still working on building friendships, but have reassigned some of my attention to writing.

3. Search for windows.

Windows of time, I mean. In every mom's day, there are little chunks of time that are not filled with motherly duties. Others refer to these as pockets of time or margins. Whatever you call them—they're there. Your job is to identify them.

Not only do you need to find those windows, you need to figure out what's filling them right now. Then decide which matters more to you—the thing you're currently doing that uses up your chunks of time, or the thing you wish you were doing.

Building friendships—I decided that this was something I could incorporate into daily living. I didn't need to set aside a special time or make crazy childcare arrangements. I could invite a new friend and her kids over virtually any day. It just meant that sometimes I had to plan ahead as far as housework. Just because it was cleaning day didn't mean I couldn't have coffee, it simply meant I needed to clean around the coffee date—either before, after, or on a different day that week.

4. Schedule.

If it's important to you, schedule it in. Most moms these days have a day planner or a smart phone or something to keep track of appointments on. Use that same tool for allowing yourself time to add that one thing.

If it's in the calendar, it feels less like wasting time or stealing time (from the ever-present housekeeping needs) and more like time well-spent. Scheduling things, even fun things like singing lessons—if that made the top of your list—makes it feel more intentional and less frivolous. It's a mind-set thing.

Writing—I realized that I spent a lot of time on Facebook and reading blogs. Hours spent entertaining myself that could be spent crafting words. So I gave myself a rule—no reading until after the writing. The first thing I do in the mornings (following my quiet time) is write my blog post. Then I reward myself with a quick skim of FB status updates. After lunch, I try to do a bit more writing-related stuff, then I get to read up on other people's blogs.

5. Don't live by the schedule.

Yes, I did just contradict myself. The thing is, you can't be so married to your schedule that you become inflexible. It's okay to skip a day of knitting—if that's what made your list—in order to babysit a friend's child. Life happens, children get sick, emergencies come up, time gets away from us . . . The best way to handle life's interruptions is to be flexible.

So go ahead. Make your list. What's stopping you?

What activity (or activities) make top priority on your list for today?

Just a Mom—3: Practical Tips for Getting Out of the Slump

We moms are not often known for our busy social lives. In fact, once we have children, many of us abandon all attempts at a social life. It feels too impossible to get out for the necessities (like grocery shopping), let alone for our own pleasure.

Those of us who get all cooped up, though, discover a few truths. First, being a socially isolated mom is lonely. Second, being a socially isolated mom is hard on our husbands. Third, we were made for community; there is something within us that craves fellowship.

If you are weary of feeling like "just a mom" and desperate to get out and get connected, here are a few things you can try that will help you get out and about:

1. Make friends with other moms.

Nothing is more enjoyable and chaotic than a visit over coffee and the cacophony of children playing together. So next time you spend even a few minutes chatting with another mom and you think to yourself, "I think I like her," just invite her over.

And please, do yourself (and her) a favor by not cleaning your house before she comes over. She will be more comfortable if you're real from the get-go. Why waste time pretending? Just be the real you in your real house with your real children.

2. Help out your mom friends.

Hear a friend mention she's got a doctor's appointment later in the week? Offer to babysit for her! (I know, you're wondering, "How in the world can I add two more children to my day?! I can barely survive with this one!") Here's the deal, though. In order to have good girlfriends, you need to be a good girlfriend. A few busy hours could result in both a lifelong friendship *and* a girlfriend who offers to watch your kids.

3. Hire a sitter.

I know how tight finances can be after a new baby arrives. And I know it's not easy to leave your precious little one in the hands of a teenager. But you need to do this! Here's why:

— If you take your time with a new sitter, teaching her how you want things done and letting her get to know your child(ren), you will have someone you know and trust to babysit.
— If you never take time away from your little ones, they will object (painfully, dramatically, and loudly) at the age of two and a half when you try to leave.
— If you and your hubby don't leave the house for dates every now and then, he will begin to feel like he's playing second fiddle to the kids.

If there are no creative ways for you to set aside funds for a sitter, go back to #2 and try doing a childcare swap with a friend.

4. Boss your feelings around.

Sometimes, us moms feel guilty for enjoying time away from our kids. We see other mommies who can't bear to be apart from their progeny, and we think perhaps something is wrong with us for *not* missing them. Can I tell you something about those mommies? They are either: 1. lying, or 2. unhealthily attached.

It is not healthy for mother or child to never experience periods of separation. It can be damaging to your marriage and it totally ties your identity to your child(ren). But that is not who you are! Who you are is:

— a child of God
— a daughter of the King
— a princess and heir in the most royal of families
— a woman with a calling (only *part* of which is being a mother)
— a woman with needs, dreams, and desires
— a women created by God to have needs, dreams, and desires

So if you feel guilty for leaving the kids, tell your guilt to take a hike. If you feel guilty for wanting and enjoying time away from the kids, give your guilt the boot. The enemy is called *the accuser* for a reason—he twists everything into an accusation, hoping to cause feelings of guilt, and expecting us to let those feelings dictate our actions.

But you've got victory on your side! *Resist the devil* (and his accusations) *and he will flee!*

It is okay for you to want more. In fact, God designed you to want more. He created you in His own image; He created you for fellowship and companionship and relationship. Yes, He created you to mother children, too. But not at the exclusion of all else.

There's one more facet to address in this series—ministry (or service) as a mom. We'll tackle that one tomorrow.

So hey, do you struggle with feelings of guilt when it comes to taking time away from the kids? How do you deal with it?

Just a Mom—4: It's Not About You

That feeling of wanting more than being *just a mom* was put in you by the One who created you. But He didn't place that longing inside your spirit for you; He put it there for Him.

You were created to serve God with your life. Each and every one of us was. Yes, everyone. Not just the Christians.

If you're not a Christ-follower, just consider this for a moment . . . Have you ever asked yourself what the purpose of life is? Have you ever wondered why you're here? Have you ever felt like there's more to it? Like something is missing? Just a little fyi, sweet friends, that empty hole was left in you by the God who created you, and it will only ever feel full and complete and satisfied once you know Him and serve Him.

If you are a Jesus girl, but you still feel that achy emptiness, might I suggest that you've only got one piece of the satisfaction formula? Fulfillment comes from both knowing Him *and* serving Him.

We are healed to help others. We are blessed to be a blessing. We are saved to serve. (Rick Warren, The Purpose Driven Life: What on Earth am I Here For?, pp. 229)

Warren describes two different ways of serving God, and says that each of us has both: a ministry and a mission.

Your ministry is simply serving others. Ministry is asking, "Whose needs can I meet?" and then meeting them.

Your mission is your specific, unique, God-given way of serving. Your mission is the combination of your skills, abilities, gifts, talents and personality with the people group that you have a love and a passion for.

For example, when I "do ministry" it may look like: delivering a meal to a new mom, offering to watch a friend's little ones, joining the women's ministry team in our church, signing up for a Sunday of helping in Sunday school, turning my husband's socks right-side-out when I do laundry (I assure you, that *is* ministry).

When I think of my mission—the specific thing God created me to do—I see women. A sea of beautiful faces, looking for hope and encouragement, desperate to experience the reality of Jesus in their everyday lives.

Too often, we make excuses to avoid being stretched. We don't want to be too busy (and most of us already feel too busy in filling our roles at home), to deal with the challenges of childcare, to try something new and fail . . . So we say things like, "I'll start serving at the church when my children are a bit older," or "I would have like to help that person out, but I just can't afford it right now," or "For this season, I need to put all my focus on my children."

Here's what God's Word says on the matter:

Now you belong to Him . . . in order that we might be useful in the service of God.
Romans 7:4 (TEV)

Because of God's great mercy . . . Offer yourselves as a living sacrifice to God, dedicated to His service.
Romans 12:1 (TEV)

Your attitude must be like my own, for I, the Messiah, did not come to be served, but to serve and to give My life.
Matthew 20:28 (LB)

For we are God's workmanship, created in Christ Jesus to do good works, which God prepared in advance for us to do.
Ephesians 2:10 (NIV)

I don't know about you, but I'm tired of making excuses.

What's holding you back from serving God?

Just a Mom—5:
Finding Your Calling

Let me start by asking you a question. **Do you know what it is that God is calling you to do for His Kingdom?**

If you don't, or if you're not sure, may I suggest four questions to ask yourself that will help you figure it out?

1. What am I good at that I also enjoy doing?

Seriously, it begins as simply as that! Ask yourself what you do well *and also* love to do.

As moms, we sometimes lose sight of our other skills and abilities. You may need to think back a ways to something you used to do that brought you pleasure.

Before kids, were you artistic, painting or creating things of beauty? Do you miss it? Is it possible that you could create art as a means of bringing God glory and sharing His love with others?

Before kids, did you have plans of being a social worker, helping families heal and repair? Do you miss it? Is there a way that you can help families now, even if you're not working in the social work field?

Another possibility is that you can't think of anything that gave you great pleasure until you became a mom. Perhaps you are absolutely gifted as a mother or a homemaker, and you find your joy in creating a beautiful home and teaching your children. Can I ask you, then, why you're keeping those skills to yourself? There are millions of us out there who are desperate for a patient mom to mentor us in the fine art of discipline, for example. How can you use your mothering skills to help others for His glory?

2. What am I passionate about?

Is there a certain topic that, when it comes up in conversation, you are utterly unable to resist voicing your opinion? Do you worry that you come across too strongly, simply because you feel so passionately about it?

Some examples . . . When teen sexuality comes up, do you go wild about the importance of teaching abstinence? If folks are talking politics and it turns to foreign aid, do you lose yourself in ideas of how to help impoverished countries? Are you gripped by the plight of a certain people group—either at home (homeless, abused, drug addicts . . .) or abroad (the Delits in India, the restavecs in Haiti, the child prostitutes in Thailand)?

Whatever puts a fire in your belly is probably related to your calling. Maybe you can't fly over to Amsterdam and hand out tracts to the drug dealers, but if you're passionate about it you can do something. Learn all you can, educate others, raise funds, send funds, PRAY.

3. What are my spiritual gifts?

Spiritual gifts are special gifts given by the Holy Spirit to believers when they accept Christ. These gifts don't necessarily manifest themselves immediately, though. Sometimes they take years to develop and grow in you.

There are a lot of gifts (I can't give you definite number), but some include: hospitality, healing, prophecy, administration, leadership, speaking in tongues, interpreting tongues, giving, music, writing, encouragement.

If you feel clueless about your spiritual gifts, I suggest taking a survey to help you get a clearer picture. Two of my favorites are: Finding Your Spiritual Gifts (a printed inventory by C. Peter Wagner) and Spiritual Gifts Test (an online tool).

4. What difficult things have I experienced in life?

You didn't think those hard things in life happened for no reason, did you? No way! We walk through hardship for two reasons: our own spiritual growth and to offer hope and encouragement to others.

When you've suffered the loss of a child, who brought you the most comfort? Likely someone else who had experienced the same thing. Depression? Abuse? Divorce? Teen pregnancy? Ask yourself which of your life experiences may have happened so that you could minister to others.

The hard part is being willing to share openly, so ask God for the courage to share what He wants you to and the wisdom to know how much or little to reveal for each situation.

After you've answered these four questions for yourself, you should have an idea of where God is calling you to serve. If you're still feeling clueless, just jump in and try something! **Sometimes you don't know what you're good at until you've experienced it.**

I once said those words to my mom, so she decided to try leading a women's Bible study. She's been doing it for at least five years now, leading one group and assisting three or four other leaders as they also facilitate groups!

On a final note, I also want to encourage you to re-evaluate periodically. Maybe every 3 years or so. While your spiritual gifts will never change, over time you may find certain gifts developing more strongly. And though we're all called and commissioned to bring the message of Christ to the ends of the earth, our individual specific roles in that commission may change over time. Sometimes a calling is for but a season . . .

In 2003, I wrote that I felt called to minister to young women and teens experiencing unplanned pregnancy. I served in various capacities at our local Pregnancy Care Centre for a number of years. More recently, I wrote that I feel called to be an encourager of women, drawing them into a deeper relationship with Christ using my gifts in writing, speaking, and mentoring. Pretty big shift, eh?

Do you know what you're called to do for this season of your life? If not, what steps are you going to take to figure it out?

Just a Mom, Q & As

After I wrote the preceding series I received a number of questions. Following are just a couple:

I agree with the things in this series . . . . a lot of it has echoed what God has been teaching me.

Once you embrace being more than just a mom, how do you make sure you don't cross over into becoming neglectful of your family? I know moms who are so busy doing good things they love, but their family, no their husbands, suffer. He's the one who ends up being just a dad who works.

Wow, what a great question! To be honest, I'm not sure I'm the best person to answer this question. Remember, I'm an over-committer. But I'll give it a shot.

As a chronic over-committer, I've come to learn a few things about taking on too much. Generally, I can detect the warning signs and slow down before it hits crisis point. Sometimes . . . not.

Warning Signs:

1. You're a "yes" woman.

Does it pain you to tell someone, "No, I'm sorry. I can't help out with that."??? If you were to measure your response ratio, do the "yeses outweigh the "nos? Do you find yourself constantly worrying about letting someone down?

2. You're frozen.

You know that feeling when you have so much to do that you just don't know where to start? So you do nothing (except maybe mindlessly surf Facebook)? Yeah, that usually means you've got too much on your plate.

3. You're crabby.

Sometimes crabby just means overtired or PMS. But sometimes it can mean too busy. If crabby happens and you catch yourself saying, "I'm never going to get all this done!" it's the second reason.

4. You're told.

Has someone from your inner circle recently told you that you're too busy? Has someone you loved complained that you're too busy? Has your husband been inexplicably grumpy with you, especially when you're leaving the house?

An Ounce of Prevention:

A. Learn to be a "no" woman.

Your default response should be "no." Or at the very least, "Let me take some time to think and pray about it."

Remember that you are not responsible for meeting everyone's needs—you are responsible for meeting your family's needs and for obeying God. And if you agree to do everything, you may actually be stealing someone else's blessing. That's right, because by taking on things you're not called to you are essentially stepping into a calling that belongs to someone else. Stealing from them the blessing of serving.

B. Submit to your husband.

Ouch! That one pinches a bit, doesn't it? God gave your husband the overwhelming responsibility of leading your family. God asked you to be his helper. If your man needs more help, asks for more help, or shows signs that he's feeling overloaded—that's your #1 calling.

I try not to agree to taking on new things without talking to Pat first. (If I'm honest, sometimes I say yes and ask later. But when I do so, I try to start out with an apology for not talking to him first.) If your husband is a part of the decision-making, he's more likely to feel supportive of the things you're taking on.

C. Be in tune with the Spirit.

This is the ultimate way of assuring that you don't take on too much. Being in tune with the Spirit works two ways.

First, the Holy Spirit guides our paths (Proverbs 3:6) and tells us whether to turn to the right or the left (Isaiah 30:21). That way, we sense Him leading us toward a "yes" for certain things.

Second, the Holy Spirit gives us strength (Philippians 4:13), so that when it might seem we have a lot going on—as long as they are things ordained by Him—He can keep us moving forward.

A Pound of Cure:

Though you didn't ask this question, I'm sure you were thinking it (I know I would be) . . .

What should I do or say if I see a friend who has become too busy and is neglecting her family?

I. Pray.

I know it "feels" like doing nothing, but prayer is the absolute most important thing you can ever do for anyone.

II. Speak the truth in love.

If the right opportunity arises, and *if* your friendship is such that you can do so without causing permanent damage, and *if* you have a definite sense that God is nudging you to do so—speak the truth in love.

Love, grace, and understanding must permeate the whole conversation, or your words will fall on deaf ears and a hard heart.

III. Help.

Sure, her busy-ness is of her own making, as are the consequences. But true friends don't judge the motives of others to determine whether or not we should help. True friends help regardless of the motives, decisions, and consequences.

IV. Know when to step away.

True friends try and try beyond the point of exhaustion. But wise women also know when it's time to step back, remove yourself from a situation (or even a relationship), and leave things in God's hands.

You are not responsible for saving her family. You are only responsible to do the things God has called you to do for her and her family. Sometimes, we need to get out of God's way. Sometimes, He isn't able to do the work He needs to in a person's heart until they are alone with only Him for help.

Are you at risk of being "too busy?" Or do you see it in someone you love?

Just a Mom, Q & As—continued

And just a couple more questions:

I really liked part 4 and 5—and here's my question: How do you know when it's time to move on?

I have lead Bible study now for 5 or so years but it really was more because I took a leap and just did it, versus feeling called to it. I do think it was affirmed as a calling because God totally equipped and led me. However, over the last couple of years God has repeatedly called up others to lead (not necessarily to take over my areas of administration) but it does make me ask, "Is it time to move on? Is God equipping others?"

I don't have a sense that I'm being told to move . . . but it does make me wonder. So how do I know?

This is probably the toughest question to answer, because your calling (and your moving on) is so very personal between you and God.

Change is inevitable.

I don't think there are many of us who are called to a lifetime of service in one ministry area. Even folks who look like they've done one thing their whole lives (Billy Graham, for example) have seasons in their ministry. They may do the same thing (such as preaching), but feel called to reach out to different groups as time changes. Even those who know they've been called to be Pastors move on eventually, to the next church family that God calls them to.

Sometimes God closes a door.

Sometimes, God does dramatic things to move us from where we are in ministry to the next step. For example, when it was time for me to move on from women's ministry . . . I'll be honest, I had a sense that He was preparing me to let go for over a year. But I was arguing with Him. He knew I was attached and invested, so He need to do something big to move me (literally) onto the next thing.

Sometimes God opens a window.

Sometimes, God puts new opportunities in our paths to show us that He is calling us onward. He doesn't always clearly tell us, "Time to quit this. Let go. Move on." But you may find yourself noticing new possibilities; little things that grab your interest. It very well could be that God is giving you tiny, gentle nudges in a new direction.

Sometimes God leaves it up to you.

I also really believe that, for many of us, there is no "one thing." It's more like "anything." Take, for example, when someone has a job opportunity and they need to choose between two great jobs. He prays and prays, but doesn't get a clear sense of which job God wants him to take. Could be that God is telling him, "It doesn't matter which job you take, as long as you serve Me with your whole heart wherever you work."

Sometimes, you just "know."

There are times, though, when it's time to move on even though you don't really have any of the indicators. God isn't closing any doors, He's not opening any windows, and there are no options for you to choose from. There seems to be nothing new for you to do, but you have an unsettled spirit.

I have a friend who felt unsettled in her job. She felt that she was supposed to free herself up for other ministry opportunities. She bravely gave notice to her employer, not knowing what was next. There was nothing wrong at her work, and no new opportunities were in front of her, but she just knew.

I've been asked before, "How do you know when you're done having babies? How can you be sure that this is the last one?" When I answer those women, I always reply, "The fact that you're asking and not sure tells me that you're not done. Not yet." {and then I wink at her} But I also suggest to her that the way she's thinking could be indicative that her heart is being prepared to be done soon.

So I think . . . You're not done yet, because you're not sure and you haven't heard a clear directive from God to move on. But your heart is being prepared for that inevitability. And when it's time, you'll know.

Preventing Road-Trip Rage

If you have small children and have attempted to journey any farther than a couple hours in your vehicle, you *know* the definition of road trip rage.

When will we be there?

Stop looking at me!

Mooooom, she's on my half!

How much longer?

The DVD player's dead!

He's not sharing the markers!

Are we there yet?

Moooooom, he keeps breathing on me!

You try counting . . . 1-2-3-4-5-6-7-8-9-10 . . . But all that does is give you more time to think about what to say as you lecture/yell/scowl/threaten the little beings in the back seat (or in my case, back seats).

A couple years ago, we tried something that has forever changed how we approach road trips. (Which is good, because we can't afford to fly seven people next door, let alone anywhere fun. Which means road trips are likely to be our means of transportation for a long, long time.)

We began our road trip by handing each child a roll of quarters in a Ziploc baggie. They were informed that they each had $10 in their hands, and it was theirs to use for buying a souvenir once we reached our destination. They were also informed that we would "match" their $10, ultimately giving each kid $20 for a keepsake (because we all know how far ten bucks goes at Disneyland).

However, they were warned that their souvenir fund would be reduced, one quarter at a time, for bad behavior. I listed some example behaviors that they'd have to pay me for: whining, arguing, disobedience, asking the same question every 10 minutes, etc. For any behavior that was out-of-line, they'd have to pay Mom. With the exception of being unkind to a sibling—then they'd have to pay that sibling.

Within the first hour or two on the road, each kid had probably lost a dollar. But for some of them, that was all they lost.

As I collected more money, I also began discreetly paying out quarters. If I saw kind, unselfish behavior toward a sibling, I slipped a coin into that child's Ziploc baggie.

When we arrived at our destination, one child was able to purchase a memento that cost $20. Another child had to search high and low to find a trinket that cost about $9. The child with $9 whined about the unfairness of it all, until I collected another quarter AND took back one of mine, leaving only $8.50.

Can you believe that a Mini Mouse on a key chain (two inches tall) cost over $8?!

If you don't want to rage while you're on a road trip, try it out! You'll be surprised how easy it is to keep your cool (even when the kids aren't). And if the kids are particularly bratty, that's more money back in your purse. It's win-win.

Wrestling with God for my Broken Marriage

When folks ask about my marriage, I usually tell them, "I've been married nearly twelve years, the last five or so happily."

Lest you think it's all rainbows and puppy dogs around here—happily does not mean blissfully. We've still got our issues. But those first five years . . . the only word that truly captures their essence is *miserable*. (Now, you're thinking that five plus five only equals ten; those two years in-between are what I fondly refer to as **the wrestling years**.)

Here's a little background for you:

I accepted Christ as a little girl, and renewed my commitment to Him each summer at Bible camp, but I lived through the school year no different than my unbelieving classmates and friends.

Living my life as I did, it's not really a surprise that I found myself pregnant at nineteen. Unlike many teen moms, I was lucky to be dating a guy that planned to stick by my side. As most of you parents probably know, there's nothing like having a child to bring someone back to their faith.

Enter five years of misery . . .

My husband tried to be supportive of my faith. He didn't complain about me taking our son to church. In fact, I think he appreciated the silent morning of sleeping in each week. We had a church wedding. He agreed to it because it was important to me. My faith was okay, **as long as it didn't affect him**.

Honestly, I think that he tried to be a good husband to me. I know he wanted to please me and make me happy. But I couldn't be pleased. Instead, I picked and prodded, begged and cajoled, fighting for him to join us at church on Sunday mornings. And as I grew in my walk with the Lord and was convicted of my sin, **I decided to act as the Holy Spirit in my husband's life**, convicting him of all his sinful ways.

They say that women go into marriage thinking of all the ways they can change their men, and men go into marriage hoping that their wives never change at all.

The change in me was probably a frightening sight to observe. I shifted from liberal thinking to deeply black-and-white conservative. I jumped from wild and free living to rigid, rule-driven, legalistic, and judgemental. And all this with a husband who was raised to believe that Christians are all brainwashed, and their goal in life is to brainwash others.

The turning point for me was the day my husband packed his bags. He had overheard me praying on the phone with a friend. The praying was, let's say, a little bit charismatic. He was freaked out! Who can blame him?

I had an epiphany in that moment. I knew, without a doubt, that there was no way I could change my husband. There was no way I could make him happy. There was no way he could bring me satisfaction. I could not change him or fix him or save him. **I could not save my marriage.**

All of those things were under God's area of responsibility. The only tasks placed under my care were: love my husband and obey God.

In an instant, I was released from my misery. My husband was released from my tyranny. I stopped wrestling within my marriage and began wrestling with God.

I would grab on tight and cry out, *Lord, save my marriage!*

He assured me, ***Trust me, your marriage is in My hands.***

I dug in hard and prayed, *God, reveal Yourself to my husband!*
He soothed me, ***I will, I am, through you and your obedience.***

When I felt pinned, I would ask *God, Why don't you change him?*
He replied, ***Why don't you let Me change you?***

When I felt like I was being attacked by a tag-team I would wail, *But God, it's not fair! I deserve to be treated better. I deserve to be happy!*
He answered, ***Find your happiness in Me.***

I would be mad and storm around the house, thinking to myself how I was NOT going to do his laundry. And God would tell me to **serve my husband**.

I would be hurt and determined that I had to speak my mind. And God would tell me to **shut my mouth**. (I cannot count the number of times God had to tell me to shut up!)

I would be lonely and depressed, entertaining fantasies of divorce or death, and then doing things *the right way* with a Christian husband. And God would tell me that the right way was to **honor the husband I was given**.

I wrestled and struggled, crying out, *I will not let go until You bless me!*

My husband began to attend church with us occasionally. Then more regularly. He agreed to attend a church-led marriage retreat. He agreed to join a home group through the church.

He was baptized on February 29th, 2004. He went on short-term missions trips to Haiti in the falls of 2009 and 2010. He has served in our church with the youth, the children, and the men.

My husband is the Christian husband I prayed for. He is a man of prayer. He is man of integrity. He is a man of faith. He is the spiritual leader in our home.

In a little over two weeks, I will be celebrating my twelfth anniversary. Twelve years married, the last five or so happily. Every single moment held in the hands of a loving Father.

When You Don't Agree with Your Husband

There have been times in my life when I've found myself confused (surprise, surprise).

We're supposed to love and serve God first, then our husbands, then our children, and so on . . . But what happens when those things conflict? Then what do we do? Who do we follow?

Here's a practical example for you. Early in our marriage, I was attending Church and (tepidly) following the Lord. Pat wasn't there yet—he wasn't sure about all that 'religious' stuff. I sat in on a powerful sermon about tithing, and felt called to obedience by it. But the money in our account wasn't put there by me, and we had always agreed that expenses over a certain amount needed to be unanimous. To say that Pat wasn't particularly excited about my idea of giving a significant portion of his earnings to a church he seldom attended is an understatement.

So what was a girl to do? For weeks I obsessed over this—obey God's Word and defy my husband? Honor my husband and disobey God? I did eventually work this out . . . I found other ways to tithe (of my time and talents) and waited for God to work out the money thing . . . which he has.

Every now and then, someone asks me about a similar situation. I can look up some handy scripture references for them (Ephesians 5:22-24, I Peter 3:1-5), but it can be so difficult to explain in a way that makes sense!

So, for anyone who's ever asked that question—married or not, in a Christian marriage, unequally yoked—anyone who's ever wondered how to make sense of the confusion, here is a fantastic analogy that illustrates what God is calling us to (as Christian women, wives, mothers).

Imagine a team of dogs pulling a sled over the snowy plains of Alaska. All of a sudden the Master says, "Turn right." But the lead dog turns left and the others follow. So the Master stops the team, walks around to the lead dog, shakes his little face and says, "I told you to turn right." Then he gets back in and off they go. Again, the Master says. "Turn right." But again the lead dog turns left.

Well this time the dog behind him turns right like the Master said but in the process creates chaos. So the Master stops the sled, walks around to the lead dog, shakes his face and says, "I told you to turn right." Then he walks to the next dog that obeyed his command to turn right shakes her little face and says, "I told you to follow the lead dog."

Get it? Your husband is the Lead Dog. Your job is to follow the Lead Dog because that is what the Master really wants.

Camping 101

We were camping this weekend—the first long weekend of the official Canadian camping season. Want to know what I love about camping? No? Sorry, I'm going to tell you anyway! And guess what?! I will share my thoughts in . . . you guessed it . . . list format!

* When you remember to pack the camera and its charger, you forget to pull it out and snap any photos.
* When you pack prepared for snow (because when does it NOT snow on May long?), you have amazing, beautiful weather and everyone wears the same pair of shorts (the only pair they were instructed to pack) for the entire weekend.
* When your husband thinks it's a "fun" idea to take a ten kilometer walk with six young children, two dogs, and four adults in less-than-perfect shape (one of whom is pregnant—no! not me!), the whining is guaranteed to begin at least three kilometers before you expected it to.
* Did you know that it takes approximately four-and-a-half hours to walk 10 km?
* Did you know that it is physically impossible for children ages 2, 3, and even 6 to walk an entire 10 km without being carried?
* Did you know that packing two granola bars per person and a handful of cheese and crackers is not really enough to sustain ten people for 10 km?
* Did you know that, in spite of all the grumbling, certain children (and adults) are incredibly proud and love to brag about how they walked—and survived—10 km?
* When the forecast predicts rain all weekend but doesn't deliver, you better believe mother nature will give you the entire weekend's worth of rain while you try to pack up.
* Exhausted from camping children are adorable.

* Exhausted dogs from camping are immovable.
* Post-camping laundry is estimated to take 3.2 days to complete. (While only one pair of shorts was worn, countless hoodies—that's Canadian for hooded sweater, sweats, jeans, socks, bathing suits, and towels somehow made their way into the pile.)
* In spring, Canadian lakes are VERY cold, and mountain-fed lakes even more so. This fact will not stop determined children from swimming in those frigid waters.
* It is utterly impossible to resist eating your body weight in snack foods whilst camping.

Never Say No

We wives tend to joke about how our husbands are always *in the mood* . . .

It's true. As a general rule, men are more easily turned on than women. A man can come home after a long day at work, catch a glimpse of cleavage while we serve dinner, and he's pretty darn excited.

We women, on the other hand, are quite the opposite. I mean, we just served dinner. It's a dinner that we prepared and will be cleaning up after. Prior to that dinner we worked, cleaned, planned, refereed. After that dinner we'll be making the bedtime rounds. So the fact that he's excited is actually pretty annoying.

Sound familiar?

Life is busy, and most women (men, too) are flat-out exhausted at the end of the day. It's so easy to tune out, veg out, then roll over and just go to sleep, giving our men the big shut out.

The thing is, if we say no enough times (even if we're not saying it with words), we launch a vicious cycle.

She says no —> He feels rejected —> He begins to isolate —> She feels rejected

The cycle goes round and round until **nobody's interested in anything**. No sex, no dates, no closeness, no communication.

Years ago, when Pat and I were in the early (and difficult/unhappy/miserable) phase of our marriage, we found ourselves in this cycle of rejection. I felt alone and unloved, so was not interested in doing anything that might make him happy (from turning his laundry right-side-out to fooling around). He felt rejected and unneeded, so he wasn't interested in doing anything that might make me happy (from helping around the house to cuddling with no ulterior motive). We were stuck.

But God did that thing He does. You know—conviction. Everything I was hearing, reading, and watching seemed to be about sex. Heck, it was preached from the pulpit at church! And I read the words of a wise woman (I don't remember who, but I've never forgotten her words) . . .

I made the decision to never say no again.

She was not only referring to the word "no," but to other ways of communicating unavailability and disinterest. She chose not to avoid his touch (even if at times it bordered on the inappropriate, like grabbing her butt in the kitchen), she chose not to turn her back but to always go to sleep facing him, and she gave her "yes" to her husband every time he was interested.

Some of you are probably thinking, *But if I did that I'd never rest!* Here are a few questions, then . . . Do you sleep well after rejecting your husband's advances? Do you sleep well when you feel cold and bitter towards your husband? Do you sleep well when you're going out of your way to avoid him?

I'd like to suggest that **your rest would be dramatically improved** if you simply removed the word "no" from your vocabulary and your actions.

I haven't said no in years, and our marriage is the best it's ever been! (Not that this is the only factor that's improved our marriage, by any means. And for those who are considering the never say no method, let me put your minds at ease—it is not every. Single. day. You can breathe easy.)

Lately, God's been bugging me about the whole "who should initiate" issue. I've always figured it should be a 90/10 split, maybe 80/20 if I'm feeling generous. God seems to be hinting otherwise. So far, I've had my fingers firmly planted in my ears, singing, "La, la, la, I can't hear you!" Conviction is a funny thing, though—it just gets stronger the more you ignore it.

So let me ask you a personal question—What are you telling your man? Does he have your "yes," or is he too often getting your "no?"

Christianity hates women and so do I

An anonymous commenter said, *Christianity is such a misogynistic religion and the women are so brainwashed to be a doormat to their husbands even to the point of humiliation. Ugh.*

mi-sog-y-ny (mi-**soj**-*uh*-nee), noun—hatred, dislike, or mistrust of women

(Dear reader—this definition was more for my benefit than yours. I had to look it up to be sure of the meaning!)

Here is my reply . . .

Dear Anonymous,

Taken out of context or read by an unbelieving reader, any words written by a Christian can be twisted around. (In fact, that's true of any written or spoken word.) It would appear that you have taken my words out of context—the contextual background being a shared faith in Christ.

The fact is, my post said NOTHING about being brainwashed, being a doormat, or being humiliated. My post was written from the perspective of a regular women in a regular marriage, and suggesting that we regular women have a CHOICE to make. We can choose to love our husbands in a way that makes them feel loved, or we can choose to reject them.

If a woman were in an abusive relationship, where her husband was asking her to participate in humiliating sexual acts, my advice would be quite different. I don't condone abuse and would never encourage a woman to stay in an abusive relationship, let alone to participate in anything that causes her to feel humiliated.

The assumption is that the average married woman feels no shame in making love with her husband. The assumption is that the average married woman desires to have a great (as opposed to average) marriage. The assumption is the average married Christian woman recognizes that, by focusing on changing her own negative patterns (rather than on wishing her husband would change his), she holds the power of change in her hands.

In fact, in taking control of her choices about their intimate relationship, the Christian wife is the complete opposite of brainwashed. She is fully in control, having more influence than ever over the state of their marital relationship. She is the opposite of a doormat. Doormats shrink away from challenges and let themselves be walked on, but she rises to the new challenge of improving her marriage by taking action. She is the opposite of humiliated. Rather, she now feels empowered and has a sense of pride.

As for Christianity being misogynistic, I'd say it's quite the opposite. The Christian faith doesn't say "hate women, degrade women, treat women as second class." The Christian faith preaches love—love for God and love for your neighbour. (I'll be the first to admit that most Christians are not perfect at this. Which is exactly why we stand in need of a Saviour to rescue us from our own evil nature.)

I would like to propose that the Christian faith is, in fact, pro-woman. The Bible is filled with accounts of strong, Godly women changing the world. Esther, Rahab, Mary, Ruth, to name a few. The gift that is given to us when God created us is difference—we are each unique. The world would have you convinced that everyone is the same (they use the word 'equal') and should be treated the same. The Bible, on the other hand, says that we are each unique and should be treated as such. I, for one, appreciate a faith system where I am recognized for me—my own unique strengths and abilities, my own genetic makeup—rather than assumed to be just the same as all the rest.

You, my anonymous friend, don't have to believe this. You don't have to agree with me. I won't be trying to force you, brainwash you, or humiliate you into accepting my faith. Christianity is a choice. Each one of us has the power to choose to believe or not. I would encourage you to exercise your right to choose. But, just as the woman who chooses to reject her husband's advances will remain sad, lonely, and unempowered in her marriage, those who choose to reject Christ will remain unhappy and dissatisfied in their lives.

Before I bid you farewell, I want to be clear that I will not argue my faith on this blog. I believe in Christ and anyone stopping by here can recognize that fact in an instant. You are free to disagree with me; however, insults will not be tolerated. If you feel such strong hatred for the things I believe, my suggestion to you would be to find another blog to read. I write here to encourage Christian women in their walks with God, to help them build their faith and to be the women, wives, and mothers God calls them to be. My purpose is not (and never will be) to debate Christianity.

As well, might I encourage you to put some credibility behind your opinions by not hiding behind the veil of anonymity? When a comment such as yours is posted anonymously, its intent is clearly to stir up dissension rather than to engage in conversation. I am open to having a conversation with you about my faith and how it differs from yours, but I am unwilling to engage in an insult-throwing exchange.

That said, for future reference, any anonymous comments that are disrespectful, contentious, or insulting will be deleted. As I said, my purpose here is not to debate, and my readers do not come here to be insulted by mysterious commenters. This is not to say I will delete comments that disagree with my point of view. If you have the courage to put your name beside your comment, and you have the ability to share your point of view without being denigrating,

I am glad to engage in dialogue with you. I'm sure my readers will be, too.

While the comments on this post are open, and I am certainly expecting to see words left by those who disagree, let me reiterate that there is a way to disagree without being unkind or insulting. And those words left by real people with real names and faces will be treated with the respect due any person.

Thanks for hanging in there for my monologue. Now, let's let the conversation begin.

P.S. My statements about Christianity being freeing, about Christian wives having great power and influence, about making choices putting us in control—those are not ideas found in some book or simply Biblical platitudes. Those are factual truths evidenced in my own life.

Being treated as unique rather than 'equal' makes me feel free to be myself rather than trying to fit some mold.

Making choices about my sex life causes me to feel powerful, sexy, and much happier than I was when I allowed my emotions to decide for me.

And I feel more valued, appreciated, and necessary as a woman in the church than I ever have out in the workforce.

The only times I feel like a doormat, feel humiliated, or feel as though someone's trying to brainwash me is when I forget the truths I've learned and instead seek approval and affirmation from the rest of the world.

Perhaps that's just me? I don't know, let's ask the readers to weigh in . . .

Is your faith misogynistic, do you feel like a brainwashed and humiliated doormat?

Getting Over Myself

I was feeling a bit sorry for myself yesterday.

You see, my ideal Mother's Day involves a big, fancy breakfast, maybe a bouquet of spring flowers, children working hard to get along all day, others cleaning my house for me, and either family time or Mommy time.

My Mother's Day reality looked a little more like this:

— The children wake me at 6:30 with their bickering over what to watch on TV.
— My hard-working husband stumbles, bleary-eyed into the house at 7am after a night shift.
— Everyone says the obligatory "Happy Mother's Day."
— Pat tries to get everyone to list the things they love about me; they ignore him.
— Sleepy man heads to bed. Mommy gets kids ready for church.
— Half an hour before we need to leave, two children engage in an all-out blow-out, screaming "I hate you at one another and going to their rooms until we left.
— Church. Home. Make lunch. Kids fight. Kids are disciplined. Repeat . . .

Granted, I did get a nice, little nap on the couch. And when Pat woke up he took the kids and dog to the playground to let me continue my nap in peace.

I know I don't have it all that bad. I wasn't ignored on Mother's Day. I wasn't treated badly. I wasn't alone. But when reality doesn't quite line up with fantasy, disappointment still comes.

Once the kiddos were in bed and my man was back at work, I decided to release my pent-up tears by watching a good chick flick. The thing is, as I tried to let them flow, the tears tasted bitter. Selfish. Self-centered. Ridiculous.

So I hung out on Facebook instead. As I read through status updates, I noticed a couple friends in my list who probably hadn't had a very good Mother's Day either. They're single Moms, working hard to fill the roles of two parents each day. Few have actual, practical support. Some don't even receive financial support. And I can't imagine how lonely these kinds of days must feel to them.

I couldn't let the day go by without each one of them feeling a small bit of appreciation and recognition for the work they do, tirelessly, day in and day out, on their own.

As I poured through my list of friends, praying that not one would be overlooked, I discovered that out of more than 300 people (probably 200 or so women), thirteen of them are single Moms. Nearly 7% of the women I know on Facebook are raising their kids alone.

My little pity party ended with a healthy dose of shame at my attitude. And as I worked through that list of thirteen, jotting words of love and encouragement on their walls, I forgot all about my *ideal* Mother's Day. I have my Mother's Day dream all year round.

Do you sometimes feel sorry for yourself when you know it's not really justified?

What do you do to get over it?

Is there someone in your life that could use an encouraging word today?

For the Overworked and Overwhelmed Woman—1

I live my life in a constant state of internal battle—either I am feeling too busy or feeling too lazy. I don't do middle ground. I tend to function pretty well when I'm on the busy side of the spectrum . . . at least for a while.

But there comes this inevitable moment in every busy season where I find myself on the brink of destruction. At that moment, everyone who looks at me is sure to recognize me as the classic overworked, overwhelmed girl with a Superwoman complex. I may be a little slower to catch on, but I do eventually clue in.

If you, like me, have the tendency to get a wee bit too busy, here are three warning signs to watch for. Picking up on these signals and acting on them may help keep you just this side of the brink of destruction.

1. Irritability and/or emotionalism.

I like to write off my moodiness as PMS. And, unfortunately for my family, I really do suffer from terribly emotional PMS. However, I've discovered that this excuse is not valid for every week of the month.

Do you have an irrational desire to scream at people when they annoy you? Does your tone of voice sound sharp and angry, even to your own ears? Do you feel frustrated with the requests and needs of your family or co-workers? Do you find yourself in tears when a friend asks, "How are you?"

Your emotions are trying to tell you something. They are saying, *I can't control myself because life is too far off-kilter.*

2. Physical symptoms.

Tummy upset, headaches, cold sores, acne breakouts—these symptoms are often brought on by stress. Not only do the stress hormones in your body bring on certain physical reactions, but being stressed brings on bad habits that also elicit these same symptoms.

I don't know about you, but when I get all stressed out, I feel too busy to cook or choose nutritious snacks, so I fill up on junk. I also feel too busy to sleep, so I stay up too late. Add poor diet, lack of sleep, and a barrel full of stress hormones together, and you'll end up with a woman who *appears* to be suffering illness.

3. Missing appointments.

Girls like us, we live by the schedule. We pride ourselves on our ability to manage a full calendar . . . and punctually! Sure, everyone gets overbooked occasionally (you do, don't you—everyone else?), but missing a couple appointments over a short period of time is not "normal."

If you need a good laugh, here is a beautiful example of an overworked and overwhelmed day in my life.

So, what's an imbetterbusy kinda girl supposed to do to stay in balance? When we see these warning signs creeping up on us, how can we stop the momentum before we plunge over that cliff and come crashing down?

I'm sure you guessed that I have a few suggestions (based on numerous crashing experiences). Come back tomorrow for part two. But while you're here today, let me ask you a quick question.

What are some other warning signs (in yourself or that you've seen in others) of being overworked, overwhelmed, and on the brink of destruction?

For the Overworked and Overwhelmed Woman—2

Knowing the warning signs of being too busy is a good start, but that won't necessarily help eliminate the stress and the related symptoms of juggling too many balls. It's what we do with that knowledge that will make or break us.

Too often, I will recognize the fact that my life is beginning to spiral out of control, and then continue along the same path thinking, "Well, there's nothing I can do about it. I just have to *get through it* somehow." So I move from being a busy, stressed out woman to a woman who knows she's busy and stressed out. (I think there's some truth to the old adage *ignorance is bliss*.)

It's a hard place to be—feeling overwhelmed and over-committed—because we feel trapped by our obligations, responsibilities, and our promises. I mean, we can't let anyone down! They're all counting on us! Right?

Here are five steps to getting un-overworked and un-overwhelmed. (Yes, I made those words up. Thankyouverymuch.)

1. Recognize the lies.

We have an enemy whose goal is to destroy us. And if he can't full-out destroy us, he'll do everything he can to destroy our effectiveness for the Kingdom of God. The oldest trick in his book is to make us believe that we're more important than we are. Trick #2 is to convince us that we're incompetent. Any of these sound familiar?

If I don't do it, nobody will.

I am the only one who can do it right.

If I don't do it, I will let everyone down.

I can't believe I agreed to do this! I am going to fail and everyone will see what a loser I am.

All the other women (or moms, or wives) can do this; why can't I?

Lies, all of them!

2. Offload responsibilities NOW.

We tend to think that if we can just cross this one thing off our lists, we will be able to manage the rest just fine. So instead of acting on the knowledge that we're about to crash, we push ourselves. This is the surest way to crash h-a-r-d. The moment we recognize that we're in over our heads, we must take action.

Delegate responsibilities to others. Get your family to pitch in with the housework, ask someone else on the committee to handle making the phone calls, cancel that meeting. Do what you need to do, and do it right away. I assure you; everyone will not be mad at you and think of you as a failure! (Yes, someone might. But most people will understand, because they've likely been there too. Just don't make a habit of over-committing and then offloading. Learn from your mistakes and say "no" next time.)

3. Say an emphatic "No!" to all things new.

No new responsibilities, no new committees, no extra volunteer dates, no new play dates or activities for the kids. It's hard, and there will be guilty feelings, but remember that guilt is just another lie. Your children will not be deprived if they don't get to go to so-and-so's birthday party. Your workplace will not fall apart if you don't work on the weekend.

4. Sometimes you need to stop everything.

This one even sends a little shiver down my spine! The very thought of flat-out cancelling everything our family is involved in has me wracked with guilt. But let me tell you this—the idea of letting my family down by being a chronically over-committed, overworked, and overwhelmed wife and mother is even more bone-chilling.

Sometimes, the only way to break ourselves of a bad habit is to go cold-turkey. Make a clean break from all commitments and simply say, "I'm taking this season to be fully present where I am with no outside commitments." It's okay. Pastors, professors, and all sorts of professionals take Sabbaticals—you can too!

5. Re-establish right priorities.

I don't remember his name, but I once heard of a pastor who prayed for three hours at the start of every day. When asked how he could possibly have time for that, his reply was, "How can I *not* have time to prepare my heart to lead my flock every day? Without those hours of prayer, I would get nothing done!"

All the good things we do in the name of God and for our families and ministries will amount to nothing if we are not *with* God. And if we take on things without His direction and approval, those things will be meaningless.

You know what else . . . sometimes God has someone else in mind for a particular job. As do-ers, we tend to see a need and fill it. But that may mean we are, in essence, stealing someone else's blessing by robbing them of the joy of serving the Lord.

Friends, I am preaching to myself here! My prideful tendency is to take it all on by myself and then ruminate on how all these people are counting on me. I let my calendar get more and more full, until there seems to be no time for the basics. I wake up stressed and anxious, and plunge into my many duties with nary a thought about skipping my quiet time with the Lord.

Let us stop this vicious cycle of busy-ness together. Let us keep our priorities in order and our focus solely on God's voice. Let us be free from the Superwoman curse. And let us leave room for God to use others to accomplish His purposes.

How to Bring the Romance Back

A friend was talking about romantic fantasies on her blog and I decided to pipe in with my two cents!

I'll be honest; I'm not too familiar with the phenomenon she's referring to. I can't say that I notice a lot of women mooning over certain celebrities or athletes. What I do notice, though, is a whole lot of women fantasizing over their girlfriends' husbands.

I'm not talking sexual fantasy, but emotional fantasy. *I wish my husband would bring me flowers like hers does. Why won't my husband ever watch the kids and give me a day off like hers? Oh, her husband is so spiritual, such a leader—how I long for my husband to be that way.*

How about this one: *I'm so unhappy in this marriage, but I don't believe in divorce. I wonder what it would be like if my husband were just . . . gone? If he died, I would be free to marry someone really right for me.*

Perhaps that last thought isn't as common as the earlier ones. But it's not as uncommon as you might think.

Here's the deal, friends—the grass may look greener over there on the other side, but in reality **the grass is always greenest where it's been fertilized, watered, and mowed.** Tending to the lawn takes time, effort, money, attention, and some hard work. If we want our marriages to look like hers—the one who gets flowers and is always smiling and touching—we need to put in the same effort she does. Maybe more.

Here is one small thing we can all do to bring the romance back to our marriages—be his biggest fan.

Cheesy? Maybe a bit. Effective? Absolutely.

How to be his biggest fan:

1. Thank him when he does something around the house. EVEN if it's something that you expect him to do (like taking out the trash).
2. Brag about every sweet thing he does for you to your girlfriends. Eventually, it will get back to him and he'll feel like a superhero.
3. Ask him to help you solve a problem (whether a discipline issue with the kids, something at work, etc.), and actually use his advice.
4. Greet him when he comes in the door! Kiss optional, but recommended.
5. Hang out with him, side-by-side, doing something he enjoys (fishing, fixing the car, watching hockey).

If you're like me, you're probably wondering how the heck this is going to help bring the romance back. You're thinking, *Sure, I'll do all that. What's* he *going to do for* me*?*

Guess what? Marriage is not a 50/50 partnership, where you take turns doing your share and keep score. **Good marriages are 100/100.** The secret to getting him to give his 100% is deceptively simple. Stop keeping score. Focus on giving your 100% and nothing else.

If you become your man's biggest fan, he will feel valued, appreciated, worthy, and respected. His chest will puff out in pride, because his wife adores him. A man who feels respected and honored is satisfied, filled up, and he will then be ready to pour out. And he will become your romancer.

You are Loved

Well, it's the end. The end of our journey together, seeking God, asking the questions on our heart, and listening for His answers.

I asked God a lot of questions:

— Lord, what do you want me to do when it comes to the writing/speaking ministry?
— Father, will you point out anything in me that offends You?
— Lord, what is one thing I can do to be a better wife?
— Lord Jesus, how can I be a blessing to my brother and sister?
— Lord, am I supposed to be seeking an income?
— How much should I spend on groceries today?
— Lord, how can I get my focus off myself and better honor You in my life?

The answer that resounds with me, out of all those 40 days, is from the one day I had no questions to ask . . .

I prayed, *Father, I don't know what to ask You today. What do You want to talk to me about?*

He replied . . .

Let's talk about how much I love you; you need a reminder.

Before you were formed in your mother's womb, I knew you. I shaped you as you grew in the secret place.

I have a special plan for you and your life. It's a plan for hope and prosperity.

I know every hair on your head. I know every desire of your heart. In fact, I placed them there.

You are more precious than rubies, more valuable than gold. I am enthralled with your beauty.

I want to dance over you with My love. I want to bless you. Your joy brings me joy.

My great love for you cannot be measured. Listen to My love in Psalm 139. Do not forget how much I love you.

All I desire is for you to love Me in return.

That, for me, is the one thing I want to remember from this time of listening to God's voice.

And you know what, I think that today God wants you to read those words and take them for yourself. You are His treasured bride, and He's telling me that you need to be reminded of how precious you are to Him.

So why don't you go back to the words in red, put your name ahead of them, and read your Abba's love letter to you?

Don't Put The Kids First

Mothers today are Superwomen and martyrs. The more sacrifices we make, the better we are at our job. While this little rule is more unspoken, the proof of our mindset lies in our standard answer to the question, "How are you?" The response I hear most often from my mom friends isn't "Good" as you'd expect. Nope. Us Supermoms love to be able to say, "Busy!"

Another symptom of Supermom syndrome is the classic phenomenon we refer to as *the kids come first*. This translates into putting the care, feeding, attention, and activities of the children ahead of one's own needs. However, this phenomenon also frequently translates into putting the children's needs ahead of their Daddy's needs.

Here are three reasons to adjust your family priorities and start putting the kids last . . .

1. We have but eighteen (or so) short years with each child. With our men, Lord willing, we have a whole lifetime. If all of our time and energy is poured into the children, we will be lost and without purpose when they're gone.
2. Putting your man first is, technically, meeting your children's deepest desire. No one wants you and your husband to stay married more than your children do! Pour your energy into keeping the marriage healthy, and they will be the beneficiaries.
3. Modeling for our children how a healthy marriage works will prepare them to look for and be a good spouse. In a household where Mommy and Daddy's relationship comes first, the children learn how to honour their spouse above all others.

The priorities of the typical Superwoman look something like this:

- — Kids, kids, kids
- — House
- — Friends, family, ministry, work
- — Marriage
- — Self

The priorities of the "new" Superwoman look a little like this:

- — Self (*Because I'm worth it!)*
- — Work
- — Kids, house, family, friends, ministry
- — Marriage

The priorities of the Godly Superwoman ought to look more like this:

- — God
- — Marriage
- — Kids
- — Other relationships (friends, family)
- — Other stuff God calls her to (house, work, ministry, self)

Healthy marriages make healthy families. Healthy families build healthy communities and churches. Healthy churches and communities grow healthy cities, countries, and so on.

So I say, if we've got kids, we stop putting them first and instead pour that energy into building up our men and our marriages. We could change the world right from our own living rooms.

Are your priorities in order?

(I know mine need some work . . .)

Laughter, Sunshine, and Joy

I have the tendency to take things pretty seriously. Too seriously. I can get so focused that I forget to take time for fun. I overlook the simple joys.

In my times listening to God this week, He's been talking to me with that theme—joy. I feel like He's been telling me to take time each and every day to enjoy something. Just stop whatever it is I'm all serious and intent about, and enjoy. Have fun.

We walked down to the park after dinner the other night. The snow there was still knee deep (on an adult), but the sun was shining and the slides were snow-free. I spent the entire time laughing. Loudly. Hysterically. The dog looked like a dolphin swimming through an ocean of snow. The kids lumbered around like baby elephants, their feet crashing down deep every third step or so.

Pat and I howled at their antics from our perch on top of a picnic table. My heart was ready to burst with all that joy of living.

And I felt God's whisper to my soul . . . *Find the joy every day. Live fully. Live now. Enjoy My gifts.*

This morning, I woke late. It's spring break, so I turned off the alarm and snuggled in. When I awoke at 7:48am, I breathed a prayer of thanks and smiled. Knowing that the kids had likely already taken over my quiet time spot, I stayed horizontal and talked with God.

He told me, "Tyler, I have a gift for you today."

What is it?

"Look out the window."

I turned to find clear, blue skies and blinding sunlight.

I felt my Father smile as He said, "That sunshine is for you, daughter. Enjoy."

I will. I most definitely will.

What has God been saying to you lately?

And my heart turns violently inside of my chest . . .

I tend to be performance-oriented. Measurable progress motivates me. Crossing items off a list satisfies me. So it's not surprising that, to date, most of my questions for God have revolved around what I do. I've asked Him things about my writing, my parenting, my actions towards friends and strangers.

Today, I could think of nothing to ask. So I asked God what He wants to speak to me about today. In my heart, I sensed a whisper . . .

Let's talk about how much I love you; you need to be reminded.

And He told me that He loves who I am, not what I do. He told me a hundred ways how He loves me, and the only reason He offered was because I am His.

Not once did He mention the work that I do at home or outside of the home. He didn't bring up my roles as a wife and mother. He didn't talk about my weight, the cleanliness of my house (or lack thereof), my volunteer work.

But over and over again, He washed His waves of Scripture over me, loving me simply because I exist.

Suddenly, the weight of all that pressure—the self-imposed pressure—to *do* is lifted. I am reminded that the most important thing is not to do, but to be. To be His, to be in His presence, to be in His love.

Psalm 139
How He Loves (David Crowder Band)
* *The title for this post is a line from the song.*

Listening to God—Where to Start

Then you will call on me and come and pray to me, and I will listen to you. You will seek me and find me when you seek me with all your ~ Jeremiah 29:12-13

My sheep listen to my voice; I know them, and they follow me.
~ John 10:27

Whether you turn to the right or to the left, your ears will hear a voice behind you, saying, "This is the way; walk in it."
~ Isaiah 30:21

In His Word, God promises us that when we seek Him we will find Him. He tells us that we can hear His voice. And He assures us that He will guide and direct us.

Lately, I have sensed the Lord nudging me to toss out my old routine. To change things up. To seek Him more than I seek to complete a series of tasks.

He wants to speak to me—personally, practically, and continually.

I need to hear Him.

Instead of completing my Bible study assignment, practicing my Scripture memory verses, and then praying (if I have any time left), I am starting my morning time with Him in prayer, ready to listen.

I close my eyes and sing to Him from my heart (if anyone else is awake I sing in my head) . . .

All who are thirsty
All who are weak

Come to the Fountain
Dip your heart in the Stream of Life

Let the pain and the sorrow
Be washed away
In the waves of His mercy
As deep cries out to deep (we sing)

Come, Lord Jesus, come (x3)

Holy Spirit, come (x3)

(lyrics by Brenton Brown & Glenn Robertson, also sung by Kutless)

I wait for the quiet to overtake my heart, for the sense of the nearness of His Presence and the filling of His Spirit . . . and then I ask, I listen, and I write . . .

How has He been speaking to you?

Crave God, Not Food—1

This week I learned something. It's nothing ground-breaking or revolutionary, yet this knowledge will revolutionize my weight loss journey. Here is what I've discovered:

When I don't pray about making choices that honor God, I tend to forget that my choices have anything to do with Him.

Riding on the success of last week, I became confident. Which is not necessarily a bad thing, except when self-confidence overtakes God-confidence. Too much self-confidence leads to "I" thinking. *I did great this week! Look how well I am managing my eating! I worked out hard. I lost weight. I did it! I, I, I . . .* All that "I" thinking left no room for God—no room for His glory and no room for Him to work.

It's risky to say that my eating (and thus my weight) is tied to my spiritual walk. Because if I fail at getting my eating under control, I am essentially failing God. At least that's how some people may view it. But I know that I cannot fail God. Whether I have success or not, whether I lose weight or not, whether I learn to manage my anger or not, whether I use swear words or not . . . I cannot fail Him.

The only way I fail is if I give up. If I give up my efforts to know Him better, to understand Him more clearly, to honor Him in more areas of my life—then I will have failed.

So this week, though I did not lose weight (I didn't gain either, and I did lose 1% body fat), I neither failed myself nor God. I had a momentary distraction and lost my purpose. I got to thinking that this was all about me, forgetting that it's truly about Him and me—our relationship.

Today, my prayer is that what I put in my mouth will be beneficial for my body, for my calling, and for those I'm called to serve. I pray that I will remember to come to Him for help when I face temptation. Mostly I pray that I will feel more intimately acquainted with Him and His love as each day passes.

"Everything is permissible"—but not everything is beneficial. "Everything is permissible"—but not everything is constructive.~ 1 Corinthians 10:23 (NIV, 1984)

Is there something you feel called to do—something that is permissible, but not beneficial (whether change your eating habits, give up TV, start a daily quiet time, get organized, etc.)—that you were distracted from this week?

Crave God, Not Food—2

What's the difference between the person who successfully loses weight and keeps it off and the rest of us?

Is it strategy? I don't think so. I've seen people succeed on all sorts of plans, from Weight Watchers to South Beach, from Curves to P90X. There are "how to" books, videos, and programs to be found around every corner. We are not lacking for information on *how* to lose weight and get healthy.

For those of us who struggle and whose weight sometimes comes off but often returns, the missing ingredient seems to be the "want to." We lack the motivation to do what needs to be done, or the commitment to keep doing what needs to be done over and over. We fabricate excuses so that we can blame external factors for our struggle (I can't find time to exercise with all these small children . . . Eating healthy costs too much . . . My body just prefers to be this weight . . .) instead of looking for the internal issues that are holding us back.

I've identified a few of the things that keep dragging me back to my old habits (of eating bad foods and living a sedentary life):

Perfectionism
I tend to think "all or nothing," so when I have a small slip-up or a weak moment it's easy to convince myself that I am incapable of getting it just right. *If you can't do something well, don't do it at all.* Sound familiar?

Comparison
I watch others who are succeeding, or who have never experienced this struggle, and I hold up my measuring stick. Mine is always shorter. Beautiful friends who've had numerous babies still looking

as amazing as they did before the first pregnancy . . . Contestants on The Biggest Loser who rock out dropping ten plus pounds in a week . . . And then there's me. And I feel about two inches tall. And I think, "Why bother?"

These two internal issues reveal the third . . .

Wrong Motivations

Am I losing weight to be skinny, to see a certain number on the scale, to wear a particular size of jeans? Do I believe that, by losing weight, I will somehow "measure up" in a new way and feel more beautiful? Or more worthy? What, really, is the goal that drives me?

So I need to remind myself of some truths. Maybe you need a reminder today, too.

The number on the scale does not define me. That number is simply an external indicator of an internal problem.

While looking great and wearing those size eights hidden away in the back of my closet would be fantastic, my appearance is nothing more than a side-benefit (the icing on the cake, if you will). The real benefit is how I will feel, not only physically, but spiritually and emotionally.

The goal is not measurable in pounds, inches, or sizes. Rather, my daily measure of success needs to be obedience. Moment by moment, decision by decision, asking God what He desires for me and then doing it.

For me, carrying this extra weight is symbolic of the burden I am hauling around that weighs me down from serving God and my family fully, completely, wholeheartedly, and with supernatural energy.

I hope you needed a pep talk this morning, in whatever area your struggle lies. What is your struggle today? Did any of those truths resonate with you, too?

Making Your Faith Real

Sometimes, faith in God becomes a routine of faith activities lacking in a heart connection. We can "do" everything right: attend church, join a small group, do group Bible studies, do personal Bible studies, have daily quiet time, teach Sunday school, tithe, and more . . . yet still feel as though something is lacking.

Do you know what I'm talking about?

Seasoned Christians often refer to it as a time when God feels far away. Newer believers may describe it simply as not "feeling" God or not really knowing if He's real and working in their lives. Either way, there's a lingering emptiness inside.

So how can we get past that point and rediscover (or discover for the first time) a true, living, active, life-changing faith that comes from having a relationship with the one true God?

I'd like to suggest that there are two steps we can take that will ignite our faith, both in ourselves and in those around us. And teaching these things to our children could make the difference between them growing up with a *real* faith of their own.

The Holy Spirit

When we believe that Jesus is our Saviour (that the only reason we have a chance at a fulfilling life here and in eternity is because He chose to rescue us) and accept Him as our Lord (we decide to let Him be in charge of our lives), God fills us with the Holy Spirit. The Holy Spirit is given to us to guide us, to lead us, to counsel us, and to pray for us. The thing is, we don't always stay "filled up"—we leak!

If God is feeling distant, chances are good that we need to take some time to get refilled. My favourite way of filling back up is to pray a brief prayer, "Lord, fill me with Your Spirit," and then crank out some worship music and sing along with all my heart. Others may prefer a quieter, more reverent approach like meditating on a verse that's meaningful to them or listening prayer. Regardless of the approach, we need to ask for and expect to be filled with the Holy Spirit.

Be Radical

The other thing we can do to fan the flame of our faith is get a little bit radical. While for some people radical might mean selling everything, living in a hut in Africa, and preaching the Good News, for most of us it's not nearly so wild. (Phew!)

In my life, radical means listening when I "hear" (sense in my spirit) the nudge of the Holy Spirit to do something. (Which explains why we need to get filled up first.) It's often a little something, a thing that makes me a bit uncomfortable. Like paying for the $5 of groceries belonging to a homeless man who's lined up ahead of me at the grocery store checkout. Or maybe volunteering to babysit for a friend in desperate need of a break. It's frequently as simple as turning the kids' and hubby's socks right-side-out as I put them in the laundry without complaining and/or delivering a lecture.

Radical is, by definition, revolutionary. For some of us, the only revolution we need to start is in our own hearts and homes.

If you're feeling a little faithless these days, if your walk with God has become routine (boring, even), I challenge you to try taking these two steps. Every day for one week, start your day by asking for the Holy Spirit to fill you up. Then go through the day ready to respond to those "nudges." At the end of that week, ask yourself if your faith feels more real.

I am willing to bet money (if I were a gambler and had money to bet) that your answer will not be no! How can I be so sure? Because it works for me, every single time I need a little personal revival.

Father, may we not become "dull" Christians with boring lives and little faith! Let us be women who are alive and on fire for you, so that we can in turn fire up those around us. Help us to teach our children, through example, how to have a relationship with you that is revolutionary. In Your Name, Amen.

"We are settling for a Christianity that revolves around catering to ourselves when the central message of Christianity is actually about abandoning ourselves." ~David Platt

Messed Up

I am a spiritual mess.

Do you know that inner sense? The one that says, "God is doing some work here. Be ready." I'm feelin' it.

Have you ever felt all choked-up and teary-eyed at church, during Bible study, while listening to someone share, or during worship? It's this inexplicable feeling of being on the brink of sobbing. Mmmm-hmmmm. Every single time I walk through the church doors.

Do you sometimes feel as though there should be something you're hearing or learning from God that isn't quite getting through? Kinda like having a word on the tip of your tongue, but not being able to locate the word. Yup, you guessed it. I've got it.

Our women's group is studying Priscilla Shirer's *Jonah: Navigating a Life Interrupted*. Naturally, our discussions surround the life disruptions we are currently or have recently experienced. One woman's husband has decided to leave his long-time career in order to pursue farming. Another woman was surprised with an unexpected, late in life pregnancy. Cancer. Moving. Financial strain. Everyone's lives are rife with interruptions.

Except mine. I've got nothin'. My thoughts go back to a year and a half ago, when we felt God leading us to move. Now THAT was an interruption! Career change, school change, find a new church, give up a ministry, new house, new friends . . . Virtually every aspect of my life was cut short. But currently, everything is cool, mellow, settled, comfortable.

Uh-oh. I know what that word means. I remember . . . In my walk of faith, I long ago decided that comfortable would be a dirty word.

There are no current interruptions in my life. Except for that unsettling sense that God is working. And until I spoke these words aloud yesterday, I had no idea they were in my heart.

I don't want more change, further life alterations, additional upheaval! I can't take it. Not now. A season of rest is in order, surely. But God, we uprooted our whole family for You! Isn't that enough? What more could You possible want from me?

Oh dear. True, I'd rather not have any sort of interruption right now. But I'd rather have the security of knowing that I'm walking in obedience than the security of "sameness." I think.

I need God to change my heart. I need God to change my mind. I need to remember that it's not about me.

It's Not About Me

I have been blogging for three full years now. That's three New Year's Days, three years of "resolutions," 1095 + days worth of thoughts, convictions, inspirations, and self-evaluation. To be honest, that much accountability is a little bit terrifying!

Coming into 2008, I resolved to put an end to my Procrastination. *No more putting off the things that should be done today, or right now. No more ignoring God and listening only to myself. No more laziness and procrastination.* My self-report card: C. There has been definite growth and improvement in some areas, like things that need doing around the house. But there are some things undone today that I know could have been done long ago (*ahem*, updating my book proposal).

As the calendar page turned for 2009, My New Year's Resolution was captured in a passage from the Word: Psalm 25:4-5. My self-report card: B. It was a big year of spiritual growth, change, hearing from and listening to God.

I declared 2010 to be The Year of Consecration, *because if there's anything I want in this life, it's that I will look different, sound different, and BE different . . . set apart for His high purpose.* My self-report card: D. Many of the things I had in mind at the writing of that post are unchanged. Potty mouth—still there; over-emotional—yup, nothing new to report; eating/weight issues—let's not even talk about it; parenting struggles—some good strides made in that department, I *think* (this is the only reason I didn't give myself an F).

What a relief that I don't have to write myself a report card, because my inner perfectionist can only see how I've fallen short. My inner spirit, though—the Spirit of the One who lives within me—He writes report cards akin to those brought home by Kindergartners. There is no A-F scale, no percentage points, no red ink. His report card gives "E" for effort, "I" for the heart's intentions, and "G" for grace.

As I stand on threshold of a fresh, new start once again, I will resist the urge to base my self-worth of my Kingdom value on my own report card, and instead accept His evaluation of who I am (not what I've done). It is only through His lens of grace that I can possibly imagine, for another year, placing before myself goals and hopes and dreams that I may or may not achieve.

The year of our Lord, two-thousand and eleven, is going to be my year of "It's Not About Me." I want to filter each action, each reaction, every decision, every circumstance through the lens of "How can I bring God glory?"

Here's what I *think* that may look like, lived out:

An invitation to speak—how can I let God's light shine through my feeble words, so that women will want to know Him better?

A house that needs cleaning (when doesn't it?!)—how can I go about my work as an act of worship and service to Him, so that He can be glorified in my home?

Children that misbehave—instead of plain old discipline "because they need to learn," how can I teach them to desire better behaviour so that they might bring honour and glory to God?

Too busy for a social life—how can I learn to see not only the value I get from taking time for friendship, but how my friendship might be used to bless someone else and offer her encouragement in His Name?

Working on (again) my food/weight/health issues—how do I want to treat my physical body (His temple), not just for me and my well-being, but for His glory and His use?

Bring it on, 2011. Because with Him, I know that I will never be graded lower than a G.

Do you make new year's resolutions or come up with a theme for your year? What's yours?

Side note: my theme phrase for this year has been borrowed from a Max Lucado book of the same title.

Too Comfortable?

I am a blue jeans, t-shirt, and running shoes kind of girl. Even as a child, the prospect of dressing up did not appeal to me. It's just never made sense to me—why would someone deliberately choose to wear clothing and footwear that pulls and squishes and needs to be adjusted all day long? Why in the world would I want to go to all that effort, just to see those nice clothes get dirty before I walk out the door?

As a stay-at-home mother, my uniform consists of stretchy yoga pants, tank top, and hooded sweater—socks are optional. For Church, I go to the effort of putting on make-up, styling my hair, and wearing a "nice" pair of jeans. Back when I was a student, I elevated my wardrobe choices as far as corduroy overalls (they were black, therefore considered "dressy"). Even during my brief time in the workforce, I was lucky enough to be in positions where "office casual" was considered dressed-up.

Comfort is important to me.

Every now and then, though, I have cause to be uncomfortable. Christmas parties, special events and the like. For certain occasions, my regular uniform is simply unacceptable. So I primp and preen, iron my clothes, purchase a pair of nylons, and get myself all gussied up. On these occasions, my new look garners a reaction from every. single. person. who knows me.

The compliments of others, and maybe even the look itself, transform me. I stand taller. I hold my tummy in (well, I try to). My shoulders are back. There's a big smile on my face. I'm confident, friendly, social. My feet ache in the heels, I can barely eat for fear of popping the buttons at my waist, I feel the need to obsessively check my lipstick, I am secretly praying that the little hole in my nylons doesn't turn into a giant run for all to see. Yet all of my discomfort fades into the background in light of my "new persona."

Perhaps all my comfort has not been as wonderful as I thought it should be. I realize that, in my comfy sweats, I feel a bit shy . . . reserved . . . insecure . . . sloppy . . . ugly even. In my comfort it has been easy to let things go. The waistband of sweatpants doesn't tell a person nearly as much about their weight as the waistband of a skirt. Comfort has become so important, that I've forgotten to push myself.

Sometimes, it's good to be uncomfortable—it changes you in ways you would not have expected. It helps you to realize that you were, in fact, stuck.

The same is true of our walk with the Lord. Settling down into a comfortable routine feels good. It feels secure. It feels safe.

But God is far from safe! He's strong and bold and adventurous. (What greater sense of adventure than to lead the Israelites on an exodus from their slave masters, part the sea to allow for their escape, then dramatically allow the sea to close and swallow up the enemy?!)

If we get too "settled" in any relationship, we begin to lose that sense of adventure. Take marriage, for example—get comfortable, feel safe, little by little you forget to do those special things for your spouse, lose the sense of romance, feel "stuck."

If, like me, you are feeling a bit too comfortable in your relationship with the Lord, maybe it's time to change out of those sweat pants. Get dressed up, and try something different. See what God will do in you . . . in me. Let Him unsettle you from the rut you're stuck in, get a little uncomfortable, and be transformed.

Do not conform any longer to the pattern of this world, but be transformed by the renewing of your mind. Then you will be able to test and approve what God's will is—his good, pleasing and perfect will. ~Romans 12:2

Hosting a Banquet

Then Jesus said to his host, "When you give a luncheon or dinner, do not invite your friends, your brothers or relatives, or your rich neighbors; if you do, they may invite you back and so you will be repaid. But when you give a banquet, invite the poor, the crippled, the lame, the blind, and you will be blessed. Although they cannot repay you, you will be repaid at the resurrection of the righteous."
~Luke 14:12-14

As a general rule, I believe the Bible to be the straightforward and literal Word of God. I don't think that most passages are intended to be ambiguous strings of words that required "interpretation" in order to be understood. I believe that God created the earth in a ***literal*** six days and rested on the seventh. I believe that people ***literally*** lived until they were 800 years old. I believe that Noah really did, ***literally***, live on a big boat containing two of every kind of [stinky] creature for months. And so on . . .

This means that I also understand the words of Jesus to mean exactly what they appear to mean. I don't see the above passage as an allegory of some sort. No, Jesus is ***literally*** saying that I am supposed to invite the poor, crippled, lame, and blind into my home.

I'll be honest, I struggle with this. The idea of inviting, for example, the unpleasant smelling homeless man outside the grocery store to my house—very uncomfortable . . . and a little scary! Especially in this day and age, where tales of horrible things done to kind strangers are everyday fare on the news channel.

So I've been asking God how I can obey Him in this in a way that also protects my family. He showed me that I don't need to drive downtown and look for unknown homeless people (not that He someday won't ask this of me—or you—but perhaps not during this season of young children at home). He showed me that we already know a number of poor, crippled, lame, and blind people whom we can welcome and show His love to.

A sibling . . . certainly not considered poor by the world's standard . . . spending money like it were going out of style on all kinds of items for personal enjoyment . . . feeling an emptiness and trying to fill it the way this world says it can be filled . . . but poverty-stricken in spirit—no hope, no joy, no love, no Jesus.

An old friend . . . strong legs and back, employed and hard working . . . struggling with depression and unable to break free . . . aching, empty, lonely, and unable to step out of the quicksand that is pulling and sucking . . . crippled and without the freedom that comes only from Christ.

Another friend from days gone by . . . addicted and strangled by the grip of drugs . . . grasping for something—anything—to break free, yet unable to move forward . . . injured . . . lame.

Another sibling . . . searching for meaning wherever it can be found . . . spirituality in any possible form—yoga, new age, meditation, positive-thinking-power-of-attraction . . . completely blind to the Truth, unable and unwilling to see the Source of Real Spiritual Meaning.

We're surrounded by those who are poor, crippled, lame, and blind. And we hold the key to their healing and freedom. All it takes is a simple invitation to the dinner table.

Life, Interrupted

In the shadow of the wintry morning I sit, waiting.

Children, out long past the sun, continue in their slumber.

I feel it rise up in me—the impatience. We must move! Go! Hurry! Get there! There is work to be done. Ministry. School. Errands.

I resist the urge to awaken Sleeping Beauty and her brother. This rest is needed. For them. For me.

In the frantic of this life, God interrupts. *Rest,* He whispers. *Be still, and know that I am God.*

I struggle against the rest, like an angry child pushes away from her mother's embrace. Like the child, I come to the crossroads, the decision point—pull away, run away, ignore the warm comfort or release a shuddering breath and sink into mother's arms.

One last thrash of resistance. Then release. Sweet rest. Life, interrupted.

Thank-you, Lord, that you love enough to intervene in my chaos, stop me in my tracks, and return my gaze to Your face.

Tapping into His Strength—I

I can do all things through Christ who strengthens me. ~Philippians 4:13 (NKJV)

We all know these words are Truth, and I'm sure we've quoted them in reference to one situation or another, but do we truly believe them?

I find myself saying these words, praying these words, then turning around and attempting to do the work in my own strength.

For example . . .

If you've been reading for a while, you know I struggle as a mother. I lose my cool. I yell. I throw tantrums. I cry, repent, ask forgiveness (from God, my husband, and my children), I commit to changing, and for a few weeks or months it's better. But then we have one of those days, and it starts all over again.

Don't get me wrong, I have no unrealistic goals of being the perfect mother all the time. But I do have a reasonable expectation that I can be free from the bondage of anger, which would dramatically change the way I parent.

After years of this cycle, why am I not free? After all, I **know** that I can do all things through Christ who strengthens me!

I suspect that my freedom lies in the method. My current method involves two steps: asking for God's help, then trying to be more patient and loving. Sure, the praying aspect is good. But from there I operate under my own efforts. **I try.**

Sometimes, though, trying is just not enough. So what does it really mean—**through Christ**?

I'm going to ponder this some more, later in the week. But I'd like to know your thoughts. How does one move from their own strength into Christ's power?

The God Chronicles

Nearly two years ago, I was burgeoning under the weight of carrying my fifth blessing in my womb. *Ahem, I realize there are some of you doing the math—Malakai is 16 months old, 20-some-odd months ago I was probably only 5 months along. You go ahead and do it a few times, then you'll realize that the burgeoning phase begins earlier each time. Back to the story . . .*

At our women's time out event (which has saved my life almost every Wednesday morning for the past five years), we participate in "Secret Sisters." The basic idea is this—draw a name, bless the girl who's name you drew, pray for her, encourage her . . . anonymously.

I was sitting at a table with my coffee (no lectures about pregnancy and caffeine, thankyouverymuch) and having a little bit of a pout fest. You see, Mother's Day was coming up, and I desperately wanted to be spoiled with a ~~spa day~~ pedicure. Since one of my jobs in our family is to track the finances, I was well aware that my wish would not be coming true.

The guest speaker began, so I stopped whining and temporarily forgot about my woes.

A while later, one of the girls running the SS program brought me a gift bag. Yay! I loved getting stuff from my Secret Sister—she was awesome! I began digging through and found a wonderful little "pregnancy relaxer kit," as I fondly call it—herbal tea, aromatherapy candles, bubble bath, lotion, and a card.

I opened the card, and a paper fell out onto the table. My girlfriend scooped it up, looked at it, smirked, and handed it to me. A gift certificate for a pedicure. I burst into tears—not the sweet, adorable tears; more like the hiccuping, snot dripping kind. (I don't think I ever did read what was written in the card.)

God knew the desire of my heart, and knew that it wasn't within my means to pursue it, so He found another way. My Secret Sister was beyond generous (pedicures are darn expensive). I was so blessed. And there was no doubt in my mind that God had provided.

Delight yourself in the LORD, and He will give you the desires of your heart. ~Psalm 37:4

Pondering in my Heart

In my quiet time this morning, I felt the Lord leading me to the book of James. There is so much wise counsel on those six pages, I had a difficult time deciding what to underline. I decided to pick a couple small sections to ponder throughout my day.

Trials and Temptations
Consider it pure joy, my brothers, whenever you face trials of many kinds, because you know that the testing of your faith develops perseverance. Perseverance must finish its work so that you may be mature and complete, not lacking in anything. ~James 1:2-4

Right from the beginning of his letter, James packs a punch. I know I want to be mature in my faith, not lacking. I even accept that oftentimes maturity is only developed through adversity. But to consider it pure joy? Whew.

Listening and Doing
My dear brothers, take note of this: Everyone should be quick to listen, slow to speak and slow to become angry, for man's anger does not bring about the righteous life that God desires . . . If anyone considers himself religious and yet does not keep a tight rein on his tongue, he deceives himself and his religion is worthless. ~James 1:19-20, 26 (also read all of chapter 3)

It seems straightforward—watch your mouth. But how? God needs to remind me of this command often. You know, "thou shalt not gossip/yell/complain/nag." That one. It seems I'm a bit slow in learning, or forgetful. I think the tongue is an area that a lot of women stumble in. Isn't it? Please tell me I'm not the only one!

Are there any passages that God has laid on your heart lately, that you are taking the time to ponder?

The Daily

Because I'm still feeling slightly frazzled/frantic/crazy/nutso, I am going to share my morning gymnastics routine with you in point form. Imagine me talking really, really fast, and breathing too loud.

— Abbey is sick—joy
— Kai is grouchy (and naughty)—excellent
— Shea is home today—is kindergarten really still two whole years away?
— getting Meg out the door for school without her sister—fun; chasing after her halfway down the block to put her lunch in her backpack—even more fun
— having tummy troubles that keep me running—wonderful
— seeing Braeden's bus pull up, when I have not yet seen the boy—fantabulous
— going out in sub-sub-sub zero weather to start the beast—great
— putting grouchy boy to bed for morning nap, in spite of the fact that I know he will not give me an afternoon nap—totally worth it
— plugging in a movie for sick girl and little girl and letting them munch granola bars in my bed—even more worth it

In spite of what my "self" wants to feel, I will have joy. These are things that could break my day, if I choose to allow them. I won't. I will laugh at the silly crazy morning. I will enjoy a few minutes of slow-breathing and sipping my steaming coffee. Then I will throw the peed on sheets in the wash (from two beds) and set to my daily work. This work that God has called me to do—no matter how mundane.

This is the day the LORD has made; let us rejoice and be glad in it.
~Psalm 118:24

Questions on the State of Our Hearts

This is love for God: to obey His commands . . . for everyone born of God overcomes the world. ~ 1 John 5:2b,4a

In our lives, do we show others that we love God? Are we really God's children? Do we obey His commands? Are we overcoming the world? Or do we simply pay lip service to the Holy One of Heaven?

God is light: in Him there is no darkness at all. If we claim to have fellowship with Him yet walk in the darkness, we lie and do not live by the truth. ~ 1 John 1:5b-6

Are we walking in the light, or are we lying to ourselves?

Anyone who claims to be in the light but hates his brother is still in the darkness. ~ 1 John 1:9

Are we in the light?

Do not love the world or anything in the world. If anyone loves the world, the love of the Father is not in him. ~ 1 John 2:15

Do we allow our hearts and spirits to be so full of love for the things of this world, that there is no room for the love of the Father?

If anyone has material possessions and sees his brother in need but has no pity on him, how can the love of God be in him? ~ 1 John 3:17

Do we view those in need with concern, or have we allowed our hearts to grow hard? Does the love of God reside in us?

Whoever does not love does not know God, because God is love. ~ 1 John 4:8

Are our lives a reflection of God's love to those around us? Do we **really** know Him?

All the Growing Up

We have entered into a new phase in our family—one where mom no longer has to do everything.

Today, I was able to send Abbey to the downstairs fridge to bring up a jug of milk.

Braeden's new daily job is to take out the garbage and recycling.

All four of the bigger kids are taking their plates to the counter after a meal. Whoever is done last takes Kai's plate (that's usually Meg, she's a good eater).

Shea likes to help me with the Windex.

Meg loves to dust with the little electro-static Swiffer duster.

Every job I do has become less mine, and I love it! To be honest, I don't completely love the help all the time—let's be real, kids helping is often more like "teaching hour" than anything resembling productive. What I do love is seeing the pride on their faces at a job well done. Each child is developing a sense of ownership over his or her chores. And seeing a sibling working hard at a task inspires the others to do likewise. What's not to love? Well, except for that nasty part of step-by-step training them in the tasks . . .

I also discovered another great idea today! It's very crazy to try to do three kids completely different homework at once. With Meg just learning to read, she needs my full attention as she reads her book. But I really needed Braeden and Abbey to practice their spelling words. So, I handed Braeden Abbey's list and Abbey Braeden's. I told them to take turns reading each other a word that they could spell out on their paper.

Not only did this ingenious idea save me time and energy, it was amazing for Braeden's speech! He had to concentrate so hard on pronouncing each word clearly enough that Abbey would know what it was, and if she couldn't understand she just asked again and again until he said it in a way that she got it. Never again will I do spelling practice with my children.

I must say, the mourning period over the "I'm never again going to have another wee, tiny, beautiful baby" might just be coming to an end. This growing up, it is neat stuff!

An Important Reminder About Priorities

I heard a story once about a woman in ministry who had a dream one night. In her dream, the Lord came to her and took her up on a hill overlooking a valley. Standing in the valley were the thousands of people who had come to know the Lord through her ministry. As she stood there beside the Lord, surveying all the people, she thought, "It doesn't get any better than this." She looked over at the Lord and tried to imagine what He was thinking. Eagerly, she waited for Him to lavish her with praise for a job well done. Imagine her surprise when He extended His hand, gesturing to the mass of people below and asked her, "Where are your children?"

Be Glorified

I want my children to love God. I want them to love His Word and discover the life, healing, and power within it. I want them to love people and treat them with compassion and kindness.

But more than anything on earth—tears fill my eyes as I write this—I want glory to come to God through them.

I want a thousand things for my children, and I ask without hesitation, but I want nothing more than that God would be glorified. Life is just a breath. All that will matter forever in our heavenly state is the glory that came to God through their lives and ours.

* Taken from "Believing God Day by Day: Growing Your Faith all Year Long" by Beth Moore (a devotional book).

Time is in His Hands

Just a quick follow-up to yesterday's post about allowing God to schedule my time.

First—It is waaaaay harder than I thought it would be to pause after each activity and ask God what to do next! I'm in the habit of running my own days, so when I complete one task I keep catching myself just flowing into the next logical thing. It is taking a conscious effort to take that minute and seek God.

Second—I sometimes like my own plan better than God's! He keeps telling me, "no, today is not the day to plan out your trip." I really just want to sit here for a couple hours, plot out my map on MapQuest, find hotels/cabins/vacation rentals, book, and have all the details settled. But it wasn't on God's list either yesterday or today.

Third—It is totally amazing to me how God can ensure I get all the important and urgent stuff taken care of in one short day! Amazing . . .

Here is yesterday's list . . .

- ~~pick up fresh produce~~—*not today*
- ~~go to bank~~—*not today*
- ~~write for book~~—*not today*
- exercise—*yes*
- meet with ministry co-worker—*yes*
- sort out ministry binder—*yes*
- ~~mail out e-News~~—*delegate*
- put away laundry—*yes*
- ~~vacuum~~, sweep & wash—*just s&w kitchen*
- ~~plan out Disney trip~~—*not today*

— retreat meeting—*yes*
— send out reference letter—*yes*
— Bible time—*of course, first*

* Of course, a few things not on my list of "to dos" came up throughout the day—dealing with emails, phone calls, feeding people, etc. I tried to take a moment each time another task popped into my head to ask the Lord about it.

It was neat, because during my quiet morning time, I really felt I needed to go exercise before the kids needed to get ready for school, but God told me to just stay and hang out with Him a while longer. He assured me He'd provide time to exercise later. Once two kids were off, the other three settled in for a movie and I was able to go for a good 20 minutes on my new (to me) recumbent bike. If you can believe it, there was time for me to do all of the "yeses" **plus** do lunch, play "Guess Who" with kiddos, do supper, receive and reply to more than 50 emails, and I even read a novel for 15 minutes!

I am a bit frustrated and confused that He has told me for two days in a row NOT to write, as I have also felt nudged that I'm supposed to be spending some dedicated time writing. When?! I know He can make enough time, and give me the words so the writing goes quickly, but I'd just like to have it all mapped out a little more clearly. Ha! I guess He'll tell me when to write.

Now, as much as I would like to surf the net and plotting out my map, I just took a moment to seek guidance and it's time to get something ready for supper. Then I'm interviewing 2 potentials for childcare providers, and God did tell me to vacuum today . . .

Fourth—Now I know why the Lord commanded us to take the Sabbath day and rest! He wants us to busy working all day. After six days like this, I am going to savour a day of rest!

God Makes Time

Have you ever wondered, "how will I ever get it all done?"

We have so much to do in each day, so many activities and obligations packed into our weeks. It's a symptom of our ADD, over-stimulated, immediate gratification society. Some would argue that we need to remove ourselves from society's mindset, but I'm not sure that would solve the problem. In fact, if we aren't keeping up (in our work, ministry, family life) with the rest of society, we're likely to encounter other problems.

So how can we live IN this world (and function at the level required to do so), without becoming OF this world?

I believe the first distinction is how we establish our priorities. I have found, by trial and error that setting my heart on God and His ways first thing each morning has the power to alter my entire day. If I start out taking time with Him, the many other things that require my time that day tend to get done. If I start out my day on my own strength, though, I spend the next fifteen hours feeling as though I am one step behind.

Romans 12:2 says, *Do not conform any longer to the pattern of this world, but be transformed by the renewing of your mind. Then you will be able to test and approve what God's will is—His good, pleasing and perfect will.* Taking time each morning to renew my mind helps establish His priorities for my day, rather than my own.

This week I am taking an experiment in life. Each morning, after my coffee time with Jesus, I am going to make a list of all the things I think I need to accomplish for the day. Then I'm going to ask the Lord to show me what to keep, what to move to another day, what to toss altogether, and what to add. Once I have turned over my list into His (much more) capable hands, I am going to ask Him, "Lord, what do you want me to do now?" At the conclusion of each activity, I'll ask that question again. I can't wait to see how He uses my time!

Criteria for Choosing a Husband

Pat and I don't "do" Valentine's Day. We came to the agreement a few years ago that it seemed foolish to make a big deal about a random day. (Don't worry, we still buy heart-shaped candy for the kids and make heart-shaped grilled cheese sandwiches. They're not deprived.) At some point in our relationship, though, we both realized that we are not the kind of people who are big on showy displays as a means for demonstrating our love and affection.

Don't get me wrong, I love a good gift! I melt for a special date that has been all planned out (right down to the childcare) by my love. But to insist that it needs to happen on a particular day in February seems like a waste of time and effort. And money. I mean, we just did Christmas for seven, then my birthday!

That being said, there was a time that these types of traditions and trappings were very important to me. The amount of effort a boy would put into planning out a special Valentine's surprise was a clear indication of his love and devotion. Wasn't it? For fun, I am going to share the tale of my worst Valentine's day ever.

I was just out of high school, dating a guy who I was thinking might be "the one" *(who was I kidding, every guy I ever met between the ages of 12 and 18 was measured against my list of criteria)*. We had been dating about four months, and I just knew that he would have something special up his sleeve for me.

It was not a good sign when, at 4pm on Valentine's day, he asked me where I would like to go for dinner. In my most sugary-sweet voice, I suggested that we should probably go to whichever restaurant he had made reservations at two weeks ago (when I not-so-subtly reminded him of the upcoming day of love). He assured me that he had an infallible plan, and I should just go get dolled-up and ready to go.

He picked me up an hour later, and we proceeded to drive, stopping at each and every restaurant in our path. For two hours I endured the torture of his impromptu plan. Eventually, he accepted the inevitable—we would not get in to a restaurant on this particular evening. *I was right and he was wrong (story of my life, ask Pat).*

His next grand plan, "Why don't we just go hang out at the bar?" I suggested that the fool drop me off there, where I would spend the remainder of my Valentine's evening waiting to meet my new boyfriend—one who would love me enough to plan ahead for special days! *(All the nice guys are found in the bars, right?)*

Our break-up came close on the heels of this ill-fated Valentine's date. Now, I'm not saying that I am the kind of girl who just dumped boys willy-nilly on the basis of shallow things such as forgetting to plan ahead. But, we did break up. I'm just sayin'.

Anyone else got a great (terrible) Valentine's story? If not, I am willing to accept submissions of wonderful Valentine's dates, as well. Share your story in the comments.

He Equips

Is the Lord calling you to do something for Him? Do you put it off, saying "I'm not qualified . . . I'm not prepared . . . I can't . . ."? Here's His response to me and my excuses.

May the God of peace, who through the blood of the eternal covenant brought back from the dead our Lord Jesus, that great Shepherd of the sheep, equip you with everything good for doing His will, and may He work in us what is pleasing to Him, through Jesus Christ, to whom be glory forever and ever. Amen. ~Hebrews 13:20-21

The Heart of a Man, The Heart of a Woman

Today I'd like to share some things I learned at the Break Forth Conference last weekend. Specifically, from John and Stasi Eldredge. I've read their companion books, "Wild at Heart" and "Captivating," and they really changed the way I thought about men and women. When I heard them speak on these topics on the weekend, their words resonated for my children.

The foundation of their message rested in "male and female He created them" in His own image (Gen 1:27). The deep down heart of a man, his passions and desires, the things that drive him—those are given by God. The very spirit of a woman, her longings and loves, the things that bring her to tears—given by that same God. We were both created in God's image, and both are good (Gen 1:31).

The Heart of a Man (and Boy):

Eldredge shares three longings of the heart of a man . . . Man longs for a an **adventure to live**. An adventure is the man's answer to the question of his soul, "do I have what it takes?" Living the adventure brings him alive. He desires **a battle to fight** (Exodus 15:3 says the Lord is a warrior). For some the longing for battle is not obvious (for example, the man who doesn't love paintball), but shows itself loud and clear in other situations (such as when a "stupid person" is driving ahead of him. The third cry of a man's heart is for **a beauty to rescue**.

If these desires are not filled, a man (or boy) will go underground to fulfill them. *(This statement rocked my world.)*

For my sons, I understood this to mean that they need to be allowed to experience adventure. Even when my mother's heart may want to keep them close and safe, I need to encourage them to try new things, to challenge themselves and push their personal limits. I need to send the message, "you have what it takes."

The Heart of a Woman (and Girl):

Stasi E. tells us that there are three core passions straight from a woman's heart . . . She wants to **be wooed and won,** pursued and fought for, wanted, seen and delighted in. *Isn't that the truth?! I found myself nodding a lot during her talk.* A woman longs to **play an irreplaceable role** in a heroic adventure. The key here is not the adventure (as it is for the man), but the irreplaceable role—a woman does not want to be merely "useful" in her role, but vital. A woman's heart cry is to **unveil beauty** and bring it to the world. Every little girl puts on a dress, twirls in a circle, and says, "Do you see me? Don't I look beautiful?"

If these desires are not filled, a woman (or girl) will turn to the men/ boys around her to fulfill them.

For my daughters, this tells me that when they are asking for my attention it is because they need me to look at them—they need to be seen and admired. Their hearts long for affection. Even in the midst of the busy life, I need to stop, turn around, look, and answer the question, "Yes, I do see you. You are so beautiful."

As much as I can do to foster my children's hearts, though, the role of their father will be what changes their lives. He is the one who teaches our sons to go to battle in the face of injustice, he is the one who's affection brings our girls delight. He is the one who shows them who the Father is. I can direct them in the way of the Father, I can encourage them and cheer them on, but he can actually **show** them who the Father is.

What does this mean for the fatherless among us? (I was one of them . . .) For me, it brings home the importance of the role a man plays in the development of our children. It means that if their father is gone, we need to pray and seek a "surrogate" father for them. What about Grandpa, or an uncle? Maybe a friend's husband?

All I know for sure is this—men and women, boys and girls have these built-in desires, given by God. Somehow, we need to find a way to direct them to Christ for their hearts' fulfillment. Because if their desires are not met in Christ, they will seek to fill up through the filth of this world.

Life Changing

I was struck this weekend, when Pat sent an email to a friend and mentor, and he used the words "life changing" to describe a conference. That phrase came and whacked me upside the head.

God was speaking, ministering, soothing, and calling to us. Yet that phrase hadn't sprung from my lips. When and how did I allow the experience of intimacy with God become a routine thing? The guilt came . . .

In the solitude of the hotel morning, I talked to Him about this. Have I allowed my faith to become rote? Is my relationship with Him stale? Why am I not knocked over in amazement as I hear Him speak?

His truth came . . .

Are you surprised by the voice of your best friend on the phone? Do you feel shocked and amazed that she called you? Or did you simply know that she would—because you speak to her all the time?

Life changing has become a way of life. I expect to be changed. I count on it and claim it. And He never lets me down.

Each person's faith walk is characterized differently. Some have those "ah-ha" moments, some hear the rolling thunder, some have ups and downs like a roller-coaster ride, and some walk quietly, slow and steady. "It's neither right nor wrong, just different."

What does your walk with God look like these days?

Equilibrium

* **e·qui·lib·ri·um**/⊂ēkwə∪librēəm/

Noun:

1. A state in which opposing forces or influences are balanced.
2. A state of physical balance.

Synonyms:
balance—equipoise—poise—equilibration

My life of late has been sorely lacking in equilibrium. The forces on one side of the scale greatly outweighed the forces on the other side. The heavy side has consisted of medical stuff. Endless, relentless medical stuff. Not life or death stuff, not even emergency stuff, but all-consuming, overwhelming, exhausting nonetheless.

Normally, I like to write about those seasons in life. My desire is to let you in, so we can journey through it together. But my longing to share life with you was no competition for the time-sucking, brain-devouring succession of medical appointments. (Even the dog has had issues!)

I've written so many posts in my head. Imagined myself sharing the glimpses of God's hand in the midst of this rather chaotic season in my life. But at the end of the day, I couldn't muster up the energy to write it. Oh, how I have missed writing! How I have missed meeting with you here!

Last night, I finally felt the scales tipping. The opposing forces in my life are beginning to level out. There was no miraculous shift, no dramatic revelation. There were simply two acts that, when added together, indicate the reemergence of my sanity.

#1. I baked.

For those who know me well, you may see this as a sign of insanity. I'm not a baker (that's definitely understating the situation). It's been about two months of the Celiac journey for my girl and I, and we've been muddling through. But the cost of those pre-made snacks is shocking. A loaf of bread—$8. A six-pack of blueberry muffins—$7. Gluten-free cake mix (in a box)—$6. I've known all along that I will eventually need to learn to bake in order to save our budget. Last night, I pulled out the marshmallows, the gluten-free Rice Krispies, and the microwave.

Let me tell you—I killed those Rice Krispie squares! And it felt so good. I felt like I was taking charge of a situation that had felt out-of-control. I felt competent. I did not feel overwhelmed, tired, or stressed. At all.

#2—I collaged.

Again, if you know me, you're even more convinced that I'm losing it. I hate crafts. Crafts hate me. My art is words, not esthetics. But my little Kindergartener had an "All About Me" page due at school. (We all know that's really homework for Mommy, not the Kinder.) And I wasn't going to settle for anything less than awesome. So I printed photos and typed words. I used colors and fonts (okay, it was all in Times New Roman, but I used different sizes and some words were bold). I cut and glued. And I was not ashamed of the result (in my world, for a craft, that's close enough to awesome)!

At the completion of those two tasks, I caught myself smiling. I did it! It wasn't a struggle. I didn't feel like crying or giving up. There was not a crushing weight on my chest. For the first time in several months, I did not feel overwhelmed by my circumstances. My lopsided state of disequilibrium is no longer quite so lopsided. And I thank God for His divine hand in rebalancing those scales.

This morning, my "writer's block" broke. I wrote an article for a newsletter. Then I sat down and wrote here. It feels like I could write a thousand posts! If I didn't have to go to work, that is. Funny thing—I feel a bit excited about work today, too. For a while there, work was feeling more like an obligation than a privilege. Today, I feel that glimmer of joy again—that I get to be a part of a ministry that had a huge impact on my life.

It's funny (ironic, not "ha ha") that we often don't see how we're allowing our life circumstances to steal our joy until we're coming out the other side. I was being mugged, and I didn't even put up a fight . . . I just handed my joy over and watched the scale tipping all off-kilter. It wasn't all the medical stuff that brought unbalance; it was the loss of joy.

Joy has been returned to me. A gift. I feel like me again. I'm back.

Ahhhhh, it's so good to be home!

* definition from dictionary.com

Hard Lessons, Soft Blessings

I'm pretty sure that when I reflect back on the summer of 2012 I will un-fondly remember it as the "summer of no."

Check out our summer plans! (The strike-throughs show plans that did not come to fruition.)

— *Sneak in a weekend in the mountains with my man, followed by several days of hard labour in our rental house* while the kiddies camped with Grandma.
— Spend *thirteen fifteen-hour days and a whole lotta bucks* fixing up our rental house between tenants.
— Watch a special person (our babysitter for the past few years) get married, and watch my children be part of her special day.
— One of those camping weekends *driving the countryside frantically searching for a good 4G or wifi connection to meet print deadlines for work*, celebrating my dad's upcoming 60th birthday. (I was present for the birthday dinner and cake, thank goodness.)
— Pat heading off on his "guys' weekend" of camping and quadding in the bush, while I . . .

You may notice a couple things missing between the plan and the reality. That's where the "summer of no" comes in.

We had to say no to the Dominican, to several camping weekends, and—sigh—to Manitoba. That one's particularly difficult, as it's going on right now. The reason(s) we had to say no . . . well, because God said no to us.

There is a part of me that believes in the whole reaping and sowing principle. So I believe that one of the reasons God gave us His no to several of our plans was simply a natural consequence for other decisions we've made with our finances. After all, money can only be stretched so many ways before you encounter thin air.

But I don't believe God is vindictive, wanting to "teach us a lesson" all the time with no room for grace. So I know that there was more to His "no"s this summer than our discipline. *(And I also know it's not proper to start sentences with conjunctions, but clearly I don't feel inclined to follow the rules.)*

In the midst of this summer of no, God has cushioned every hard lesson with a gentle, soft blessing.

We didn't get to go to the Dominican and hang with Pat's family for a week. If we had, we'd have never had the funds available for the emergency (and expensive) truck repairs that were required in order to have an operational vehicle this summer. We also would not have been able to afford the extensive (far beyond what we anticipated) repairs required on our rental house. As well, who knows where we'd have found the extra days required to labour over the house!

Truck repairs and rental house repairs stink—big time! But God knew they were coming, and He protected our resources (both financial and time) so that they'd be available when they were most needed.

We didn't get all the camping weekends we had hoped for. However, because we saw the way our summer was playing out (ahem—housebound), we realized we would have the freedom and availability to host a Japanese exchange student in our home for 4 weeks. Megumi (16) became very special to our family, especially to her sister/roommate Abbey (10). What a cool experience for us and our kids!

The kids and I didn't get to go to Manitoba . . . missing out on ten days of fellowship with my extended family. I'll be honest, I'm still really bummed about this one. The photos cropping up on Facebook from yesterday's wedding are bittersweet for me. In the original plan, I was working all day Wednesday, packing up the six of us Wednesday night, connecting up with my mom Thursday afternoon, and driving straight through to Winnipeg. On Wednesday night at about 9pm, I was struck with the stomach flu. It attacked me fiercely for about 16 hours, then left me weak and listless for another 18 or so. In the wee hours of Friday morning, Megan appeared at my bedside and spoke the dreaded words, "Mom, I think I'm gonna throw up." Praise the Lord that her battle was less than half as long and painful as mine!

I can't name many things I hate more than being sick to my stomach while being the sole care provider for four children. One thing that would probably be worse, though, is travelling under those conditions. Even worse, cancelling travel plans at the very last minute due to those conditions. But God knew these unpleasant conditions were coming, and He made sure we were right where we needed to be when they struck.

Other side benefits to being home . . . My kids won't miss the first week of school; Malakai (almost 5) won't miss the first week of Kindergarten. Shea (7) was able to get the cute, bob haircut she desperately wanted before school started. Braeden (14) was able to go with his Dad on the guys' weekend. The other kids and I still have two days on our docket to do some household organizing before school starts. Everyone (except Braeden) should be well-rested for the first day of school. I decided to keep my days off next week, and will use the time for meal planning, shopping, and cooking with a friend. Just tryin' to see the silver lining . . .

I believe that God could have prevented all the crappy stuff from happening. He could have kept our truck and our bodies healthy. He could have kept our renters from being such poor caretakers. He could have made life circumstances and finances work out so that we could have all that we wanted. **But would I have seen His hand in that?** Through this sucky, yucky, crummy summer of no, I've been able to see His hand of protection in new ways. And if

I'm perfectly honest, I am learning some cold, hard lessons that I probably wouldn't have if I'd gotten only "yes"es.

Have you had a circumstance, a day, or an entire season of hard lessons, but where you can see that God was providing soft blessings in the midst of it?

We Never Walk Alone

I had the privilege of sitting under the teaching of Beth Moore—in person—this past weekend. She was speaking to us about walking. More specifically, our walk of faith.

My notes make it clear that I had a number of "ah-ha" moments, with words circled, underlined, and asterisked all over the place. Today, I just want to share one thought . . .

We are ***never*** walking alone. Never. In everything we do, everywhere we go, every single day, we are either walking with God or with His and our enemy—the devil.

That's a sobering thought. One that might be hard to swallow for some. Bear with me for a moment as I try to take you on the path that Beth took us on . . .

1. From the beginning of time, God has walked among His people. He walks with us and we walk with Him.

And they heard the sound of the LORD God walking in the garden in the cool of the day . . . ~Genesis 3:8 (ESV)

I will walk among you and be your God, and you will be My people. ~Leviticus 26:12 (NIV)

2. Satan tries to replicate everything God does, including walking among his people.

[Satan] said in [his] heart, "I will go up to heaven. I'll raise my throne above the stars of God. I'll sit as king on the mountain where the gods meet. I'll set up my throne on the highest slopes of the sacred mountain. I will rise above the tops of the clouds. I'll make myself like the Most High God." ~Isaiah 14:13-14 (NIRV)

And the Lord said to Satan, "From where have you come?" Satan answered the Lord and said, "From going to and fro on the earth, from walking up and down on it." ~Job 2:2 (ESV)

3. We make a choice whom we will walk with (serve). For some it's a life choice, for others it's a choice that changes in our day-to-day.

But if serving the LORD seems undesirable to you, then choose for yourselves this day whom you will serve . . . ~Joshua 24?15a (NIV)

No one can serve two masters. Either he will hate the one and love the other, or he will be devoted to the one and despise the other. ~Matthew 6:24 (NIV)

4. We must be careful that we don't allow ourselves to default into walking with the enemy.

Be on your guard and stay awake. Your enemy, the devil, is like a roaring lion, sneaking around to find someone to attack. ~1 Peter 5:8 (CEV)

5. We are never walking along; we're either walking with God or the devil.

I have seen this play out in my life, in the very few days I've had at home since Beth taught it. I'll tell you all about it in my next post.

Today, let me leave you with a question to ponder . . .

Who have you been walking with?

Taking the Longer Walk

In my last post, We Never Walk Alone, I mentioned that I had some good ol' life application for the whole concept of "we're either walking with God or the devil."

What's interesting (to me, at least) is that I came home solely focused on a different point I learned at Living Proof Live—the concept of losing ground in our walk with God. I saw where I had allowed the enemy to push me back in the area of my calling (writing and speaking to encourage other women in their walk with the Lord). But when I sat down to write about that, instead the thoughts about not walking alone poured from my keyboard. (God does that sometimes; when I'm writing something, He just takes over.)

Anyway, to the point now!

About once or twice a year, we find that the kids get a little "rangy." (I know that's not a word.) When this happens, Pat and I clamp down to reign them back in. Recently, though, the struggle has been dragging out. We're getting worn out. And it seems a couple of the kids are just getting started. Needless to say, a great deal of my morning prayer time has been spent on this.

After LPL, and during my morning time with the Lord, I was reminded of the concept that we never walk alone. As I was praying over the frustrations with kid behaviors and infighting, I sensed God asking me, "Who is your family walking with?" Suddenly, I saw with great clarity what was happening; why the disrespect and disagreements were continuing—we were not walking with God together as a family.

Our twice a week family Bible time had dwindled to once a week . . . some weeks. We were dealing with behaviors by clamping down in discipline, but not getting down to our knees in prayer. Where I had thought we just wandered off the path a bit and were "not walking closely with the Lord," He showed me that the enemy had snuck in, and he was walking among our family, stirring up dissention.

I saw an image of someone leaning in beside one of my kids, whispering in the child's ear, "Go punch your siblings. They deserve it." and "Your parents are idiots, don't listen to them." This someone was wandering to and fro among my household, up and down across my family. (Job 2:2)Because we weren't walking closely with the Lord, we were walking with another travelling companion. One whose mission in life is to steal, destroy, and kill all that is good and Godly. (John 10:10)

So I spent an evening in my front living room, folding laundry and praying. I talked to God and asked Him to walk with us and among us. I talked to the devil and told him that he had to get out—he is not welcome to walk anywhere near us. I prayed for spiritual protection for each member of our family. And the next day, I started praying with the kids when we encountered struggles.

Life didn't become perfect overnight. But peace came into my heart, and I saw that same peace infusing the hearts of my children.

We're still clamping down on the problem behaviors. But we've added an important layer to our discipline strategy—prayer. And I do believe we're finally beginning to turn the corner. We took the long way to get there, but now we're walking the right path.

As for me and my house, we will serve (and walk with) the Lord. (Joshua 24:15)

Marriage Builders

Last week I mentioned five Marriage Busters—behaviors and attitudes that contribute to marital problems. There's nothing worse than someone telling you what not to do without offering alternatives, so here are five Marriage Builders to help build a strong relationship.

1. Embrace Differences

You've heard that Men are from Mars, Women are from Venus . . . Men are like Waffles, Women are like Spaghetti . . . women need Love & Respect is what men need . . . Well, it's all true! Men and women are inherently different—in their needs and in their primary means of communication. Not only do we need to invest the time to understand these differences, we need to learn to embrace them.

Just the other day I was watching our four-year-old son pretend to shoot passing vehicles with an imaginary shotgun (seriously, a shotgun—he went, "Chck, chck . . . Boom!"). How does he know this? He's male, and God created him to do battle, be a protector, be tough. Ever seen a little girl cradling a baby doll saying, "Shhhh, Baby. It's okay. Mommy's here."? She's female, and God created her to nurture and love.

Too many couples waste valuable time and effort trying to convince their spouse that he or she is wrong and does things the wrong way. The fact is, though, that neither way of being is wrong. They're just different.

2. Speak your spouse's love language.

I can't say enough about The Five Love Languages! If you figure out what someone else's love language is—and then use it—you will see that person transformed before your eyes. I use the love languages when dealing with my kids, in ministry, at work, and in my marriage.

How does your husband show kindness, love, or appreciation to you? Does he buy you a gift or flowers? (Gifts.) Does he thank you? (Words of affirmation.) Does he snuggle you? (Physical affection.) Maybe he does some jobs around the house to ease your burden. (Acts of service.) Perhaps he takes you out for a date or an evening stroll. (Quality time.) The way he expresses his love is most likely his love language. Try speaking that language to show love to him!

3. Prioritizing.

In a child-dominated society, we tend to feel guilty if our world doesn't revolve around the children. We spend hours on activities the children are involved with. We plan our meals based around what our children will (hopefully) eat. Or maybe children aren't the focus, but our jobs are. Or our ministries. Or our friends and extended family. The sad fact is, you seldom see married couples whose marriage is their priority. Spouses too often get our leftovers—whatever bit of time and energy is left at the end of a busy week.

It takes effort and intentionality to put marriage first and give our spouses our best. But it's so worth it! Imagine how great you'd feel if your husband came in the door, cell phone to his ear, and said, "I need to go. I'm home and I can't wait to see my wife!"

My mom shared a great quote with me recently . . . *In today's society women tend to live as though their job is to serve their children and train their husbands, but the Bible says that women ought to serve their husbands and train their children.*

4. Get rid of selfishness.

Many a marriage breaks down under the burden of "equality." *I deserve this . . . Or I'm owed that . . . Since he got time away to do ________, I'm entitled to time away to.*

This isn't about equality. It's about selfishness. Constantly thinking about 'me' and 'I' will get us nowhere but disappointed. But reversing that thinking will bring joy and fulfillment!

Try thinking, *He deserves . . . I want to do this for him . . . I can make his life easier by . . .* Not only will acting in kindness to your husband bring you joy, but chances are good that it will motivate his heart to act in kindness to you. Eventually, it's no longer a competition to win what we deserve, but a contest to see who can give more generously to the other.

5. 'It' matters.

You know what I'm talking about! Sex means something to men that it doesn't to women. It truly is more of a need than a want. (Kinda like how women need to talk and share emotions.) So let me ask you a tough question—when is it okay to deny meeting one of your husband's genuine needs?

Would you deny your dog the exercise that it needs? Would you deny your children the affection that they need? It strikes me as odd how many couples are more concerned about meeting the needs of their offspring and their pets than they are about meeting the needs of their spouse.

If you're feeling like your marriage isn't all it could be, take stock. Do you notice a lack of marriage builders in your relationship?

If so, don't be discouraged! There is hope for change (Pat & I are living proof). Next week, I'll share a surprising truth about what's required to turn a failing marriage into a thriving one. It's not nearly as hard as you might expect!

How can I pray for your marriage today?

Unbalanced . . . 2

For some time now I've had a little ache inside. I'm quite certain that ache is caused by the emptiness I feel when my relationship with God isn't as rich and full as it's been in the past. When you've had "great, fantastic, wonderful, amazing" it's hard to settle for "mediocre."

All I knew was that I had to escape from the work of the retreat so that I could hear God's voice speaking to my heart.

My afternoon hours were spent in the prayer room, in my bed, and outside walking. The entire time—even those 15 minutes of the most restful, refreshing nap I've ever had—spent in intimate communion and conversation with my Daddy. Oh, how I'd missed that! The funny thing is, no one else on the retreat team even noticed I was gone.

Mostly, I talked to God about finding balance in my life. About putting Him and His priorities first. About how I've been feeling overwhelmed ever since I started working, and it just seems I can't get on top of everything. About how disappointed I sometimes feel that I'm not yet seeing growth in the speaking and writing ministry that He called me to.

One question Sandy encouraged us to ask God was, "What is it You want me to prayerfully neglect for this season?" So I asked Him. Here are some of the things He said to me . . .

Do not neglect preparing a healthy supper for your family. You know that this is important to your husband, and you will bless him and your marriage by taking care of your family in this way.

I kinda argued with God about this one. It's been my biggest struggle since I started working, and it feels impossible. He told me to stop whining, discipline myself, and do a meal plan. (Don't you just love how God speaks to us in a way we understand?!)

Do not neglect writing and speaking, but especially writing on your blog. I did call you to a ministry, but I'm the one who will determine its growth rate. Continue to be faithful to minister to the women I place in your path, both in person and online. The growth will come in My time.

Again, I tried to argue. It's so hard to find time to blog, and I've been having trouble focusing my thoughts in to something worth writing. He reminded me that I didn't have this problem when I was rising at 5:30am instead of hitting snooze until 6:30am. (Ouch!)

Do not neglect your work, which is also an important ministry I've called you to. Do not allow a spirit of confusion to divide your attention, distract you, and keep you from giving your all at work.

I didn't argue with this one. I've been feeling torn, like a failure at home and wondering if I should even be working. Yet knowing that God placed me in this job and that I love it.

Finally, I decided to remind God that I was asking Him what I should prayerfully neglect and He kept pointing out things that I wasn't giving my best to. You know, in case He didn't notice that. LOL!

Clear as day, I heard these words in my heart; *I didn't ask you to plan this retreat. In fact, I didn't ask you to become involved in the leadership of your church's women's ministry at all. That, my daughter, is an area you can prayerfully neglect for this season.*

With those words from Him, a weight lifted from my soul, and my heart jumped with thanksgiving and praise for His name. He is the God who speaks!

In case I needed reassurance of God's call on my life, He offered it. The sweet woman who prayed with me in the prayer room later came and shared a verse that God had placed on her heart for me . . .
Jeremiah 1:5 (NLT)

I knew you before I formed you in your mother's womb. Before you were born I set you apart ***and appointed you as my spokesman to the world****.*

I've never read those last nine words before. Not once have I noticed them! God's Word, it never goes stale; it's fresh and new every time you read it and take it to heart.

And so, as I continue through this season of life—a season that looks unbalanced in many ways—I do so with the assurance that God's got every bit of it in His hands.

Question: **In what ways does your balance appear unbalanced?**

There is more than one Path

Have you ever gotten completely hung up, trying to figure out what God's will is for your life? Which path you should take?

I know I have . . . It's especially easy to get snagged when there's a decision to be made, and neither option is clearly wrong or bad.

Should I continue working as a stay-at-home mom or should I step out into the workforce? Which school should my kids attend? Should we stay where we are with a good job, good friends, good church or move to a new place where things will be different but still good? Do we have another baby or not?

I have good news for us all—it doesn't matter!

Now hold on . . . before you get upset with me, please don't misunderstand. I'm not saying it's not important. I am not saying that God doesn't care. It is important. If it's important to you it's important to God (and vice versa). And God cares about every detail of your life. His caring is deep and intimate.

But sometimes—dare I say oftentimes—we become tied up in knots worrying about whether we're heading the right direction and walking in God's will. The thing about God's plan for our lives is that it's not a static thing. His plan shifts and changes. I said that wrong—His plan doesn't shift and change, He has always known the plan and will stick to it—but He reveals His plan to us one tiny step at a time, and it is not a continuous path in the same straight line.

Proverbs 3:5-7 says *Trust in the Lord with all your heart and lean not on your own understanding; in all your ways acknowledge Him and He will make your paths straight.*

The word is PATHS, not path. This means that there will be more than one path; there will be different paths; the path will change. I didn't say the path might change—the path will change.

Think of the path of your life, walking in God's will and plans and purposes, as a road map. Very rarely can you get from point A to point B by sticking to one road. You'll need to head East for a time, then turn your car onto a different highway heading South. Eventually, you'll probably need to turn again, onto another road.

But here is the coolest thing about a road map . . . Have you ever noticed that there are often several possible routes that will get you to your destination? You could head halfway across the world on the wrong road, yet there is still a way to turn yourself around and get back to where you're supposed to be headed.

It doesn't really matter which route you decide to take. One path will have more bumps, more construction, more twists and turns. Another path will be more direct and straightforward. On one path you may have an easy journey; on the other you may learn invaluable lessons that equip you for your destination.

Too often, we allow ourselves to be filled with worry. We fret and we stress, overthinking each decision. We make ourselves sick with anxiety, and we remain unmoving, completely frozen by the fear of taking the wrong path and stepping out of God's will. We stay parked on the shoulder, analyzing the map until we have a headache, going nowhere. Which, quite frankly, is exactly where the enemy would like us to hang out in this journey of faith.

Sometimes, sweet friends, we just need to go. We need to make a decision, pull out onto the road, and drive forward. We need to release the fear and worry of heading the wrong direction, and move ahead in faith and trust. Faith that God can get us where He needs us even if we make the occasional wrong turn. Trust that God is with us no matter which path we're driving on.

In Joshua 1:9 God says to His people (that's us) *Have I not commanded you? Be strong and courageous. Do not be terrified; do not be discouraged, for the Lord your God will be with you wherever you go.*

So if you feel stuck between two choices that could both be good, don't allow the enemy to hold you frozen in terror. Instead, be strong, be courageous, and decide which way you will turn. Trust God to be with you wherever you go. Have faith that He will make your paths head straight to the destination that He has pre-determined for you. But keep moving. No one ever got to their destination by thinking about it and planning it out. I guess that's why they call it a *walk* of faith . . .

Sometimes, the decision doesn't seem clear because it doesn't matter. Either path will bring you to where you need to be. And either way, God will be there.

** Photo courtesy of bigour.blogspot.com.*

Asked and Answered

One question I've been asked several times (thanks to the re-entry letter sent out by our mission's coordinator) is, "What is the ONE thing in Haiti that impacted you the most?"

At first, I struggled to come up with an adequate answer. To narrow it down to only one thing felt impossible. There were so many stories! But I began to notice a common thread running through all my favorite stories. Prayer.

We prayed in Haiti, in a way that we've never prayed here. We prayed for everything, about everything, over everything. And we saw our prayers answered—repeatedly, immediately, consistently.

Our prayer journey began a few weeks before we left, as team members began to struggle against attack. The enemy was hard at work trying to discourage us from stepping out in obedience, and failing that he was happy to distract us from our true purpose. Our team began praying together with the expectation that God would answer. After all, we were heading out into the world at His calling, so there were no doubts that He would give us victory over our struggles.

I can't speak for everyone on the team, but for Pat and I, as well as a few others that we heard from, those last couple weeks before we departed were a time of inexplicable calm and peace in our lives. Which, considering that the last weekend of January is the culmination of a year's worth of efforts at my work (requiring a good month's worth of fuller-than-full-time, focused work), is quite amazing. Co-workers and friends would ask me if I was having crazy, restless dreams about Break Forth and Haiti and I would reply—honestly—that I was experiencing the most restful sleeps of my life for the entire month of January!

Next came the bins of supplies. Fourteen bins, needing to weigh less than 50 lbs each, with enough supplies donated and purchased to fill twenty. So we told God that they were His supplies, and He needed to make them fit. He did.

We stored the bins in the garage of someone's home until our departure. Unfortunately, we forgot the keys to that house. And the homeowners were away on the night/early morning of our flight. And their house was alarmed. So we reminded God that they were His supplies and that He needed to help us access them. He did. Of course, when you're attempting a break-in at 3am—the exact hour you're supposed to be gathering with the team—it can be a little stressful (especially for those of us who like to be on time). So we reminded God that we needed to arrive at the airport on time. We did.

Those supplies must have been very important, because some of them were inspected in Calgary, some in Miami, and more at the Port-au-Prince airport. There was one bin containing medical supplies, including syringes and morphine (things that Customs doesn't take well to being brought across borders). Thirteen of our fourteen bins were opened and searched. When Customs officials put their hands on the last bin, we prayed. They left it sealed and stacked it on our pile.

We brought with us about a dozen bright, green soccer balls. Our hope was to get out in the community, play, and then give away some of those balls. We were cautioned that doing so could be unsafe—that we could be overrun by desperate children, teens, and parents . . . that small children could get hurt in the process . . . that turning people away would break our hearts. Our team was confident, though, that God wanted us to give those balls away. So we prayed, we played, and we gave. No mobbing occurred, apart from what is typical (the "Pied Piper" effect). No one was injured. No one was turned away in tears. And one boy, tears leaking down his cheeks, thanked us, "Today, you blessed my life."

Our team held a rice distribution on the campus, serving the families of the local church. The leftover rice pile was massive! We were brought to a nearby community—what could be called a slum, with huts, houses, shacks, tents, and lean-tos pressed tight together, streets littered with trash, and children barely clothed—and told we would take the rice door to door. When our truck filled with rice pulled up, fear set in. Dozens of Haitians approached from all sides . . . We prayed. They stood back, many returning to their homes. And we delivered our packages down alleyways and laneways, through tin gates and doors that were merely curtains. Safely. Successfully. Beautifully.

The stories don't end. God provided goats and families to give them to. He provided the exact school supplies that the school was in need of. He gave us joy during moments of frustration. He provided healing for a workman whose leg was surely broken, except that it wasn't. He gave a spirit of reconciliation in moments of disagreement. He provided safe travels, preventing the tire blowout until after we were safely delivered to the airport.

We asked. He answered. For anything and everything. In ways I've not seen here at home.

I wonder if it's simply that I don't pray with utter confidence and expectation. I wonder if it's because I don't ask for help in the little things as well as the big. I wonder if I'd see just as many

The Ugly Duckling

Once upon a time . . . There was a mother duck who hatched some eggs. Out of all the eggs came fluffy, beautiful little ducklings. Except for one. There was one egg that was larger than the rest, grey instead of white, and it took much longer to hatch. And when it finally did, instead of the duckling she expected, the mother duck was surprised to discover a chick with pokey, grey feathers. An ugly duckling.

We all know the classic tale by Hans Christian Anderson. The duckling's childhood was a sad one, with all the other animals (including her siblings) pointing out how ugly she was. She didn't fit in with her family. In fact, she didn't seem to fit in anywhere. Until one day, she grew up to discover that she wasn't a duck after all! She was a swan. The most majestic of birds, admired by people and animals alike.

She knew who she was, where she belonged, and she realized that she was truly beautiful.

Sometimes, we feel like ugly ducklings. *I'm overweight. I can't bake. I have no special talents. I don't know what I want to be when I 'grow up.' I don't fit. I'm not sure who I am. And I sure don't feel beautiful.*

Sound familiar?

The problem with these thoughts is, like in the story of the ugly duckling, they're not true.

The duckling didn't feel like she belonged because she was looking for her identity in the wrong place. She was trying to understand who she was in the context of the wrong family. Had she discovered the swan family right from the beginning, she would have been assured of her inherent beauty from the moment she hatched.

When we feel like we don't belong, we're allowing the wrong family to define who we are. We may look to the family of stay-at-home mothers and see how we don't quite measure up (especially in the housework department). Perhaps we hang out in the family of fitness buffs and find ourselves falling short of the standard of health and wellness (as we sneak Twinkies after midnight). Some days we try to identify with the super-spiritual, service-oriented, perfect-appearing church volunteer . . . Next to all these families, we kinda look like an ugly duckling.

But if we could only go to our true family from our infancy! If, instead of looking at various people and people groups for our identity, we sought to understand who we are in God's family, how different things could be. No matter how diverse we are from our siblings, no matter how different we are from the rest of the world, our Abba would tell us how beautiful we are every day.

And if we chose to listen to His words of affirmation, rather than the opinions of the outside world . . . We would be transformed! Women who are confident and peaceful shine beauty from within. Whether they are big or small, quiet or loud, funny or serious; whether they stay home to care for their family or work outside the home; whether they do Scripture memorization or talk to God like a casual chum . . . They appear beautiful because they feel beautiful. And they feel beautiful because they find their identity in the right family.

Ask God if He thinks you're beautiful, and listen to what He says.

The King is enthralled by your beauty. ~Psalm 45:11

The unfading beauty of a quiet and gentle spirit . . . is of great worth in God's sight. ~1 Peter 3:4

He has made everything beautiful in its time. ~Ecclesiates 3:11

How beautiful you are, my darling! Oh, how beautiful! ~Song of Solomon 4:1

The LORD your God is with you, He is mighty to save. He will take great delight in you, He will quiet you with his love, He will rejoice over you with singing. ~Zephaniah 3:17

You are precious and honored in My sight, and . . . I love you. ~Isaiah 34:4

Riding the Roller-Coaster

My time in Haiti has been marked by roller-coaster emotions. There have been tears of sorrow, tears of joy, moments of laughter, and vents of frustration—all squashed together into a big melting pot covered by prayer. I hope you'll indulge me as I share some of those experiences . . .

Things that brought sorrow:

Seeing people in want—no, in need—of basic necessities. Children playing in the community are clothed in filthy garments (probably their only outfits for the week, with special church clothes set aside for Sundays). Often these children have only a dirt-encrusted shirt and no pants or underwear. Those privileged enough to go to school also have a school uniform, but many are mis-sized, torn, stained, and tattered.

Children at school who do not receive their hot lunch for two days in a row, due to lack of funds.

Children sitting at their desks with no school supplies, while their peers write in notebooks with freshly sharpened pencils. Women who say they cannot come to church because they have no shoes to wear.

Men who carry cell phones and ride motorcycles, but cannot provide food for their families.

What struck me the most in these sorrowful moments was how, in some ways, our cultures are very much the same. (With the exception that North American children don't generally go bottomless, and for about 8 months of the year, they couldn't!)

Things that brought joy:

Yesterday, the foreman of the Haitian work crew was injured at another work site. Obviously, not a joyful thing. But every single worker on the Haiti Arise property gathered to pray for Moncello. Fifty or more people stood in a circle, held hands, and cried out to the Lord for Moncello's healing. Many of the Haitian men could be seen wiping tears from their eyes after the prayer time.

I had the humbling honor of delivering the message in church on Sunday. I was terrified! I've never spoken with men in the audience, nor have I spoken with a translator. I stepped up to that podium fully under God's strength. And the joy that surged through my soul at serving within my gifts kept me floating for hours after!

Laughter:

Our team has had such fun together. We truly enjoy each other, and there is a genuine love among us. Our evening card games can get pretty rowdy. And with a group of fairly competitive people on our team, you can imagine that most every project turns into a challenge. There was a lot of smack-talk going on between the two groups who were preparing the rice distribution bags.

Frustrations:

The most frustrating experience has been how often we are told "No." Our hearts are to serve in the community, not just on the Haiti Arise campus. But most of our community outreach ideas (such as a soccer game ending with the handing out of soccer balls or the distribution of shoes) are gently shut-down by the leadership here.

Don't get me wrong—I understand their reasoning. They are looking long-term, with a vision to help the people of Haiti get on their feet and for them to reject a handout mentality. They are also protecting our safety, as they don't want us to be mobbed by a throng of desperate people. Every "No" has been justified and explained. But it's still frustrating. And disappointing.

The sketchy internet service here was also a source of frustration for me. I live life twice—once for the experience and again in writing so that I can process the experience. And I love the community of friends that has come around me as I share. I absolutely hate that I've barely connected with you throughout this trip. (Apparently the internet was upgraded this morning. Total bummer that it was a week too late for me.)

Prayer:

The highlight of the trip—for me, at least—has been the way we've witnessed God's answers to prayer. We pray, He answers. Over and over again. Every project we've embarked on, every supply we've unpacked and distributed, every moment of frustration or heartache has been bathed in prayer.

The spiritual lives of our team members are being (and will continue to be) transformed by our time here. People have prayed aloud for the first time. People raised their hands in worshipping the Lord for the first time. People prayed for the healing of others for the very first time.

Pat and I, as leaders, have grown so much! We've discovered the blessing of servant leadership by putting the needs of the team before our own needs, and we've grown into prayer warriors, who step into every new situation armed.

We all came to Haiti hoping to do some good here, and hoping to be changed by our experiences. I honestly cannot say how much good we've done. We did some construction, we equipped some teachers, we played with some children, we prayed over properties and plans, we shared our testimonies . . . In all these things we've no idea what impact they will have. But I am quite certain that all fourteen of us will return to Canada changed for the better.

Will I return to Haiti? I cannot say for sure. I'll wait on God to provide that answer. Will I do another mission trip? Absolutely, unequivocally, YES.

And for those who are wondering about <u>my biggest fear</u> . . . Let's just say we're praying about it.

Here I Come

I fully expect God to speak to my heart when we're in Haiti (in less than a month—wow!). I know, with absolute certainty, that this trip will change me. I look forward to it with eager anticipation . . . in addition to a healthy dose of fear and trepidation.

While I desire a closer walk with the Lord, I'm not so naive to think that a heart change would come without a cost. If I want to be in step with God, it will require personal sacrifice. Not out of obligation, but because of my love for Him.

My eyes are going to be opened to the suffering and heartache of the Haitian people in a way that can only happen through a personal encounter. My heart will be broken wide open. I know it, because my heart is already aching with the raw tenderness that comes with brokenness.

How will I be able to leave that place? How will I be able to walk away from the hungry bellies, the desperate eyes, the outstretched hands, the empty hearts desperate for a Savior? How will I ever return to my comfortable Canadian life?

The prospect of what God might ask of me is daunting. What if He asks me to sell everything, and give the money to the poor—whether here or in Haiti? What if He asks me to uproot my life, my family, my everything in order to move in among the people of Haiti? What if He asks me to open up my home, my life, my heart to a passel of orphaned Haitian children?

Or what if He asks me to do none of that? What if He simply calls me to come home? What if He asks me to leave there, to walk away from the orphaned children? What if He asks me to take what I see there and use it to change who I am here? I think the former might be easier.

Either way, I'm as ready as I'll ever be. Thrilled. Terrified. Willing.

Change me, Lord. Less of me and more of You. I am willing.

And at this very moment, with the writing of these sentences, my theme for 2012 becomes clear to me. The heart attitude that I hope will direct my year. Two words. Two actions.

Listen and Go.

Speak, Lord. I'm your servant, ready to listen. (1 Samuel 3:10, Msg)

And then I heard the voice of the Master: "Whom shall I send? Who will go for us?" I spoke up, "I'll go. Send me!" (Isaiah 6:8, Msg)

About The Author

Tyler holds her Bachelor of Arts degree in psychology, is a two-time graduate of She Speaks (speaking/writing conference), has been mentored in writing and speaking by best-selling author Shannon Ethridge, and recently spent six years as founder/director of a thriving women's ministry. Her desire is to see women experiencing the freedom and fellowship that comes from leading trasparent lives, developing strong spiritual habits, and discovering the power of Christ in their lives and ministries.

Tyler spends her time hopping between the roles of wife and mother, writer/speaker/artist coordinator for BreakForth Ministries, and speaker/writer/women's ministry consultant. Good thing she thrives under a full calendar!

In 2008 E. Tyler Rowan started on a venture of blogging that resulted in a ministry. In a down to earth style, Tyler writes to women wherever they are in their spiritual walk and offers practical insights, encouragement, and a whole bunch of laughs as she uses her life as life lessons to share with others. You can read more of Tyler's writing on her blog http://etylerrowan.ca.

Tyler is married to her best friend Patrick and together they have five children, Braeden, Abbey, Megan, Shea and Malakai . . . . and Daisy the dog.

CPSIA information can be obtained at www.ICGtesting.com
Printed in the USA
LVOW11s1835020914

402060LV00001B/307/P

9 781477 297629